CALLED

THE MAKING & UNMAKING OF A NUN

ALSO BY MARGE ROGERS BARRETT

My Memoir Dress

CALLED

THE MAKING & UNMAKING OF A NUN

Marge Rogers Barrett

Antrim House

Simsbury, Connecticut

Library of Congress Control Number: 2016934643

ISBN: 978-1-943826-05-6 (paperback)
ISBN: 978-1-943826-06-3 (ebook, epub)
ISBN: 978-1-943826-07-0 (ebook, mobi)

First Edition, 2016

Book design by Rennie McQuilkin

Cover design by Jeremy Gilbert

Author photograph by Linhoff Photo Finishing

The people and events of this book reflect the views and interpretations
of the author. A few names have been changed to protect
the privacy of certain individuals.

Antrim House
860.217.0023
AntrimHouse@comcast.net
www.AntrimHouseBooks.com
21 Goodrich Road, Simsbury, CT 06070

for my family

TABLE OF CONTENTS

III. CALLS

AFTERWORD / 305

CALLED

THE MAKING & UNMAKING OF A NUN

FOREWORD

I have called you by name; you are mine.

— Isaiah 43:1

In late winter of 1963, my senior year at Our Lady of Peace High School in St. Paul, our class went on a silent, three-day retreat. We didn't speak to each other. We didn't chatter going home after school, and at home, we didn't converse with our families—a herculean task for teenagers. We truly tried to focus inward.

I remember sitting on a gray metal folding chair, on the last day of the retreat, a Friday afternoon, with the sun pouring in the windows of the school auditorium. Those enormous windows reached to the ceiling. Light streamed in, as it did in the paintings of the angel appearing to Mary the Blessed Virgin, asking her to be the Mother of God. I was sitting in the middle of long rows of girls, listening to the Retreat Master. His words echoed in my head: "You were put on earth to make a contribution; God wants you to give something back; this is God's purpose for your life. He saved us and called us . . . Now you belong to Him . . . "

And, suddenly, I knew. Knew that God had chosen me. I wanted to cry out, "No. Not me. Why me?" I didn't want to be chosen, but there it was. He had called me, and what was I going to do? I couldn't say no to God.

I. SOUND OF BODY, MIND, AND SPIRIT

*O*nly *morally, mentally, and physically sound persons may be admitted into the postulancy. . . . When a candidate applies . . . the provincial superior . . . shall prudently question her regarding her parents, age, health, habits, and motives.*

– 1963 "Constitutions" of the Sisters of St. Joseph of Carondelet

QUEEN OF EVERYTHING

Whenever Monsignor Neudecker visited our classrooms at Holy Redeemer grade school for a talk about Jesus, he ended with a big smile: "All right, let's see today, hands up, how many boys want to be a priest? How many girls want to be like Sister?"

I never raised my hand. In fact, I'm sure mine was the only sour face: wearing that heavy habit, going to church, praying, teaching kids? *Not that!* I liked that Monsignor at least mentioned the three different vocations open to women: religious, married, and single. I figured I'd either be single or married like my mom, but I didn't worry or even think about it much. I had things to do.

That was in the 1950s, when my family lived on the edge of a small farming town in southwestern Minnesota, close to the Iowa and South Dakota borders, *Little House on the Prairie* land. My parents believed nothing would harm us and let us wander the neighborhood, and, as we grew older, roam all of Marshall. Raised with legroom and breathing space, we'd be off for hours discovering, marching to places that no longer exist.

We were in the mud on that first day of Easter vacation. My brothers, Jim and John; my sister Mary; and I had dug our boots in, sinking them with a squish squish. We smelled fresh dirt as we pulled one foot and then the other out of the sticky earth. I stomped water straight up. "Hey, you guys, Old Faithful."

It had been winter a couple of weeks before. The wind had blown snow so high around our house we couldn't see out the windows and had to tunnel out the back door, but on this day the phoebe called, "Come see, come see." The sun in the green-blue sky shone so bright it hurt our eyes; it sparkled off the last melting snow. The backyard, crisscrossed with our tracks, looked like a relief map of holes and hills. We watched the holes fill up with water and splashed around some more; then we needed to go farther out.

John said he had something to show us, but it was really far away. Mary asked Mom if she'd pack us a picnic lunch with peanut-butter sandwiches and apples. We left on our journey, walking single file. Jim and John, their caps over their eyes, were old, ten and nine; Mary, carrying our lunch, was seven; and then me, the tail end, just five. The boys walked fast, and Mary skipped to keep up. She turned back and shouted, "Hurry up, Me-Too." She called me that sometimes. My brothers' friends called me *Little Rogers*. I shook my head, scowling; I wasn't just a Rogers, not just a Too.

I followed the others down Minnesota Hill and across Highway 19. We walked on its shoulder out of town, past the auto repair shop, listening to the workmen shouting orders: "OK, Gus, go ahead, bring it in." "Check the motor on this one." "Whoa. Whoa. Back it up."

We passed the flower nursery in its milky white bubble of a building. Steam poured out from two holes on its top—a giant ghost breathing. The ghost wore black patches covering holes made by hail and heavy snow.

We walked past the Van Maes farm. There was no sign of Mr. or Mrs. Van Maes. He wouldn't let us sled down his hills in the winter, and she would say to me, "Are you *another* Rogers?" or "Is your mom wearing an *eternity dress* again?"

Their cows stared at us from behind the fence. "Hey, hey, dumb cows," we shouted. They mooed and moved away. The sheep had already bunched together in the pasture. We walked on, kicking an old Campbell's pork and beans can back and forth. The sun was warm. I looked right up at it and then remembered that my grandmother wouldn't be happy with a new batch of freckles. "Clear fair skin, that's beauty," Muzzy always said.

Soon tall thistles scratched my face and big burrs caught on my pants and jacket. I lagged behind looking for a fallen branch, a walking stick, a cane like my daddy's shillelagh. I found a perfect one and named it Howdy, my partner for the road, my friend. "I'm tired," I told it, "let's stop and rest." I looked up at the floating clouds. "Look, Howdy," I said, "whipped cream and marshmallows. Would you like some?" But Mary turned around, calling, "Come on, slowpoke." "Come on, tag-a-long." I caught up and didn't complain because I wasn't a baby.

After a long time, Jim shouted, "Over here."

"Look! It's a slough," John yelled.

I peeked through high, skinny buffalo grass—carefully separating blades to look through because they could cut. What I saw was something strange in our dry, flat prairie land: open water. Brown and gold foxtails with their caterpillar buds, and black soggy logs, smelling fishy and moldy, surrounded the pond. Chunks of ice floated in its center.

On the bank, I stooped to pick some crazy grass, the reed kind I usually tore into pieces. One green-and-black striped piece would fit perfectly into the ragged edges of another—until I pulled it apart—then I couldn't get it back together again. Like Humpty Dumpty. The boys could get these reeds to whistle, but I couldn't.

The grass was tough to drag out because its roots were buried in magic ice, rubber ice that bends, bows, but hardly ever breaks. Under sheets of it, clear as glass, I saw sticks, leaves, and stones. In some places, it reflected trees back up to the sky. I noticed myself in the ice, a bundled-up figure: dark pants; red jacket with black buttons; black, furry hat tied over long black braids; big, heavy galoshes; and red, homemade mittens from

Muzzy. A pale face with tons of freckles, blue eyes that watched me teeter-totter on the ice, dipping the wet ends, the bubbles gurgling underneath my feet. I swayed back and forth: a trickle, a trickle, then—crack—it did break. The hole swallowed my boot. I leaned to my left side, lifted my right leg with both hands, and yanked my boot out of the ice and mud.

On firmer ground, I clomped through dried-up milk-weed pods. I tugged one out to play *He loves me, he loves me not*, picking seeds apart from the core, blowing and scattering them far, far away. A gentle breeze floated some back. Their soft puffy parts tickled my nose. I attacked big, brown cattails, squeezing the stuffing out of them, and snapped off some pussy-willow branches to build a huge bouquet. Hearing something in the mud, I knelt down to check for frogs, to see if they were still winter nesting, when the boys cried out.

I dropped everything and ran toward the water. It *was* something. A raft! A real one made out of old lumber pieces and huge nails. The boys leaped on it and with two giant sticks pushed out, leaving Mary and me behind. We watched them smoothly glide across the water. "Hey, we're Tom Sawyer and Huck Finn," they shouted.

Soon Mary begged, and then I did, too. "Come and get us. Let us go out, please. Let us try it, pleease, pleease."

The boys poled back to shore, whispering to each other. They grabbed our hands, helping us on, then hopped off and shoved the raft out. Mary and I looked over the slough. I stood tall, the Queen of the Water. Queen of ponds, lakes, rivers, oceans, and seas. The Queen of the Swamp.

Kneeling down on the raft, peering into water world, I studied slippery, stinky slime. I saw the long stems of lily pads. Too early for the flowers—either yellow or white—the dark-green, almost black stems grew deep, deep down, so deep down they probably grew all the way to China. I reached to drag one out but stretched too far, and my jacket got wet. The icy water spread to my shirt, to my arm. My knees felt damp. I looked hard at the wood raft riding low in the water.

"Hey, Mary, we got to go in. I'm all wet," I said.

Mary looked at me. "You are? Why?"

"It's getting deeper. We got to go in."

"OK, where are the sticks?"

We looked, and then I moaned, "Ohhh, nooo," realizing Jim and John had jumped off with the paddles.

We screamed, "Jim! John!"

Stickless, brotherless, we shrieked, "Help! Save us! Help!"

Crows, sweeping over our heads, echoed our cries back, their calls resounding through the slough. *Caw. Caw. Caw.*

We looked up. *Caw. Caw. Caw.*

Around. *Caw. Caw. Caw.*

Margaret Rogers

Then spun at each other.

"It's your fault. Why didn't you get the sticks?" Mary said.

"Why didn't you?" I said.

There was nothing more to say.

The sun started to sink. The only sounds now were the swishing of the grasses and the water lapping, lapping, lapping over the sides of the raft. The sky turned gray, throwing scary shadows on and off the water. Clouds grew into ghostly sheets, swaying, haunting. Wolves spied from behind bushes. An octopus peered out of the deep, tendrils sucking, ready to spray us with black ink.

Shivery goose bumps popped up on my arms and legs. I started to cry, thinking we might drown before anybody knew we were missing, this cold, dirty water covering our boots . . . our knees . . . our shoulders . . . our heads. I hollered, "I want to go home. I want Mommy and Daddy."

Then I spread my legs apart, right foot out front. I lunged. The front of the raft dipped under but moved. I did it again. The water splashed over us, and Mary cried, "Stop!" but I didn't stop. Right foot—push. Right foot—push. Right foot—push. Mary, feeling us move, began to help. We nudged the raft, pushing it down, letting it come back up. We rocked and rocked, doing our strange foot dance, until finally the raft bumped into the mucky edge. As we jumped off and crawled up the hill, we heard giggled shouts, the boys calling.

"Pickle, you're supposed to come home."

"You're late for supper, Fats."

We started marching toward home. When we met up with the boys, hiding along the path, we said nothing. We had won. Proud of ourselves, Mary turned up her nose, and I did the same. We could tell on Jim and John later. It was something to hold over their heads, aces up our sleeves. Besides, no one likes a tattletale.

DERRING-DO BUT SAVED TOO

After they got married, Mom and Dad rented an apartment across from the old senior high school. Before Jim was born, they started building a white colonial with Irish-green trim on the outskirts of Marshall. It would be a few years before the house even received an address: 300 Charles Avenue in Morningside Heights. Mom said everyone thought they were silly to spend so much money on such a big house so far out of town.

Our jumpy, staticky old home movies show a farmhouse with a barn in the distance; up close, kids crazily run around a backyard of dirt; in other directions stretch long fields of corn and alfalfa. We played everywhere. Especially on top of our hill, the corner of Minnesota Street and Charles Avenue. Minnesota was one of the only steep streets in flat Marshall; we sledded down it in winter, braked our bikes on it in summer.

It was the route to everywhere—to Mass, for instance, every Sunday. Always running behind, Dad would yell, "Alice, we're going to be late! Let's go, Alice," while Mom dressed us kids and grabbed prayer books and picture books and rosaries and veils. We'd all race out the door and hurl ourselves into the '48 Kaiser. Dad would shift through the gears at a frantic pace. We'd fly down Minnesota Hill.

One time I didn't quite make it into the car before it started to move. Jim grabbed me by the seat of my pants, shouting, "Peggy's not in!" With all the commotion, Mom and Dad didn't hear him. I could see the road rising up, little brown stones

300 Charles Avenue

and crumpled leaves scattered on the black asphalt. I smelled the rubber of the tires. Jim finally pulled me in, and I hit my head on the door, yelling, "Ouch!"

Dad turned fully around: "Goddamn it. What the hell? What's going on back there?"

Mom said, "Shh, Pat. We're going to church."

My head hurt, and I was still a bit scared, but I didn't say anything. We bulleted up the main aisle of Holy Redeemer, spreading out over several pews because we were too late to sit together. Bored, we kids snapped the hat button on the back of the pews, hearing it resonate in the quiet church. We nudged and poked each other. Dad gave us the evil eye, mouthed, "Stop it." He hated noise and disrespect in God's house. He liked to pray. You could watch his lips move in private prayer. Mom sang in the choir loft above us. We'd turn and look at her, too. Singing the hymns, her mouth opened wide. After Mass, Mom and Dad chatted with friends and then we all got into the car and drove home.

There were many trips up and down Minnesota Hill. One beautiful spring Saturday, Mary and I decided to take our doll babies for a ride. We pushed their buggies out the back door, down the sidewalk, to the big, old, blue Kaiser parked along the side of the house.

Flowers bloomed on both sides of the walk. I snapped off a yellow tulip and split some bridal wreath, tucking the tulip in my doll's hair and twining the little white flowers in my braids. Mary and I climbed into the car, swaddled Amy and Anna in their blankets, and leaned over to set the dolls in the backseat. Mary turned the steering wheel, and I spread out the map from the glove compartment on my lap.

"We'll be in the Twin Cities before lunch," Mary said, turning to me and nodding.

I pointed out the windshield, "My, but there are a lot of cars on the road. We'll be dog-tired when we get back home tonight."

"What do you think we should buy? Oh, let's not miss the sales," Mary said.

I sighed deeply. "Must we go so slowly?"

"Here, let me change gears . . . " Mary tugged the stick shift down. The car started rolling. Suddenly our moods shifted.

"We're going down the hill!" I shouted.

"I don't know how to stop! How do I stop?" Mary yelled.

We screeched, "Help! Help!"

At the steepest part of Minnesota Hill, I looked back and saw Mom, clutching her apron to her mouth, and Dad chasing us, long legs like bicycle wheels, black hair spiked like spokes. His arms beat the air. He caught up with the car, yanked Mary's door open, shoved her over, jumped in, and slammed his foot on the brake—just before we would have charged across Highway 19.

"Goddamn it!" he shouted. Breathing deeply, he shifted the car in reverse with his right hand. With his left, he wiped his sweaty forehead. Then he flung his right arm over the top of the seat, and staring over his shoulder, backed up the hill twice as fast as we had come down.

Dad parked the car, pulled the emergency brake, and ordered us out. "Girls, don't you *ever* try to drive the car again." As Mary and I started gathering up our dolls, Dad banged into the house, giving us one final, dreadful look. Mom ran over and hugged us.

The top of our world changed one spring day in 1950. We watched the colors of construction. Black, clattering plows dieseled up Minnesota Street. In a cloud of dust and sand, they tilled and turned over yellow cornstalks and green alfalfa fields. The next day, brittle bits were lifted high in the air by an orange front-end loader and dropped into heavy red dump trucks. Finally, clean white concrete trucks, their tops twirling, poured cement over the empty brown soil. Weiner Memorial Hospital began to take shape.

The hospital was a square, two-story brick building. Only a small alley separated its parking lot from our garage. The hospital fascinated us—and we used it. Lucky for us it was built so close by; we were always getting stitches and breaking bones.

On Christmas Eve of that year, Mary and I—so excited for the holiday—chased each other around the house, playing tag. I ran pell-mell into a roughed-in drywall corner of our almost remodeled kitchen and knocked myself out. When I woke and tried to open my eyes, I found them caked shut with sticky blood. I could barely see Mom and Dad standing over me. They had giant heads, enormous red mouths, the same color as the newly painted kitchen walls. Dark eye sockets stared down at me. Grotesque brothers and sisters. I squinted at the brand-new, white refrigerator; I wanted to lay my head against its coolness. The red mouths, shouting at each other, pulled me back.

"Why weren't you watching them?" Dad said.

"Me! What about you?" Mom said.

Dad scooped me up and gently carried me across the alley to Weiner Memorial. Blood continued to seep over my eyes. It smelled icky sweet, tasted bitter. It made me sick to my stomach. At the hospital, a nice nurse wiped it away, put something cold on my head, and held my hand while the doctor cross-stitched my forehead. I could hear and feel the needle punch through, then pull at my skin. It hurt, but I didn't cry. Dad said

I was a brave girl, and the nurses gave me a Christmas stocking full of candy.

At home, everyone had to wait on me. It was the best Christmas ever. Well, the best, at least, until the Christmas I got a little red cash register and *Little Women*. Santa usually gave each of us just one gift at Christmas, but that year Mary and I got *Little Women* to share. We couldn't wait to read it. We both loved to read. Mary and I traded off *Little Women* during the day—reading only to an agreed page number—and at night, until very late, we read together with a flashlight under our bedcovers.

As our family grew, 300 Charles Avenue needed to be expanded. A family room was added on next to the kitchen. We played all sorts of card games at its large table: canasta, rummy royal, go to the dump, hearts, and poker. We also did our home-work on that table, with a large, green swag lamp swaying over us. Sometimes Mom set up the ironing board in the den, open-ing a door that led to the concrete patio.

Across the room, tucked into corners overlooking the front of the house, were built-in beds for Jim and John. Because of the expense, only a slab of cement was put under this new room for the foundation, and the boys complained of it freezing in the winter—"You can see your breath when you talk"—and boiling in the summer—"You can cook an egg on the window-sill." One could sit on the thick, dark-green coverlets of their daybeds—but we didn't, because the boys bragged about mice climbing out from under the mattresses and running over their faces at night. "Who cares about some little mice?" they'd say.

Early one morning Mary got up to do John's paper route—he was out helping Jim with his that day. Hearing some-thing from the family room—maybe mice!—Mary tiptoed in and found a skinny, white-haired woman, dressed in a blue-and-white nightgown with ties in back, bent over the ironing board. She must have come in the patio door.

The wild-eyed lady turned to Mary and shrieked, "He's in his heavens!" The lady jerked back and continued to iron one of Mom's aprons, which must have been left on the table.

Mary waited a few moments. "Who are you?"

The lady snapped the cord out of the outlet and waved the steamy hot iron in the air. "Don't tell."

Hobos often came to our back door, unshaven, with long hair, dressed in overalls and dirty work shirts, cardboard stuck in their holey shoes, but they always knocked softly and asked politely, "Can you spare anything to eat?" Mom always said, "Invite them in, dear," and then fixed a bag of food while they chatted about the weather.

Mary sensed this lady was different; she must have been frightened, too, by the hot iron swinging over her head, but knowing what Mom would do, she asked the lady, "Are you hungry?"

The lady stormed, "Yes, Madam. I will have eggs with ham, over easy, toast in my coffee."

"OK." Mary nodded slowly. "I'll go fix it."

In the kitchen, Mary picked up the telephone and dialed our own number. She let it ring and ring until Mom finally woke up and answered, upstairs in her bedroom. Dad was away on a business trip.

Mary whispered to Mom, "There's a strange lady in the family room."

"What? Is that you, Mary? Where are you? Speak up. What are you saying?"

"Shh, Mom. She'll hear."

When Mom finally understood, she told Mary to hang up the phone. Mom called the hospital to ask if a patient had escaped.

As soon as the woman noticed the orderlies, she started screeching. We heard her, too, and raced downstairs. She writhed on the floor with her nightgown up around her thighs. "Don't let them take me! Save me!" she cried, reaching out to us.

Mom moved quickly to the lady, helped her stand up. She held the lady's hand, softly assuring, "Shh. Shh. You'll be all right. They'll take good care of you."

As the white-uniformed men guided the woman out through the patio door, Mom comforted us. "Don't worry; the nurses and doctors will be kind to her. Don't worry. She will be safe." We trusted what she said.

Mom always was at home. Dad traveled a lot, working hard at his insurance business. He didn't take much vacation time, but Mom insisted on a trip every summer. She would rent a little cabin somewhere. She'd pack up all the gear, and we'd load it into our regular-sized sedan, stuffing the trunk with bedding, towels, clothes, food, diapers and blankets, sun and mosquito lotions, fishing tackle, toys, books, playing cards, puzzles, and crayons and coloring books. When the car was full to bursting, we'd begin the long drive, Dad behind the wheel, Mom and the baby in the front seat, the rest of us in the back.

I have no idea how we all fit; we must have sat on one another's laps, certainly one reason for the fighting that always ensued. I do remember Dad sweeping his arm across the front seat of the car when we took trips, swiping any heads bobbing in the backseat. We had no seatbelts or air-conditioning and usually traveled on scorching days in July or August. We drove for hours, oftentimes a whole day, to that year's lake—Ottertail, Le Homme Dieu, Pelican—and stayed at the cheapest resort advertised for that summer. It would be named after alluring objects or the combined names of the Mom and Pop owners—Whispering Pines, Smooth Waves, Lil 'n' Ben.

We would haul all our stuff into one of the tiny cabins. Mom would bake and cook and clean the whole week—and still want to go the next year. How she convinced Dad to take vacations at lakes I'll never know. He always feared we'd drown. For no real reason: as a young man, he lifeguarded, so he knew how to save us; and he had insisted we all take Red Cross swimming classes at Legion's Field, so we could save ourselves.

But I didn't blame Dad for not wanting to be near

water—something always seemed to happen on our trips Up North. Like the week we spent at Little Hubert Lake in Brainerd, Minnesota, when I was about seven. As soon as we arrived and got the car unloaded, Jim and John headed to the beach with the tackle box, net, and fishing poles. At eleven and twelve, they considered themselves *sportsmen*.

I ran after them. "Can I come too?"

"Oh, go play with your dolls," John said, as he and Jim jumped into one of the rental boats.

I watched them lean over the motor, sitting on the last seat of the rowboat, their baseball caps touching. Jim, with blue eyes and freckles, looked like me, as did my younger brother Tommy. John, Mary, and my two-year-old brother, Danny, had darker skin and didn't freckle. Mary had blue eyes, but John's and Danny's were brown. Danny had long, brown, curly hair. He looked like a girl, but Mom wouldn't let Dad cut his hair because she said he was so cute. Jim and John had crew cuts under their baseball caps. Mary and I wore braids. We'd sit still while Dad braided our hair every morning. He pulled our hair very tight—so tight our eyes squinted—because he didn't want our braids to loosen. It felt like my brain stretched. As my hair came undone over the course of the day, my whole head grew freer.

I watched as Jim and John got the motor going and drove the boat out just a little way from shore, yet too far for me to see Jim's first cast—which landed a big, old, rusty hook into John's upper cheek, just inches from his eye. Jim roared back to shore, nondriving arm flailing, yelling over the sound of the motor, "Help! Help!" Dad raced to the dock, took one look at John, and told him and Jim to get into the car. The three of them rushed to the emergency clinic in town.

Mary and I knew this was our chance. We hurried down to the dock and climbed into the boat. Neither of us had ever run an outboard motor before. Somehow we got it started and then steered the boat out into the middle of the bay—where the motor stopped. We kept trying to get it going again, priming and pulling the rope as Dad did. We checked to see if there was gas. When the gas cap slipped out of my hand, it dropped into the water like a sinker, straight down. I figured I'd dive in, keep my eyes open underwater to try to spot it, follow it down to the bottom. But the water looked so deep, I changed my mind; I wasn't going in after it.

Of course the boat didn't have any oars. We had to wait. Finally, we spotted Dad running to the end of the dock. "I'm coming, girls. Just wait. Don't do anything." We watched him dash over to the cabin next to ours. He knocked on the door. He must have introduced himself to that stranger, told him the situation, and asked him if he could borrow a boat to tow us back to shore.

He rowed out to get us, his dark head bobbing up and down with the motion. He had removed his shirt—he always wore a white dress shirt, sometimes rolling up the sleeves. With only his T-shirt on, we could see his muscled arms straining with each pull. His long legs, which stretched almost the length of the boat, pushed up against the little seat in the front. As he got closer to us, we could hear the oarlocks groan. Dad jerked them almost out of their sockets, his face getting redder and redder. He finally floated up beside our boat. Throwing us a rope, he said, "Goddamn it, girls, you scared me to death."

I caught the lifeline. I tied the rope to the front of the boat as tight as could be, and then Dad towed us back to shore. He didn't say anything except that John's eye was fine and his cheek would heal quickly. Rescued, relieved, I thought how lucky we were; we'd soon be back in the cabin for one of Mom's home-cooked dinners; we'd all sit around the table and tell stories about our near disasters. Dad and Mom would be tired but happy, all their children safe and sound.

The Rogers Family

TAKING CARE

We kept a group lookout from our sunporch, waiting, watching for Dad to walk back from Weiner Memorial. Piled on the daybed, the six of us were betting on the sex of the baby.

"I bet it's a girl." Mary threw her nickel in next to mine on the pot pillow. Mary was ten years old. I was eight.

"I have a penny," three-year-old Danny screeched, throwing it in.

"Me, too," Tommy said, carefully dropping his shiny penny. He was six years old.

As Jim, thirteen, called, "A dime. Chances are it's gonna be another boy," John, twelve, said, "Here comes Dad."

Mary and I had called it: we'd spend the pot on a new toy for our baby sister, Patricia, named after our father, Patrick; born on October 11, 1953, a sunny Sunday when we didn't have go to church.

As a baby, Patty hardly ever cried. She lay on a blanket and a pink pillow on the living-room rug, her little head slowly turning to find our voices or follow our movements. Because she had fine, soft blond hair—so different from the rest of us with our thick, curly brown and black—she seemed like a tiny, fragile doll. Mary and I changed her diapers and wrapped her in blankets just as we did our doll babies. We helped Mom with bottles. We danced around Patty, calling out her name, watching her slowly respond.

Within a few weeks, I overheard Mom talking with Dad, telling him Patty was not gaining weight, that even though she had nursed all of the children, she was going to give up on breast-feeding because Patty wasn't interested. The bottle didn't seem to be the answer either; it took Patty almost an hour to finish it.

Dad had reassured her, "Honey, she's probably just a little slower than the others. She'll be all right. If you're really concerned, why don't you give Joe Murphy a call?"

I eavesdropped when Mom phoned Doc Murphy, asking if there was something wrong with Patty's tongue and upper palate. "Oh," she said, "Patty's just like some children who don't have a strong sucking reflex. Thank you, Joe."

But there were other things. And soon Mom and Dad both worried.

"She's too good, Pat. She doesn't even cry when she's soaking wet. At first I thought how lucky, what an easy baby, so mild, like when I was carrying her, no kicking or rolling over. But she's still the same; she sleeps all the time. I never thought I'd want a baby to cry."

"Call Joe, Alice," Dad said.

Mom called Doc again the next day, asking first about medicine for John, who had the flu and a very high temperature, and then bringing up Patty. Doc said Mom and Dad should take her to specialists in the Twin Cities.

"Why? Don't you know what's wrong?" Mom asked.

Doc had to strongly suspect Down syndrome at birth, based on a few distinguishable physical characteristics: the slanting eyes, flat-bridge nose, and curved little finger, but it was difficult for a good friend to deliver the diagnosis.

Because the tests couldn't be scheduled at any other time, Mom and Dad left Patty at Northwestern Hospital in Minneapolis during Christmas week. Our friends, the Flynns, invited us to their home in Canby, a small town about an hour from Marshall, for Christmas dinner that year. "I'm so grateful, Helen, for your invitation," Mom said to her friend on the telephone. I was glad to go to the Flynns, too. Their daughter Sheila was my age. Busy with her brand-new Christmas doll, Sheila let me play with all her old ones. It was fun but strange; I missed baby Patty.

Mom and Dad returned from Minneapolis on December 26, Mom's forty-fourth birthday. Her eyes appeared swollen and red—"Because of the cold weather," she said. Dad called for us all to sit down in the living room, on the good davenport, a clue that something was seriously wrong. The six of us squeezed together. Dad's strong voice sounded weak. Mom started to cry—which was shocking—we had never seen her cry.

Dad told us Patty was a gift to our family. She was different and she wouldn't learn like the rest of us because she had Down syndrome. He said God loved Patty very much, that she was special, very special. God had given her to us to help us love one another more. Blessed with a little angel, we had the opportunity to take care of her.

"Is she sick?" Tommy asked.

"Does she have to go to the hospital?" Danny asked.

My younger brothers looked scared, their eyes big and round like glass marbles. Patty looked up from the floor with tiny, blue, steely eyes. Somehow I knew Patty wouldn't be a sister like Mary, knew we wouldn't share clothes or secrets or fight over jacks or canasta melds. I didn't understand it all, but I knew I'd always take care of Patty.

We all helped her grow up, taught her to walk, and talk, and dress herself, tie her shoes, play marbles. She was slow but eventually learned. Some things she learned really quickly, like how to get up on a chair to unlatch the back door. She never wanted to miss anything. Tommy and Danny pulled her along in their games, forcing her to keep up with them. Mary and I babysat her, kept track of her. Jim and John trucked her around with them, joyriding through Marshall in their Woody car. They taught her to say, "Cool, man. Cool."

Mary and I tried to keep her in our room at night—she had a single bed next to our double. We coaxed her: "Be a good girl." But she'd roam around at night, wanting to sleep with everybody; starting out with Mary and me, she'd go on to the boys' room, then Mom and Dad's.

Taking care of Patty wasn't always easy. All of our neighbors knew her really well because she'd just walk into their houses. We would find her hiding under their kitchen tables, scooping out ice cream she had lifted from their freezers. A chair in front of the refrigerator always gave her away. No one ever yelled at her, but we kids had to clean her up—as well as the neighbor's kitchen—and then pick her up, because she always plumped down on the floor refusing to go. It was a good thing she was a skinny little kid, but, skinny or not, she was still heavy. She'd throw up her arms like a rag doll, and it was almost impossible to hold onto her. Often, as a last resort, I'd threaten: "I'll pull the pillow over your head when we get back home." That scared her. She reluctantly got up then.

Patty loved to hide. Her favorite places inside the house were the closets, the basement pantry, and under the piano in the sunporch. Outside, she loved to hide in the fields behind our house. I remember the first time she hid there. Jim and John were supposed to be babysitting for the weekend.

Usually Mrs. Kaczrowski stayed with us when Mom and Dad went away on business or vacation trips. Mrs. K loved to cook, and she loved us because we'd eat all of her kolaches and bismarks. At night, she would talk with her friends on the telephone in Polish. You could tell she was telling on us because she looked right at us and whispered something, forgetting we wouldn't know what she was saying. Before she went to sleep, she recited her rosary in Polish.

Mary and I were the ones who discovered Patty was missing. She wasn't in any of the beds or her usual hiding spots. We yelled for the boys to help. We all looked outside in the yard and the garage, then started knocking on our neighbors' doors, asking if they'd seen her. Soon all of Morningside Heights was searching.

We would have given anything for her to be somewhere, anywhere. We were almost ready to call Mom and Dad, when we heard one of the neighborhood kids shout, "Found her!" Patty was sound asleep, curled up on the floor of our cornfield fort. We had bent dead cornstalks down to the ground for the floor, stomping with our shoes to soften them, knowing we still couldn't go in barefooted because it never got really soft except right after a rainstorm. New, growing corn served as the borders of our fort, forming fresh and sweet-smelling walls, and the sky was our ceiling.

Patty's light pajamas blended in with the khaki husks and cobs of the fort. Silken strands stuck tightly to her fine, blond hair. Like the State Fair's Princess Kay of the Milky Way, she looked like Princess Patty of the Alley.

"Pretty smart," she said, when we shook her awake. "I smart, right? Hiding in the fort?"

I hugged her. So happy to find her, I forgot to scold her.

All of us felt frustrated with her at times, but we always defended her. My good friend Mary Ann once laughed, "Gee, that Patty is dumb."

I grabbed her arm. "You're stupid. She's special. God doesn't send many of them like her."

Years later, Mom told me about the letter that accompanied the test results from the hospital. She had kept it in her top dresser drawer. The letter stated that since Mom had six other normal children to raise it would be a mistake for her to keep Patty at home. Patty should be *placed* in a state institution since "It was more constructive for the mother to give her attention to the normal children than to squander her affections on a hopelessly afflicted infant."

After Doc Murphy gave her the letter, Mom said she felt like a zombie. She couldn't eat or sleep. Barely able to get herself up in the morning, she continually pulled herself together to take care of the rest of us. She'd start to cry whenever she tried to talk to friends and was hurt by the insensitive curious people who wanted to know what a child with Down syndrome looked like. "Can I see your baby?" they'd ask when she took Patty for rides in the buggy.

Her own mother, provoked about the tests, wasn't supportive. Muzzy pronounced, "I don't believe it. She'll be fine. Wait and see."

Muzzy never accepted Patty's developmental disability, which must have been very hard and lonely for Mom. I didn't know until I was a mother myself what a wrenching experience this must have been for both my parents. Mom always seemed to take everything in stride, dealing with problems as they presented themselves. That's how I recall her dealing with Patty. Dad, of course, sought guidance from the Church. He asked advice from the director of Catholic Charities in the Twin Cities. Monsignor sided with the medical profession: "Find a home for Patty."

But Patty already had a home. Remarkably, and happily for us all, Mom and Dad decided to ignore the authorities they normally believed in profoundly. "When it comes to your kids, you ultimately make the decision," Mom said, "and with that decision, I went on with life. By that spring, we entertained the bridge group and proudly placed Patty's bassinet in the center of the living room."

Mom and Dad became pioneers in the field of educating the developmentally disabled. They helped organize a new group for parents of children with disabilities, the West Central Association for Retarded Children, which included five adjacent counties. Dad wrote a column for the *Marshall Messenger* in 1955: "Authorities claim that 3 per cent of our population falls into the category of mental retarded. Two-thirds of this group can be educated to be useful citizens. This is the group where the population must put their shoulders to the wheel and assume their obligations to society."

Mom described how comforting it was to discuss problems and concerns with other parents in the Association. When Patty was eighteen months old and still couldn't walk, a kindly father told her at a group meeting, "Don't worry. It will come."

And it did. Patty learned to walk and then run. When she was six years old, she fell off the gas tank in the backyard and broke her leg. I found her and raced for help. "Looks like a fracture," Mom worried, as she rushed Patty over to the hospital in our red Flyer wagon. I scurried alongside. They put Patty's leg in a cast, and we pulled her home. Later, she had a walking cast, which had to be replaced almost every week because she hobbled through the heel; she was out visiting all her friends in the neighborhood.

There were no schools in Marshall offering programs for children with developmental disabilities. Inspired and convinced by their chapter meetings, Mom and Dad believed Patty could learn to read and write. They did not want to send her to an institution, where children were often forgotten by their families. They didn't want to lose Patty.

My brother John had visited Faribault State Hospital with his high-school social-studies class. He returned home from that field trip very upset. Pale and shaken, he described the treatment he'd witnessed: kids tied in chairs, drooling, or sitting in vomit or feces, kids being beaten up by other kids. He demanded a promise from Mom and Dad that they would never send Patty there.

They searched for a special school. There weren't many choices, and most of the programs were in the Twin Cities. They finally decided on a Catholic boarding school in St. Cloud, close to St. John's University, where Jim and John now studied, about a four-hour drive from Marshall. The boys could visit Patty during the week. On some weekend breaks, Patty could come home with them, and for holidays, and for summers.

In September 1959, when we all took her to the children's home, Patty was six years old, the age children go to first grade. We kissed her goodbye. Mom cried. No one spoke on the way back home, not one word. There was just a big lump in my throat. That night, missing her, missing her climbing in bed with me, I cried into my pillow.

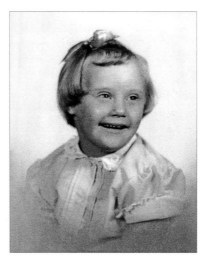

Patty Rogers

MIRACLES

In fourth grade, Sister Consuela told us about the Blessed Virgin appearing to children who took care of sheep in Fatima, Portugal. Mary revealed herself as The Lady of the Rosary and gave Lucy, the oldest of those poor peasant shepherds, a message for Pope Pius XII either about Russia converting from Communism or about the world coming to an end. We didn't know which. The Pope was supposed to open the sealed letter in 1960, but Sister said when Lucy presented the envelope to the Pope, he tore it open, read the letter, and fainted dead away over his prie-dieu. When he came to, he refused to tell anybody what Our Lady said.

During recess and after school, my friends and I worried about this new Catholic mystery. Everyone agreed it meant the end of the world coming soon. We argued over what that would be like.

After school, I didn't talk to Mom or Dad or my brothers or sisters about any of this; to talk about it would mean it could actually happen. But in bed that night, I kept waking up, seeing friends sinking into water alongside the *Titanic*. Clutching my bedcovers tightly around me, I thought of Dorothy rescuing Toto from mighty Kansas winds. Burning up, I saw arms and legs sticking out of fire as they did in the Children's Bible. I smelled hell, something like burnt pinfeathers of chickens. I thought I could hear neighbors digging shelters, metal shovels clunking on hard-packed dirt. And then this new worry—miracles. Could they happen in America? In Marshall?

I crept downstairs. Mom was up, ironing my red-and-yellow Sunday dress. It smelled baked clean, like the summer sun after a rainstorm.

"Margaret, what is it?"

"I can't sleep."

"Why?"

"I just can't."

"Well then read for a while here next to me."

She picked up one of my library books from the coffee table, a new one about Betsy-Tacy and Tib, my favorites. She handed it to me, but I couldn't read. I knew something Mom didn't. And I wasn't about to tell her. I curled up on the sofa, covered myself with the old green afghan, and watched her iron.

I often pulled up a chair close to Mom wherever she set up the ironing board, sometimes in the kitchen, next to the eating nook; sometimes on the sunporch across from the battered black piano; sometimes, like now, in the living room, alongside the white mantel and fireplace. Mom said the change of scenery helped break up the monotony. When she stood at the board, we could talk, because she stayed until all the clothes were hung or folded and stacked in nine separate piles. We had time. I could tell her about school, friends, enemies, the neighborhood games and fights.

Mostly Mom listened, but I could tell when she wasn't really paying attention—she'd turn her head to the side or stare at whatever was flattened on the board. "Hmmm, uh huh, ummm, is that right?"

Tonight I settled in to watch her iron. When she had started, I knew she would have spit on her finger and tapped the iron. When it spit back, she would have begun pressing the clothes, sprinkled and rolled in the wicker basket. She wore, as she always did, one of her flowered housedresses, the blue daisies faded almost to the color of the yellow background, and her white smocked apron, tied in back, its sleeves puffed out, stiff with starch. Her nylons, full of runs, slipping through garters, bunched at the knees and sagged over her old, arch-supported oxfords. Sweat dripped to her eyebrows, clouding the glasses that had slid to the tip of her nose. With a sudden jab of her arm, the sweat spilled to the cloth below, the iron hissing and swallowing all the steamy moisture. She complained of the heat: "It gets to me. I'm good for nothing. My legs ache." In the summer, she would iron sometimes in her underwear.

How could I tell Mom that the Mother of God, the Queen of Heaven and Earth, was going to appear to me? Probably right here in the living room.

I hid behind the couch. I needed to plan in private. I figured I'd kneel down when she appeared, say, "Hello, Holy Mary." I'd kiss her hands, place mine in prayer, fingers matching up. Would Mary speak? In Portuguese or in English? If in Portuguese, would I suddenly understand it? Another miracle? Would she wear the blue gown, the white veil, the tiara of gold or the crown of jewels? Would she smell like violets or roses or lilies of the valley? Would Mom know Mary was there? The living room would be transformed. The bright, bright light could even ignite the sofa and chairs and tables. I would have to scream "Fire!" Everyone would wake up.

Mom stopped ironing, looked up, said, "Margaret, come on out from behind the davenport."

But I couldn't come out. I couldn't tell. I crouched in the corner, knees to chin, waiting. It grew later and later.

Finally, I peeked out from my hiding place. Mom was now working on my school uniform, my navy jumper, the black iron under her reddened hand smoothing out the white crumpled emblem of Our Lady.

"Mary's going to appear to me like she did to Lucy," I blurted out.

"What?" Mom said.

"Mary's going to appear to me like she did to Lucy."

"Oh . . . " she said. Then, "Don't worry. You'll be all right."

She didn't offer any advice, just continued ironing until very late. Finishing, she came over and took my hand. "Let's go on up, honey, I don't think she's coming tonight."

In fifth grade, I was finally chosen to be an attendant for the Blessed Virgin Mary's Coronation. I had wished for it every year. Our teacher, Mrs. Malo, one of the only non-nun teachers, told us to wear pastels. I didn't know why—maybe to blend in with Mary's muted blue. But the nicest dress I owned was checkered black and white, trimmed in white lace. I thought it would do.

I woke early on May Day. I hadn't slept well because I'd set my hair in big metal rollers, and the picks pressed against my head all night. I'd also dreamed my bouquet burst open at Our Lady's feet, petals spraying like the seeds of a milkweed pod. I'd reached out frantically to catch them, but they blew away. I'd cupped my hand trying to snag one seed, and then another, as they puffed back to earth.

Instead of the homely navy school uniform and ugly ox-fords Dad made me wear for arch support, my good clothes were waiting on the chair—nylons, slip, checkered dress, and black flats. I bobby-pinned a new, white, short, lacy veil on my dark curly hair.

Mom helped me cut flowers from the garden. "Only the best will do," she insisted, picking the tallest and brightest. We wrapped the bunch in waxed paper, tying the bundle with a brown rubber band. Dad said he'd come from work to watch me attend.

When I got to school, I saw the other flower girls wearing lavender and mint and knew I was dressed all wrong. I could feel my face burning red during the procession. Dad was waiting at the Grotto, mumbling the rosary. When I glanced over at him, he quickly gave his thumbs-up sign.

He'd given me the same sign at my first piano recital when I was seven and so happy, wearing a yellow dress with rhinestones, a poofed bottom, and a green velvet sash. Mom had let me unbraid my hair; a bow held back my ringlets. I'd worn brand-new, patent-leather shoes and lacy anklets. Walking across the basketball court stiffly, like a model carrying a book on her head, I'd made a deep curtsy, sat down on the piano bench, curved my fingers over the keys the way Sister taught us—and forgot my piece. I'd tried a note with my right hand, then my left. I looked out at the audience and spotted my dad. Nodding, giving the thumbs-up sign, he seemed to be saying, "It's OK, honey, just get up." I stood and bowed again. After the recital, Mom said to everybody, "Mary practices; I'm afraid Margaret reads too many comic books." Dad didn't say anything, just took my hand as we walked out of the gym.

Now, at the Grotto, he looked so proud I decided I might look all right after all. His reassurance allowed me to become confident. As Dad continued praying, I patted my hair, straightened my veil, getting ready to present my bouquet of red tulips and yellow daffodils at the Virgin's feet. I might even have done some praying, but I doubt it. I was too filled with thoughts of making it to the Grotto without tripping, of not showing my slip when I leaned down, of wondering how long the Coronation was going to last—important matters.

STAND UP, STAND FOR

Very early on I knew what Dad believed in: friendliness, hard work, success. "Peggy, love what you do. Don't worry about how much money you make. Love to go to work because it isn't really work. Forward thinking, that's what's needed."

One summer, when I was about eight years old, he took me to see his mink farm outside town. In the car, he explained his concept of buying stock in companies. "Peggy, you gotta believe in people. And get in at ground level." He told me about Art Gunderson, the barber in town. One time, cutting Dad's hair, Art started talking about how he'd like to breed minks. Next haircut, Art told Dad that he had bought some fine-looking animals. By the third haircut, Art exclaimed how fast the minks were multiplying, and by the fourth, Dad had signed up, partners in fur.

We drove through Marshall towards the small town of Lynd, to the Mink Factory. There were stacked-up steel cages on an empty, barren field. It smelled terrible—like an outhouse on a hot day. I only got out of the car so I could see up close the sleek animals in their cages. They ran in circles until they sensed me, then playfully poked their black noses through the wires. Busy and bold, they performed an irresistible peek-a-boo show.

"Please, Dad, can I pet one?"

"Peggy, they're not pets. They're investments."

"Please, Dad?"

" . . . OK, but put him back in if it looks like he'll bite."

I reached in and very carefully lifted out the mink closest to the latch with both of my hands. The mink had the blackest, thickest, softest fur; the deepest brown eyes; the glossiest tail.

"I feel so sorry for him, Dad. I'd never kill him to make some silly coat for some stupid lady." I swept my arm through the air. "I'd like to set all these minks free, unlatch all their doors."

Dad nodded. "I see your point. Now, honey, I think it's time to go."

Reluctantly, I put Minky back in his cage. "Don't kill him, Dad."

"We'll keep him for a while."

I wondered for how long. I knew Dad wouldn't change his mind.

All the Rogers kids worked: the boys delivered and collected for newspapers, shoveled snow, mowed lawns; Mary and I mainly babysat. During the summers, the older kids detasseled corn. I always begged to go along, but Mom said I was too young. Every summer I begged and begged. I wanted to be earning money, too, spreading it out on my bed at night, stacking it in bills and coins, counting it. When I was nine, Mom reluctantly allowed me to walk to Liberty Park very early in the morning to see if anyone would hire me.

Normally I loved walking to the park, halfway to town; we played games on the sidewalk—jumping rope, hopscotching, leaping over cracks. Dedicated to soldiers who died for our country, the park was divided by the Redwood River, which ran under Highway 19. On one side, we swung and played on merry-go-rounds and teeter-totters. There would be other kids there no matter when you showed up. We would join in their games while Mom talked to their mothers. Usually we'd stay for about an hour unless Mom brought hot dogs and marshmallows; then we would find twigs for roasting the treats over barbecue pits and would picnic on Liberty's wooden tables.

On the other side of the park, we walked right down to the river and skipped pebbles and walked across its big rocks. In front of the river was the band shell, where there were concerts in the summer. We always came to listen. Mom would spread an old green army blanket on the grass and we all bunched our butts on it, arms scrunching legs, so we wouldn't get scratched. Some people listened from their cars. Instead of clapping, they honked their horns. We loved that.

But at 4:30 in the morning—the time to apply for a detasseling crew—nothing fun was happening at the park. It was the last two weeks of the harvest, when farmers, who normally hired adults and older kids, took any bodies tall enough to reach the corn. I made the second crew.

We left from Liberty Park in old school buses. We drove for a long time, bumping along, too sleepy to talk, finally ending up at some farm, where a leader showed us how to pull out the tassel of a cornstalk. He told us we could get a drink of water at the end of a row—about a mile long. He assigned a row to each of us.

The dew soaked first my shoes and socks then my pants and shirt. We lifted our arms up, over, and over, and over, plucking off those corn tufts. The stalks were dirty and scratchy. Be-

Knee high on the 4th of July

fore we had even finished one row, the sun had risen. By the end of the second row, it was already scorching hot, and I was sweating like a steam bath. Salt and dirt prickled my open cuts.

Midway down the next row, I noticed the girl next to me falling behind. I heard a strange, strangled cry. She'd fainted with the heat. On my other side, another girl collapsed. The supervisor and some helpers carried the girls away on stretchers, leaving me surrounded by nothing but corn and sun and sky. I was scared. But row by row, drink by drink, I made it through the day.

When I got home, Mom took one look at me—sunburned, exhausted—and said, "That's it. No more detasseling."

I was relieved by her decision. But glad she had let me try.

One night a stray dog appeared when we were playing capture the flag with the neighborhood kids. He limped into Red Team's circle and collapsed at my feet.

"Hey, whose dog is this?" I asked my friends.

"Don't know," Jami said, shaking his head.

"Never seen him before," Mary Ann said.

"Boy, does he look hungry," Willy said.

The dog's tongue hung out a mile, and his ears drooped to his paws. I ran home and got some of my dad's favorite food: peanut butter on white crackers and a bowl of milk. The dog gobbled them up. Then he plopped down again, and I petted him. Soon Mom called us home.

The dog followed. He plunked down on the back steps, and my brothers and sisters stepped over him, patting his head.

"Do you think he'll stay until morning?" I asked. No one answered.

I led him into the garage, a good hiding place. Mom and Dad hardly ever used it. It was too small for our car because of all the outdoor equipment stored in it—lawnmower, rakes, shovels, old tires, jumper cables, garden pots, hoses, fertilizer. The garage also held our pigeon coop and ladder fort. The dog would like it.

I filled the milk bowl with water from the hose and got him to lie down on an old rug. "Don't go away, dog," I told him. Later, when everyone was asleep, I snuck back outside. He was still there. I covered him up with my blanket. "Goodnight, Blackie dog," I whispered, "you be a good boy. I'll see you in the morning light."

The morning light showed Blackie had fleas. He had them so bad birds swooped down to peck him. We kids took turns swinging sticks in the air, screaming, "Shoo!" "Scram!" "Beat it!" Until we got rid of his fleas—and we had no idea how to do that—we decided to keep Blackie a secret. We fed him in the garage and played with him in the vacant lot next to our house. He rolled in the grass, letting Tommy and Danny jump on him and grab his fur. He let Mary tie red bows on his floppy ears. Jim and John hitched him to the red wagon, yelling, "Mush. Mush." He pulled, wearing a silly face—I think it was a smile.

After lunch on Blackie's third day with us, the boys carried their BB guns outside.

I ran after them. "Can I come?"

"No," they both said.

"Please," I begged.

"You're too little. No nine-year-olds allowed," John said.

"Please."

"For cripe's sake, no. But we'll take Blackie. He can sniff out game," Jim said.

I watched them leave. They marched through the backyard, past the sandbox, across the alley, and into the cornfield. I . . . very . . . quietly . . . followed. I couldn't see them, but I could hear them. They moved so quickly I fought to keep up. I ran so fast I didn't even see the barbed wire. I felt it, though, felt my skin ripping, saw the blood dripping down my leg. "Help! I'm hurt."

In a second, Blackie was there, licking my face. The boys raced behind him.

"What're you doing here?" John asked.

"Geez, what happened?" Jim gawked at my leg.

I was glad it looked so bad, because they forgot to be mad at me. "I ran into the fence."

"What a mess," John said. "You'll probably need stitches."

"Please don't tell."

Blackie licked my leg all the way home. The boys didn't tell. I got upstairs, splashed some mercurochrome on my leg, wrapped a rag around it, then changed from shorts to long pants before Mom noticed. I had to keep changing rags and pants until the bleeding stopped. Even though my leg hurt, I wasn't about to tell.

But Mom found out about Blackie the next day, anyway, and it was my fault. I'd just finished giving him a bath, trying to wash away his fleas. He was so funny splashing around in the metal tub, ducking his head under and slapping the water with his paws. Laughing and carrying the wet, slippery supplies back into the house, I stumbled. The glass shampoo bottle slid out of my hand, hit the floor, and broke into a million pieces.

Cooking at the stove, Mom spun around. "Margaret. What was that? What are you doing with shampoo? And towels? They're soaking wet. Why so are you, you're dripping on the floor. What've you been doing?"

Not able to think fast enough, I spoiled the secret, telling her about Blackie. "Please. Please, Mom, can we keep him?"

She frowned. "We're not going to keep a dirty, old stray dog."

"Please. He isn't dirty. He's clean, except for the fleas, and we adopted him so he isn't a stray."

"Fleas! You kids will get them."

"Please."

"We'll have to wash everything."

"Please."

"We need to get rid of him immediately."

I started to cry. "Please, Mom."

"Margaret, I'll have to talk to your father when he comes home."

I retreated to the cornfield fort in the fields, throwing myself down on the floor, watching the dust from the stalks settle on my red vest and tan pedal pushers. I thought about what Mom might say to Dad. Maybe she would say, "Well . . . we don't have any pets right now except for the pigeons." But then he'd probably bring up Pretty Boy. Our parakeet, who never did learn how to talk, froze to death in his cage one cold winter night when someone forgot to leave open the French doors of the sunporch. In the morning, Pretty Boy lay as stiff as his perching log.

"And remember Brownie?" Dad would say.

Brownie, our first dog, got shot in the leg. Mr. Van Maes, up at the farm, had only one good eye, but one was enough to spot Brownie chasing his sheep. Old Man Van Maes had warned us, but we still hated him three-legging our dog.

"And those crazy chickens?"

The Easter Bunny had delivered chicks, Henry and Henrietta, who grew up to both be Henrys, big and strong—and mean. They pecked and chased us as soon as we walked out the back door. They crowed, cock-a-doodle-dooing, early, really early, in the morning. The neighbors didn't like them either. A mangy dog finally ate them.

Mary had seen this happen from Weiner Memorial the night before she had her appendix taken out. "Light was just dawning," Mary said, "and I got up and looked out the window. On our street, this horrible dog was attacking our chickens. I buzzed for the nurses, screaming, 'Save Henry! Save Henrietta!'"

Thinking she was having a bad dream, or was frightened being away from home, the nurses got her back in bed, but as soon as they left her room, Mary climbed out the window at the end of the hallway and crept down the metal steps onto the fire escape. She was scared and sick, but she hollered and shook her fist at the dog. He paid no attention. Mary rushed back inside to frantically call us on the phone. Mom answered. We all woke up and raced outside. Too late. One mangled chicken lay motionless under the dog's legs. The other chicken swung from the dog's mouth, bloody teeth sunk into a wing. Henry's spindly chicken legs dangled back and forth under the dog's head. We tried to hide our tears and to wave to Mary, crying at the window of her second-story hospital room.

I secretly wasn't too sad—those chickens scared me.

Remembering Henry and Henrietta, Mom would say, "We'd better not chance it," and Dad would agree, "Enough's enough."

And sure enough, when I returned home for supper, Dad said, "Honey, we can't keep the dog. We found a farmer who'll take him. Come here, boy." Blackie trotted right up and jumped into the car.

Blackie pressed his big black nose against the back window as they drove away. I hid in my room and cried under my bedcovers. For a long time I cried, wishing with all my heart he would come back. Wishing and wishing, and then I thought I heard him—at my window. Wroof. Wroof. Wroof. I looked out. He smiled up at me.

The farmer phoned soon after. "That dog's gone, can't find him anywhere."

"He's here," I said.

The farmer sure was surprised. So were Mom and Dad.

"Imagine that!" Mom said.

"That old fellow made it back," Dad said. "That's got to be six, seven miles."

"He must have run all the way," Mom said.

You'd think they would have seen how much Blackie loved us. You'd think they would have understood, but no: "I'll take him back tomorrow," Dad said.

I rushed to get Blackie to the cornfield fort to hide him. Blackie and I could live in it forever. Blackie did what I wanted, and I knew he liked listening to me. I had already told him things I'd never told anyone. I told him about my very best friend, Mary Ann, moving far away to California. I told him about the Langan girl across the street getting polio. When I'd gone over there with a present, she moaned from a criblike bed far back in the living room. Told not to get close, I handed the coloring books to her mom. I explained to Blackie why he couldn't go over there, and why we couldn't run through the sprinkler. Mom and Dad wouldn't let us do that, or go swimming, because they were afraid we'd catch the disease. I didn't want Blackie getting polio. He understood. I could tell by his eyes. He had the biggest, brownest eyes.

Settling himself in the fort, he dropped his head on my lap. I hugged him and put my head on his. The next thing I heard was Mom's voice far away. "Margaret, where are you? It's time for dinner."

Then Dad yelled, "Peggy, it's late. C'mon. Bring Blackie home."

What? Bring Blackie *home*? Oh, boy! All the way back, I rehearsed what I'd tell Mom and Dad: *Blackie won't be like the others, he won't peck us, or chase sheep, or die; I'll take care of him.*

They would listen to me this time.

They didn't. They took Blackie back to the farm, not wanting to put up with an old, diseased dog. I had tried to come up with alternatives to keep him—"Forward thinking, that's what's needed"—but had to accept my parents' *because we say so.* I was learning to advance, recede, compromise.

One Christmas my whole family got together at my house. After visiting over Tom and Jerrys, my dad's favorite holiday drink, and eating a heavy turkey dinner, we gathered around the tree, sipping Bailey's Irish Cream. The soft lights of the blue spruce were reflected in the Waterford aperitif glasses: red, green, silver, gold. A deeper red blazed from the fireplace. We lounged in its warmth, in its smoky smell and crackling sound. We began to reminisce, the way you do when you're older, full of food and drink, ambiance, and one another.

"Remember Blackie?" I said, and started telling my story.

My siblings shouted me down—reminding me of how tricky writing memoir can be; what you remember can be recalled quite differently by others.

"You make it sound like Blackie was your dog," Jim said.

"He wasn't, you know," John said.

"No, he was mine," Mary said. "He followed me around."

"Yours? He was mine," Tom said.

"Are you kidding? He was mine," Dan said. "He played with me for hours."

"No. He was mine," Patty said.

We argued with one another, and then laughed, realizing how our individual memories made each of us the hero or heroine of the story. But, of course, I knew my brothers and sisters were barking up the wrong tree. Blackie was my dog. He would always be my dog.

We differed on the ending of the story as well. Jim thought Blackie died of flea infestation; John, of old age; Mary said he lived happily ever after, close to his newfound farm friends; Tom said he couldn't speculate; Dan said he had spotted him later that summer in the neighborhood, but Blackie refused to follow him home. Patty, who had learned how to compromise more than anyone else in the family, simply said, "He died happy, Marge."

A CHANTEUSE AT THE MANGLE

Mom loved to sing. She had a trained voice; if she hadn't had all of us kids, she might have become famous singing opera or appearing on the *Ed Sullivan Show*. Instead, she sang in the Holy Redeemer Choir for weddings and funerals, for us kids on car trips, and for Dad on St. Patrick's Day—always two favorites, "I'll Take You Home Again, Kathleen" and "Danny Boy."

Mom sang snatches of tunes while she did the laundry. "I wander'd today to the hill, Maggie, to watch the scene below." With a heavy wooden stick, she pulled clothes out of the boiling-hot water in the wringer washer. "The creek and the creaking old mill, Maggie . . . " She lifted the clothes and stuck them twice through the wringer, performing her own damp-dry cycle. "As we used to long ago."

Her washing song continued as she cleaned the clotheslines with soapy water and then rinsed them with fresh. She hooked the clothespin bag onto the lines to weigh them down. She had to keep jumping up until the hung clothes brought the ropes and the raggedy bag to her level. "The green grove (jump) is gone from the hill, Maggie, (jump) where first the daisies sprung. The creaking (jump) old mill is still, Maggie, (jump) since you and I were young."

Mom wouldn't hear of buying an automatic washer and dryer. "We don't have the money, and the washer won't get the clothes really clean, and the dryer, such nonsense, there's nothing like the smell of clothes hung out to dry." But one day in the late 1950s, Dad surprised Mom and had new modern appliances from Abe Electric in Minneota, a small town a couple of miles from Marshall, delivered to our house. You could tell Mom was pleased: "Oh, Pat, you shouldn't have." Still, Mom liked to hang everything out, except during winter, and sometimes even then—giant, ice-swollen pants and shirts looking like Macy's Thanksgiving Day parade balloons suspended in our backyard. Sheets and pillowcases, washcloths and towels, shirts and pants, skirts and blouses, dresses, handkerchiefs, underwear, and socks—all swung from the clotheslines, strung from the house to the garage.

To save room, and because the sun would bleach them out, Mom made us spread diapers and baby blankets on the fence and bushes around the house. I refused to put anything on the front shrubs; the backyard already looked like a camp under siege.

After they were dry enough, the clothes were fed into the mangle. With its wide-open jaw, the mangle loomed like a metal monster, its oversized roller primed to flatten anything in its path. It stood in the dank, dark basement next to the cellar with its jars of home-canned fruits and vegetables and extra cans of food, lots of extras, a hoarding, post-Depression instinct of Mom's. "Always be prepared, always have something on hand," she would say.

Mom sat on the red rusted chair in front of that big, steamy box, her knee jabbing the plate that worked the roller down over linen, play clothes, and fancy dresses. Dad's white shirts looked dry-cleaner done; Mom could press them so even the sleeves didn't have a crease. She performed a sit-down dance, her knee jerking in and out in rhythm with her hands, placing and replacing one side of the shirt, then the other, the back, front, sleeves, buttons, and collar. Her body moved in time to whatever song she hummed.

The mangle wasn't as easy to talk over as the ironing board. I had to shout while the pedal clanked and the roller whirred, but I often pulled up a chair. One day Mom and I talked about her parents and grandparents. I was working on a family tree for school.

Mom knew a lot: her father's parents, Joseph and Johanna Brewers Schreiber, came over together from Germany in 1883 with their oldest child, Gerhard. They were among the first settlers to come to Lyon County. They homesteaded land in Westerheim Township, named "western home" by its people, mostly emigrants from Norway. The farm was north of Ghent, a tiny town—less than three hundred people—about two and a half miles from Marshall. The promise of rich soil must have been the attraction for the Schreibers. They worked to grow and flourish there, using oxen for plowing. My grandfather, Edward, who we called Papa, was born in 1884, their first year in Minnesota. He and his two younger sisters were sent to the Ghent schoolhouse and then later to St. Michael's Convent, a Catholic boarding school in New Ulm, a German town about seventy miles from their farm.

"I can't imagine going away to school, leaving you and Dad for weeks and months. I'd have hated it," I said to Mom.

"But it's what you had to do back then to receive an education," Mom said.

"Isn't Wanda Gag, who wrote *Millions of Cats*, from New Ulm? Did Papa know her?"

"I don't know," Mom said, "but I guess they were around the same age. Maybe she went to St. Michael's, too. Her family was German-Bohemian. Same as Gag's Drugstore in Marshall. They must be related."

Mom continued on about Papa after elementary school, riding his horse seven miles back and forth to go to high school in Marshall. He worked: fed and milked cows early in the morning and late at night, and planted and harvested crops. And he studied, attending business college in Marshall and finishing his degree at St. Thomas College in St. Paul.

Papa's parents died young, his dad when he was eleven, his mother when he was eighteen, leaving Papa responsible for the family as a teenager. He was just nineteen when he bought the Ghent general store and named it Schreiber Hardware. It was the biggest store in the whole county, selling wagons, buggies, gasoline engines, pumps, furniture, glassware, livestock. And later, automobiles.

"An accomplishment," Mom said. "Go get the book, *History of Lyon County*, in my top dresser drawer, honey. You'll see a picture of Papa as a handsome, young man with curly black hair and almond-shaped eyes."

I found the book and the write-up about Papa: "Edward Schreiber is a Lyon county product that has certainly 'made good.' Although a young man, he has built up an enormous business and is rated as one of the most successful business men of the county accomplished through a strict application to business, an indomitable purpose, and honest dealing."

I didn't tell Mom I thought he looked like a girl in that picture—like her. In our family-album photographs, he looked swarthier, hair straighter, thick and black over deep brown eyes peering through heavy, dark-framed glasses. He always wore a dark suit with a freshly pressed white shirt, tie clasp and cuff links, a soft fedora.

In 1907, Papa married Julia Dierickx. He was twenty-three and she was twenty-one. There wasn't a write-up or a picture of Muzzy in the *History of Lyon County* book, but bits of her life were stuck in its pages anyway. There was an orchid, pressed in fraying parchment paper. Thinking of how Muzzy looked in her wedding picture—pretty with high cheekbones, wide blue eyes, and thick dark-brown hair—I imagined her placing the flower from her wedding bouquet in this book.

Muzzy raised their five children, living first in rooms behind the store and then in a large home off Main Street. "Muzzy liked both places," Mom said. "The tight quarters, where everything was stacked and layered, mixed together—schoolbooks, laundry lines, pantry shelves—because everyone was close." In the big house, Mom said they could stretch out and relax. They could store food in the mahogany kitchen cupboards, read in the living room with its built-in bookcases, entertain in the parlor with their upright piano, and work on sewing projects in the den while listening to the standing Kent-Atwater radio. There was also a big backyard for Papa to plant a garden.

"Why do we call her Muzzy, Mom?"

"Because her first grandchild, your brother Jim, called her that when he was a baby. And it stuck. Now everyone calls her Muzzy."

Mom filled me in on Muzzy's family tree, too. Her knee bumped against the plate; her hand rhythmically picked up and placed the laundry rolled in the wicker basket, the smell rising—fresh, clean, cottony, with a touch of lye soap.

"Peter Dierickx, Muzzy's father, came over from a village named Caprycke in Belgium, and Rosalie Overmeir, Muzzy's mother, came from a village named St. Margariet."

"I love that name," I said. "My name. But it has an *i* in it. The Belgian names are hard to spell."

"Yes, they certainly are," Mom said. "I never learned to speak or write the language."

Mom didn't know how her grandparents met in the United States, but the Dierickxs got married in Henry, Illinois, in 1881. Their children, Muzzy and her three brothers, all walked to a one-room schoolhouse in Atkinson. Muzzy was known for her fantastic memory, never forgetting any lessons.

"Just like you, Mom," I said.

The Dierickx family moved to Ghent, Minnesota, in 1901. Like Papa's family, they moved farther west looking for more land at a cheaper price.

"Look at the *History of Lyon County* again, Margaret. There are newspaper clippings glued to the inside cover about my grandparents."

One in Flemish and another in English, they reported that Rosalie and Peter, "both emigrants from Belgium, who for many years farmed near Ghent, died there at 78 and 94 years of age. They'd died within a week of each other." Mom thought her grandmother died of a broken heart. She remembered the bitterly cold day, the wind shearing through St. Eloi's Cemetery at their double funeral service, and the words pronounced over the two caskets: "For sixty years, they travelled life's pathways together in loyal devotion and Christian-home idealism."

Mom said everyone in town belonged to St. Eloi's parish. The Catholic Church was an enormous part of life. Like a big family, everyone worshipped, played, and prayed together. Everyone went to Mass on Sunday and tried to live what the priests preached. The sisters inspired them, not so much with lofty ideas, but by living in community with them, suffering and rejoicing with them—and teaching their children.

"That's how we live in Holy Redeemer's parish, too," I said.

When the Dierickx family moved to Ghent, Muzzy's formal education ended. At fifteen, her *higher* education consisted of sewing classes in which she excelled, becoming an expert seamstress. Mom and I remembered gifts she had given us: a hand-crocheted, popcorn-stitched bedspread; embroidered linen doilies and pillowcases; a knitted wool afghan; and oval-framed and cross-stitched pictures of a Victorian gentleman and lady. Muzzy could sew anything, from bulky coats to intricate lacy pieces. I hadn't known, though, that she had kept the books for Papa's business. And her writing always fascinated me.

"Did Muzzy learn to write letters in school?"

Whenever Mom got carried away talking, she'd mangle slower, balancing her knee right over the plate, not pushing it, just keeping it in midair. It gave an emphasis to what she was saying. "She must have. You've seen her letters, Margaret, on that white, blue-lined stationery. She used that feathery ink pen and wrote with such whorls and curlicues. You've seen her do it, sitting at her little writing desk. Such beautiful handwriting. And everything spelled correctly. Her parents' Flemish tongue—which wasn't French, or Walloon, another kind of French language spoken by Belgians—embarrassed Muzzy. Muzzy always spoke and read only English."

On another mangling day, Mom told me about herself, about going to school in Ghent's four-room schoolhouse with her brothers and sisters. St. Agnes Convent School was run by the same order of nuns, St. Joseph of Carondelet, who taught us in Marshall. The priests and nuns from St. Eloi's—named in honor of the Apostle of Flanders, a patron saint of blacksmiths—visited the Schreiber home often; they'd all go on picnics and excursions together; they were close friends. Mom said she heard a number of times from various sisters, "If you need a friend, call Ed Schreiber, and he'll help you."

Mom said she had been a strange child in school; she alternated between being very quiet and shy, and then suddenly blurting something out, sometimes not even connected to the lesson.

"Why did you do that?" I asked.

"I don't know."

Curious, I thought, but brushed it aside. Years later I'd remember this conversation with Mom . . .

She and I were playing gin rummy at the river cabin. I was expecting Mom to win. She usually did. We had had wine with dinner; I was getting sleepy.

Out of nowhere, Mom said, "Margaret, I don't know if I've ever told you that some bad things happened to me when I was young."

I looked closely at her. "What are you saying, Mom?"

"Well, there was our neighbor . . . "

"Yeah, that mean old guy. You told me his name once."

I stared at my ninety-three-year-old mother in her housecoat and slippers. I didn't really want her to go on. But I couldn't stop myself. I had to ask.

"What happened, Mom?"

Still holding my cards, disjointed thoughts raced through my mind: I needed another jack for a threesome; I should have discarded the other two when I had a chance; my mom, a young girl.

"Did you tell anyone, Mom?"

"Just your dad."

I didn't ask her when she told Dad. I didn't want to think about them discussing this. I didn't want to be there. Or here. Listening to this. But again, I had to ask.

"Was it rape, Mom? Did he rape you?"

"No. He made me do what you call oral sex. My brother, Al, too, I think."

I didn't ask her if she ever talked about this with her brother or why she thought this guy had also abused him. I didn't ask anything more at this time, because after I said, "I'm so sorry, Mom," and we finished that hand of cards, she looked directly at me again.

"That's not all," she said. "Remember when I called Ghent a Peyton Place?"

"Yeah . . . " I said. "That time we were mangling?"

"Yes. Well, Papa carried on with a woman right in our house."

"What? What do you mean?"

"Muzzy and Papa entertained a lot, and she'd come over with her husband. Several times I saw Papa and her sneaking off somewhere. They'd kiss . . . "

"Oh, Mom."

"They saw me watching them once. Papa offered me money not to tell Muzzy."

"Oh my God, Mom. Did you ever tell her—or anyone?"

"You're the first, Margaret. I didn't even tell your father because he didn't like Papa too much, and I knew this would've caused a serious rift between them. Papa was my father after all.

I still wanted him in my life . . . I think his difficult childhood was the fault. He never had any time to be young."

"But what a horrible thing to do to a little girl. How old were you?"

"Young."

I didn't know any of this when I mangled with Mom, but her remarks about acting strange in school and Peyton Place-Ghent are what came back to me in my dreams after Mom and I finally went to bed. I marveled at Mom's forgiveness: she recognized Papa's behavior as immoral and disturbing but felt his difficult childhood possibly led him to conduct himself in such a way. He was her father. She loved him.

I'll always wonder about her childhood. How had she endured? How did she get over it? She didn't get therapy. She didn't even unburden herself until her husband was dead and her children had children and grandchildren of their own. I don't know why she chose that time to tell her secrets. Was it the unburdening in old age that counselors talk about? I wish I had asked her more. How could she continue to love her father? And her mother must have known something was wrong. Why didn't she help this troubled daughter? Or did she? How long did Papa carry on with that woman? Were there others? How—when—why—did he decide to stay with Muzzy and have more children? Did they love each other? He must have been a good guy if the nuns had trusted him. Had he been?

I resisted telling this story to others. Mom was private; she breasted her secrets as she did her cards. But then, I told myself, she told me, her daughter who writes. She had to suspect I would eventually divulge the secrets she had shared. At that time in her life, with what was happening in her Church and what she was reading about in books, I believe she wanted to warn me to protect my own children from sexual predators. She was concerned about her grandchildren, the next generation.

At the mangle, we talked more about Mom's early life.

"Did you like going to school, Mom?"

"Yes, and because they strongly believed in education, Muzzy and Papa sent me to Derham Hall, a Catholic boarding school in St. Paul, for my last two years of high school. The Sisters of St. Joseph of Carondelet, who taught me at St. Agnes and you at Holy Redeemer, ran it. At that time, Derham Hall was part of the College of St. Catherine. At first, I was so lonesome there. So homesick. I cried myself to sleep every night. Just like you said you would if we had sent you to a boarding school."

"Did you tell Muzzy and Papa?"

"No. By senior year, I really wanted to go on to college, but the country plunged into the Depression. Muzzy and Papa said they couldn't afford the tuition, and I had to come back home to take care of my grandparents. That was a difficult time for me. I really had wanted to go to college. A few years later, I was able to enroll at Mankato Commercial College. I took all their courses: bookkeeping, shorthand, pre-law, rapid calculations. I could add numbers—four in twenty-five rows in half a minute! After graduation, Mr. Hall hired me to be a secretary at his law office in Marshall."

"The same Mr. Hall who comes with Mrs. Hall at Christmas and gives each of us a one-dollar bill?"

"The same," Mom said.

"What about your brothers and sisters? How did they go to college?"

"I sent money to help my sisters go to St. Catherine's. My brothers went to Notre Dame. Alfred became a seminarian there in the Holy Cross Order. He drowned at the Order's retreat center in Deer Park, Maryland." (What happened to Alfred was stored deep in my imagination as a child: almost a priest—therefore revered—who drowned somewhere far away. I envisaged him choking, not turning his head to breathe in air. I imagined him trying to save his panicked friend. Had Alfred tried the right headlock? Did he ultimately try to knock his friend out? Years

Alfred Schreiber

later, after Mom gave me Alfred's diary of his early seminarian days in St. Paul, I have imagined him possibly deliberately dying with his friend.)

Mom went on. "My brother Edward died testing fighter warplanes in 1942. His plane left what is now LaGuardia Airport in New York and crashed somewhere in New Jersey."

"Both of your brothers, Mom. And all of my uncles, because Dad's brother was killed in the war, too."

"War is horrible. It was horrible."

Mom answered my question about why we weren't supposed to tell Muzzy bad or sad news. We weren't supposed to upset her because she had already suffered so much. After barely recovering from a painful miscarriage, she almost died, pregnant again with Eddie, her fifth child, while quarantined with the flu in the 1918 pandemic. A year later, when she was thirty-five, she was one of the first to receive radium treatments for woman problems at Rochester's Mayo Clinic.

"What are 'woman problems,' Mom?"

Mom stopped mangling for a minute, staring over the top of the machine. I could smell the cloth scorching underneath the rollers. "Oh, trouble after you've had kids," she said. She shook her head. "Muzzy had a tough time."

"Why hasn't she ever told us kids any of this, Mom?"

"She believed in just carrying on," Mom said, looking at me.

"Well, can't you carry on and still talk?" I said.

Mom smiled at me, then shook her head over the burned shirt she pulled out from under the mangle rollers. She threw the shirt back in the basket, picked up another, and pressed her knee against the plate, bringing the roller back down.

"I won't tell her anything bad or sad," I promised.

Beyond the traumatic events of her early years, my mother always spoke freely and honestly about her life. I especially liked it when she chatted about her early days with Dad. "I met your father at the post office. I bumped into him by accident. We introduced ourselves. I told him about my brothers graduating from Notre Dame. I heard he'd gone there, too. I . . . don't . . . quite . . . remember . . . who called whom after that meeting."

Because she paused like that and raised her eyebrows, I wondered if she had called him and suspected the meeting wasn't by chance.

"Why didn't you get married in a white dress, Mom?"

"Well . . . my mom and sisters didn't want me to spend so much money, and they thought I was too old to wear white." She looked sad and maybe a bit angry but calmly added, "And I knew I would get more use out of the blue suit, and I was crazy about that gray fox-fur jacket."

"Why did you listen to your mom and sisters? Wasn't it your money, and how old were you anyway?" I asked.

"I was twenty-nine years old, which in those days was old to be married."

"Like the Old Maid card?"

"Oh, I had a lot of suitors. I just wasn't interested in any of them."

"When did you get married, Mom?"

"Your dad and I were married in Rochester on April 10, 1939."

"How old was Dad?"

Mom didn't answer, acting busy with the clothes; she always put off questions about her and Dad's ages. She was born in 1909 and Dad in 1914. Clearly embarrassed about *robbing the cradle* (before *cougars),* she lied about her age all her life. Dad must have known, but maybe not; she lied even on her driver's license.

Mom also hadn't answered the question about why she listened to her mother and sisters. Maybe it had something to do with the discrepancy of Mom and Dad's ages, but again, after what she had told me about her childhood, I realized she must have had some deep-seated feelings about her mom and sisters. She loved them and spared them her pain, but she must have been jealous of their lives, their innocence, and their education. Also, she was separated from her sisters by age; she and Alfred, close in many ways, were just a year apart. Her sister Grace was six years younger; Rose, eight.

But no white wedding dress? It made me sad just thinking about it—Mom loved to get dressed up. There's a picture of her in the ruffled formal she wore to the Catholic Women's Guild Installation. Beautiful with her black hair swept up, without glasses, her far-set hazel eyes sparkling like the rhinestone at her neck, hanging from a black velvet ribbon. My sisters and I, *maids in waiting*, always helped pull up her girdle, pick out her shoes, put on her jewelry. We chose outfits for the Blue Moon Ballroom. She told us about the big-name bands playing there, Duke Ellington and Glenn Miller, and how she'd want to dance the night away.

"We loved the Charleston. Your dad always danced very well. One time when we were first married, we went to a Jaycee sponsored dance, and your dad won the prize for the Best Waltzer. I was pregnant so I didn't dance; his partner was Mary Eloise Stauffacher. Sometimes I could only get your dad out on the floor for a few dances because he complained of his bad back."

They must have

Alice Schreiber and Patrick Rogers on their wedding day, front row left, then Julia (Muzzy) and Edward (Papa) Schreiber; back row, l to r, John Rogers, Rose Schreiber, Merton Rogers, Grace Schreiber, and Edward Schreiber looked like quite the odd couple: he, so tall; she, so short—5'2"—as in the song they'd jitterbug to. "Five foot two, eyes of blue / But, oh, what those five feet can do."

We talked about how Mom continued to work for the law firm when they were first married because they needed money to buy an electric stove and refrigerator. She stopped after Jim was born but then did the bookkeeping for Dad's insurance business from the house: answering the phone, setting up appointments, filing the claims. Mom, a whiz at numbers—she looked at a number once and knew it forever—had hundreds, maybe even thousands stored in her head. No one ever had to look up a friend's telephone number or address, although we had a harder time making out her messages—Mom would forget and write them in shorthand. We'd try to figure out what the lines, dashes, and circles meant.

The office work got to be too much after I, the fourth child, was born. Dad told her she had to stop. I never asked why. Did Mom get too tired? Couldn't she manage as well as Dad wished? I don't think Mom would have wanted to quit. But almost all mothers stayed home then, except for the widows and the few divorced women we knew. I'm sure Mom missed being in charge of the insurance and law offices, missed discussing ideas with Mr. Hall and other lawyers, grown-up people, but I don't think she would have traded her life. She knew she couldn't do it all, and she liked being a mom.

Talking over the mangle, like talking over the ironing board, was our time. Eventually I took over the mangling, starting with hankies, then pillowcases and sheets, the flat pieces. You could easily burn your hands or crush them under the roller, and when I mangled, Mom shouted down the steps about every ten minutes, "Margaret, are you all right?"

I was fine. But I missed our time together.

Mom didn't look back with pain or sorrow. She lived through her childhood, grew strong, independent, and loving.

Alice Rogers (l) and her sister Rose Calkins at the Silver Dollar Bar in Ghent, MN

One of my favorite memories of my mom and her sister Rose was accompanying them, along with my cousin, Rose's daughter, Annie, back to Ghent in 2000. Rose was eighty-two, Mom was ninety, but you wouldn't know it: like young girls, they pointed out and named the farms of the whole surrounding area and told gossipy stories of the former inhabitants. In Ghent, they jumped out of the car and literally raced to the backyard gardens of their old homes, their grandparents' house, St. Eloi Church and Rectory, Ted's Ballroom. We had a beer at the Silver Dollar Bar, the oldest continually operating bar in Minnesota. The bartender was amazed Mom and Rose knew the old people in the sepia pictures hanging on the walls.

But what was truly amazing to me: the discussion over our beer, about Mom's one big regret in life. For the first time, my mother told her sister how disappointing it had been for her not to go to college.

Rose said, "Well, you could have, Alice. Why didn't you?"

Mom answered, "No. I couldn't, Rose. The folks made me take care of Grandpa and Grandma. And there was no money."

Rose said she hadn't known. She was sorry. Mom didn't say anything.

I had heard this regret from my mother in another way: "I should have gone to college after I raised you children. Instead of writing diaries all my life, I might have become a real writer."

Mom gave me her old L. C. Smith typewriter. It functions beautifully; she found a place in the Twin Cities that sold ribbons for it. When I look at it now, I picture Mom's head bent over it for so many years, first with full, black hair; later with thinning, dyed-brown hair; then, finally, with wispy, gray-white hair. She had typed innumerable documents for Dad and for us kids and lists and letters—Mary said that when she taught in Taiwan, Mom sent her a typed letter every week for two years.

When grandchildren came along, Mom adjusted and sent out emails—and complained of spam. "Look at this, Margaret. I have to go through all these messages before I can find the grandkids' letters. Look at this. A lot of them are dirty. It takes so long to delete all of them. What a waste of time." But she was connected. Like her mother and her grandfather, who also lived almost a complete century, she moved through tremendous changes.

Along with her typewriter, Mom gave me her diaries, saved in dusty, cardboard boxes. Mostly her entries are short and full of mundane detail about what time she got up and went to bed, the weather, the events of the day, an occasional comment on her feelings about something or other. Her earlier and later ones, however, were quite expressive in detail and description. It makes sense: she had more time to write. She had *a room of her own*. The last diary, dated 2007, is written in red ink. Her pen is stuck in the book on March 13, the day she died at ninety-seven years of age. She had been writing in her books continuously since 1972, recording events and reflections. In the late 1960s, she described trips that she and Dad took around the world. Before that, busy with children and household duties, her writing was intermittent.

My favorite diaries are the ones she kept from her high-school years through the late 1930s. Her first Regal Note Book contained entries from her boarding years at Derham Hall. On the cover, she wrote her name, Alice Schreiber, and "Peep not for it concerns you not." The entries show:

Wednesday, Sept.16, 1925
My Diary,
I had a real hard day. Came up to St. Catherine's with the folks and Dara Hennen. Dara and I are here to attend school for the term. First time I've been in Twin Cities since 7 years ago. We went to Nazareth Hall Preparatory Seminary where my brother, Alfred and friend, Emiel, attend school and then came and got registered.

Sept. 15, 1926
Starting school again at Derham Hall High School. This year I'm a senior. Margaret Regnier from Ghent, my old hometown, is to be my roommate this year.

Margaret Regnier and my mom were best friends all their lives. I remember as a child visiting the Regnier farm near Ghent. Margaret, who never married, took care of her elderly mother and father on a huge old farmstead. I remember the house as always dark with a musty smell, but the back and front yards were bright with flower and vegetable gardens and white lawn chairs overlooking vast fields.

Margaret had a distinctive voice. A schoolteacher, she spoke with a lilt and a large vocabulary. I took Mom to visit her when they were both in their nineties. Margaret led me to the old kitchen sink. "Your mother says you're writing a memoir about this area, Margie. I want you to include something about prairie grasses. Look out this window. When my parents came from France and settled this land, for as far you could see"— she swept her hand across the glass—"tall grasses waved in the wind: big bluestem, six to eight feet tall, sometimes up to twelve feet tall. Bronze in color. There were Indian grasses with plume-like heads that turned golden. Brownish switchgrass and little bluestem that went red in the fall. An ocean of color. Unbroken. Endless swaying. Imagine."

I imagined, but it was difficult to see beyond the corn-fields. Southwestern Minnesota has rich black dirt. Every inch of land has long ago been tilled for crops: mainly corn and soybeans but also hay and grains. I can never wrap my head around the vastness of the former prairie. Minnesota once had eighteen million acres of prairie stretching across the state; the patches remaining are mostly the remnants that could not be plowed.

I find the toughness of native plants also hard to believe—greater growth below the surface than above. Deep, enormous roots, sometimes three times longer than the plant, help the plant absorb even small traces of water. I find myself in this image: a sheaf of grass taking sustenance from the inborn roots of those who have gone before me, bowing in the breeze.

I discover in Mom's "Grandma's Story" under "Who were your babies named after?" her note, "Pat had an aunt Margaret McElligott and my good friend Margaret Regnier." I never met Great-aunt Margaret, one of many unknown relatives. I hope to research her story some day. But I'm proud of being named after Margaret Regnier, who was pretty, smart, funny, and indomitable.

So was my mother. And she acted as she saw fit, even if it clashed with her religious beliefs. When I developed phlebitis after my second child was born and had difficulties again after my third, Mom called and asked if she could come over for coffee. She sat across from me at my kitchen table. "Do you believe in birth control, Margaret?" When I nodded, she said, "I think that's fine. You don't need to have any more children if you don't want to."

Mom did *not* demand perfection of herself or her children. I love that for one whole summer when I was nine she let me wear an old, buttons-missing red vest, which for some reason I was attached to; I never took it off.

I wore it learning to press the flat pieces on the mangle. Perched on the old red chair, knee hopping in and out, I was proud of my pressing power. Proud of my smooth, straight work. I began to sing like Mom, "And now we are aged and gray, Maggie / And the trials of life nearly done / Let us sing of the days that are gone, Maggie / When you and I were young."

A WORKER IN A CHAPEAU

No one got in Mom's way. Clothes and bedding, food and house—fresh was best, and it required work. She tackled the weekly cleaning with a white kerchief on her head, a mop or dust rag in her hand. She rushed through the house, swishing in every corner, swiping every surface. Monthly, she scrubbed floors by hand, pulling the pail and her knee cushions along from the front to the back of each room. Yearly, she washed windows with newspaper and vinegar. She polished them inside and out until they squeaked.

We were supposed to help; we all had our duties, but we grumbled, "It's not my turn," "I did it last time." Sometimes we really got going, pushing or shoving or chasing one another around: "I DID IT LAST TIME." "YOU DID NOT." "I DID, TOO." If we threatened to take our battles outside, Mom shouted, "Don't you dare fight where the entire world can see and hear you. You fight inside!" She wanted the neighbors to think of us as good kids, not *ruffians*.

Mom didn't like us kids to fight. As soon as my older brothers started to wrestle, she'd run for the old frying pan, the heavy black one. Pounding on its iron bottom with a spoon, she'd yell at the boys, "Stop it! Stop it, I say. Right now! *Stop it.* I'll have to tell your father." If the boys kept brawling, she ordered, "Girls, to your posts." Mary and I grabbed our assigned tables and lamps, protecting them until the boys finally quit.

Then, everything back to normal, we got on with our chores.

One of the jobs I liked was cleaning the throw rugs. I hung them over the clotheslines and whipped them soundly with the old gray wire beater. Whack. Take that. Make it a double whack. Make it a triple. Whack. Whack. Whack. When I took too long with the rugs, Mom came out to help. As she beat them, the sunlight bounced off her diamond wedding ring and broke through the dust cloud billowing above her head.

The gravel roads smelled of that same mix of dust and sun when Mom would load us all in the car and head out into the country in the spring. Sitting on pillows so she could see over the hood, hands gripping the wheel, back straight, she would stop suddenly, snapping the backseat riders into the upholstery, the front-seaters into the dashboard. "Quick, over by the fence," she'd call out. We'd sprint across the ditch to pick wild asparagus growing by the side of the road.

In the summer, we loved to go to the Van Nuytten farm to buy fresh eggs and chickens, loved swinging on the towering tree in front of the farmhouse. The swing, made of an old, soggy mattress, could hold the farm kids and all seven of us. We tumbled on it and giggled and pumped, our legs hanging over the edges. "Pump. Pump to Heaven. Pump. Pump to Heaven," we sang. We swung to the oak's top branches. We sailed into the sky.

There were also haystacks to climb and hide around. Once my brother Jim fell through the middle of one, and we ran for Mom. She and Mr. Van Nuytten carefully poked the haystack with a pitchfork to find Jim. When they finally pulled him out, he could hardly breathe. He had asthma. Mom washed his face and held his hands, all the time talking to him softly, "Breathe, Jimmy, breathe. That's it. Just relax. You'll be all right."

As soon as Jim's face had changed from blue to white and Mom's worry lines had smoothed to smiles, we hurried off to play. There were cats and kittens and dogs and puppies. And chickens. We tore into the coop with sticks; the chickens squawked and jumped and tried to fly, fluttering feathers all around. Mr. Van Nuytten chased in after us, hollering, "You can't play in the hen house."

Mom crated some chickens home. In our backyard, she stretched their necks across the stained tree stump and lifted the sharp hatchet. The still-living chickens ran around with their heads cut off. An awful act. Mom plunged them into a vat of boiling water and presented them to us, their blood still dripping on the grass. We plucked off their wet, stinky feathers. Mom finished off the massacre by setting a rolled newspaper on fire to singe the pinfeathers. Ugh. The smell. Like rotten garbage and spoiled milk mixed together. "Hold your noses, kids," Mom said. She hated the smell as much as we did, but she liked freezing most of the chickens and fixing one—very fresh—for supper that night. I never could eat it, remembering how it was killed. For years, I didn't eat chicken.

In June or early July, we'd take a trip to a strawberry patch outside of town. Mom picked fast, three boxes to our one. She then doubled back to our rows whispering, "Eat as many as you want. They're free while you pick. Eat. Eat them now." We ate and ate and rode home from those trips more sick than tired.

Mom planted two packages of every vegetable seed in her garden. We kids had to hoe, weed, water, and harvest. We hated it. Mom loved it. She loved dirt: "Isn't it wonderful, the smell and feel?" Under the spade, in her hands, she didn't care if what she was digging was dry dust or wet globs. Wearing her wide-brimmed straw hat, her apron with the deep front pockets filled with seeds, she complained about not having enough time outdoors. "The inside work keeps me too busy."

Even though we hated garden work, we liked its fresh taste: crunchy sweet peas in their shells, raw beans, rhubarb pies and sauces, cukes vinegared to pickles, swiss chard steamed in the pressure cooker.

Our corn never grew well so we carted bushel baskets home from nearby farms. The first twenty-four ears we ate right away. There was nothing as tasty as that first August feast, nothing else served but ears and ears of fresh corn smothered in butter and salt. The rest was frozen in groups of twelve, set aside for later.

We picked, cleaned, and measured all the garden vegetables into plastic bags and carried them down to the double-size freezer in the basement, which also held the butcher-wrapped side of beef, labeled in handwritten black ink, HAMBURGER, STEAK, LIVER, ROAST. The meat and chickens took up the left side of the freezer, vegetables the center, and on the right, set neatly in a row, large canisters of store-bought ice cream. I sneaked spoonfuls right out of the tall cardboard cartons, labeled like the meat: CHOCOLATE, VANILLA, STRAWBERRY. I dug through the freezer burn to the softer folds underneath. I hid my big serving spoon on the shelf above the freezer.

Every Sunday we kids got to make our own super-duper desserts. We usually used ice cream as our base, adding other ingredients: Hershey's chocolate syrup, strawberry or raspberry sauces, nuts, bananas, candied cherries. We sometimes added hot puddings or baked bars. We had the run of the kitchen. It always got messy. We tried to clean it up, but there was always a sticky residue on everything.

On special days, we helped Mom and Dad jam rock salt and ice into the ice bucket around a custard of cream, sugar, and eggs. We cranked the handle of the dasher over and over and over, until we had the best homemade ice cream.

The best and worst of all chores happened in late summer when it was hot, really hot. Mom bustled about, insisting, "I won't let the heat get me down." She lugged crates of peaches, plums, and pears into the house. She hauled up canning kettles, Mason jars, metal lids and rings from the basement. With a crowbar, she pried the tops off the wooden crates. "Girls, get the water boiling. Now lower the fruit into the water. Careful, don't let it splatter. Quick now, take it out. Use the big ladle. You're wonderful, such good helpers."

Only Mary and I canned. The boys got out of it; they were supposed to mow the lawn and do other outdoor chores.

Sometimes Mom told stories while we canned. One time, when I was twelve and Mary fourteen, between boiling and blanching she told us about her trip to Europe in 1938. I think about it every time I eat a bowl of fresh plums. I remember Mom's voice telling the story. It all blended in—the sweetness, the freshness, the bottles, the seals.

"I made that trip when I was twenty-eight years old, single and carefree. I wanted to see the world and to have fun, a last fling before I settled down. I had already bought my own car, a Model A Ford. It was a beautiful turquoise with an ivory cloth roof and a rumble seat so I could take my friends for rides. I saved over two years for it, setting aside half my paycheck, $12.50, every month. I bought it in 1933, and it cost $300. Imagine! I scrimped some more until I had saved up the $1000 dollars for the trip overseas. Mr. Hall gave me a month's leave of absence from the law firm."

At the kitchen table, Mary and I were peeling the skin off the fruit, trying not to squeeze it to death. Mom pared her plums round and whole.

"I said goodbye to your dad. It was beginning to be serious between us. There were others, but I knew your dad was the one. A tall, handsome bachelor, new in town, starting his own business—and he was interested in me. When we first met, he said he thought I was Irish. Can you imagine—with a name like Schreiber." Mom stopped skinning and smiled.

"Go on, Mom," we urged, cutting the pits out and then the plums into halves or quarters. We dropped the pulp into the jars.

"Well, we were getting close, but I wanted one last fling. I went alone. Planned the trip with American Express. They've been around forever, but they were a lot more helpful then, even sending agents to meet me at the railroad stations and escort me to hotels."

Alice Schreiber next to a life boat on the SS Gerolstein

"Did you go by train, Mom?" Mary asked. She hurried to the stove and the boiling kettles to help stir sugar water to a syrup.

"I traveled by everything. In France, it was motor coaches; in Italy, old-fashioned horse-drawn carriages; canal boats in Holland; the gondola in Venice. I crossed the span from Paris to London in seventy-five minutes by airplane. We sailed over on the ocean liner, *SS Gerolstein*, from Pier D at Weehawken, New Jersey, on June 17, 1938. After ten days on the water, we docked at Rotterdam, Holland. Girls, you would have loved it. Huge. Flags unfurling in the wind." She swung the ladle in the air. "And fun onboard—you could swim, play shuffleboard or tennis, read and lounge on the canvas deck chairs. I played bridge every morning, dined and danced late into the night. So many fascinating people to meet." Mom smiled again, lifting her head high.

I was entranced by Mom's story, which sounded like a fairy tale. Nothing was more exciting to me than travel except reading books—although they fascinated mostly by where they took me. Mom continued her magical story while Mary and I poured juice over the scalded fruit. Mom held the heated jars with a towel as she placed the metal lids on their tops and then screwed on the metal rings, tightly sealing the jars.

"Europe. I hope some day you'll get there. Girls, it was all so beautiful, the cities as well as the little towns in the country. My stay in Venice: the moon full at night, the sky grander than anywhere in the world, the lights sparkling on the water. Of course, in the daylight, the reality was dirty water in the canals and old decaying buildings. In Florence, there was a siesta from noon to three in the afternoon. The people were more deliberate there; even their speech was slower. I talked so much faster than the Italians. I liked the English. They were sympathetic to the Germans and said they liked us Americans. I got to see the King and Queen of England on their official visit to France. A British newspaperman let me act as his secretary."

"What did that mean, Mom?" I asked.

"It meant I could be part of the action. On top of the Arc de Triomphe in Paris, the parade passed directly beneath me." She took her hands from the jars and swung her towel. "The Queen looked quite charming. She wore white lace. The visit, of course, had great political significance, joining these two nations."

"Joining them for what?" Mary asked.

"England and France agreed to allow Adolf Hitler keep a country called Czechoslovakia as long as he didn't try to expand anywhere else."

Slowly, Mom's smile faded to a frown. "Some of the landscape still haunts me. I especially remember the French countryside, the battlefields of the First World War: shell craters, dugouts, and tangled barbed wire. Twenty years after, it still looked like a no-man's land. Fear of exploding shells still kept people from cultivating the land. And then there was Germany. I was in Munich the day Hitler rallied there. The papers were full of that little man shouting at mobs of people. I couldn't read German so I didn't understand."

"Sister Amatus told us about Hitler," I said. "She said he was a horrible man."

"Were you afraid, Mom?" I asked.

"No. I just never dreamed of what was to come. I didn't know much about Hitler at the time. There was a lot of building in Germany and military parades were forever going by. The Nazis had a No Cosmetics Edict, and even little children were dressed in military uniforms. I'll never forget that summer of '38, seeing all those soldiers marching and marching through the cities."

Mom wiped away any last stickiness from the jars with a wet dishrag. "I came back on the *Westernland* of the Red Star Line, leaving Southampton, England, and landing in New York. I had $17 left, enough for a telephone call to Muzzy—her birthday—and a bus trip back to St. Paul. I carried all my gifts, something for everybody, and wore the only thing I bought for myself, a floppy felt hat from Paris. Muzzy and Papa and your dad were all waiting for me at the bus station. I didn't know your dad was coming. He said he started out late from Marshall and drove like a madman. Muzzy and Pop were furious when I drove off with him. What a trip!"

"You mean your trip home, Mom, or your trip to Europe?"

"Both, dear," she said, smiling.

I already knew a lot of Mom's story. I had snooped in her top dresser drawer, where she kept important papers, and found the diary of her trip. Dad's letters were also in the drawer. I read them, hoping for romantic love letters. Nah. Mom should have run off with the German captain of the ship, who wanted to seat her at the head table with him, or the Irish Yale professor, or the guy from the State Department, or the American Consul to France. Dad wrote only about how hard he was working, signing off, "Very tired, Love, Pat."

There were pictures of Mom in the drawer, standing by her car, waving from the ship. Slim. Almond-shaped eyes. High cheekbones. Bobbed black, wavy hair. She wore high heels, silk blouses, stylish skirts and jackets. Wild hats—huge, brocaded rims; tiny-ribboned bowlers. She was beautiful. A princess.

That was not the way she looked working in our steamy kitchen, her sweaty face burning red, her old smocked apron stained by purple, yellow, and orange juices. Her hands ruined. At the beginning, when she sterilized the glass jars, lifting them to the light looking for cracks, the fingers that ran around the rims checking for chips were white and smooth. By the end, her hands were blistered shiny red from the slimy, scorching fruit, her fingernails split, blunt, and broken. Yet when I watched her canning, I could somehow see that young woman reflected in the jars.

And come winter, when she sent us down to the cellar to choose from the pantry shelves any jar we wanted for lunch, we ate the fruit with her fresh-baked gingersnaps or sugar cookies, and it was so good. Better than fresh corn or stolen ice cream. Better, right then, than Europe.

In 1994, Mom and I traveled to Germany for Oktoberfest and to Austria and Hungary with a parish group that volunteered at Patty's group home. Mom was in her eighties; I was in my forties. The trip was a mixed bag of fun and frustration: I was used to traveling on my own so this first large bus tour was difficult for me, and I found myself guiding the older ladies of the group because they clung to Mom and me. They ended up being the highlight of the trip, however, demonstrating stamina and good humor through Hofbrauhauses, museums, and long, song-filled bus rides.

This was the first extensive trip I'd taken with Mom in a long time. During the whole tour, she seemed to lose things; she'd misplace her hearing aids, her billfold, her purse, her pills in her purse. She mislaid things even in her small suitcase. "I don't know where it is; it's not here."

The last night in Vienna, I came out of the bathroom attached to our bedroom to find her stark naked.

"What the hell, Mom. Where's your nightie?"

"Packed, Margaret. I won't have to find anything or pack anything in the morning. It's all set."

Mom wrote about the trip in one of her diaries. The cover reflected Mom and her tastes: a black cotton covered with pink pansies, blue petunias, yellow cornflower, and Carolina pucoons mixed with colorful fruits and vegetables. In this multicolored cover of life, I found this entry: *This was my first time in Salzburg, Vienna and Budapest, so I'm very grateful for a fabulous trip, and I've gotten to know my daughter Marge a little better and to appreciate her more. We get along well together. And I do try not to talk so loud and unnecessarily."*

Shamefaced, I realized how impatient, how cross I must have been at times. More than anything, though, I regretted never getting to travel with her again. She was a great traveling companion, even keeled, game to try things.

Mom believed in doing good and keeping busy. She was a philanthropist and a hospital volunteer for almost fifty years. She cared for and enjoyed her daughter with Down syndrome and her son with mental illness. She spent time with her children and grandchildren and her many friends. She gave herself to others. Her giving influenced me to join the convent; I wanted to give myself to others, too. Mom also inspired me by being good friends with a number of sisters, laughing and joking with them, supporting their activities. Through her eyes, I saw nuns as normal people. I imitated my mother instinctively when I was younger, but not until I had children of my own did I fully realize her impact on my life. Now, I'm pleased when my children say I'm becoming her.

THE MICK

It was never easy to get details of Dad's life. He could, and would, talk about anything—except the past. "We never look back, only forward in time," he'd say. I have pieced together the story of his early life from the little he offered and whatever Mom told me about him.

Dad came from a poor family. At five years of age, Waldron Patrick Rogers was shining shoes at Barnum's Drugstore and digging sugar beets from fields near Glencoe, a small Minnesota town an hour west of the Twin Cities. He had only one sibling, a younger brother, John Edward.

A scrappy kid, called *Mick*, Dad took on not only the Protestant children but also the German Catholics. (Tiny Glencoe sustained two Catholic parishes: the Irish St. George's and the German St. Peter and Paul's.) Dad spent most of his elementary-school days studying outside the principal's office; in the seventh grade, Sister transferred him from St. George's to the public school.

Amazed when he told me this, I said, "Dad, you didn't practice what you preach. Imagine if any of us got kicked out of school. What would you do?"

"You kids are way too smart for that. I don't have to worry. You're not going to be like your old man."

I wondered how he could possibly have fought about religion with his young Catholic classmates; they all believed the same doctrines, received the same sacraments. I assumed these children fought their parents' battles: the German Krauts against the drunken Irish. Their second-generation immigrant experience differed from mine: in Holy Redeemer Grade School and Central Catholic High School, Catholics were now united together, different nationalities into one religious group. Dad's kind of immigrant experience had vanished.

Sports turned out to be Dad's salvation. A star in basketball, he was treated as a celebrity after Glencoe won the state basketball championship in 1931. Dad said Glencoe opened its heart to the players. The town celebrated with a huge banquet, giving each of the players a small gold basketball. "They went crazy when we won. Hell, a lot of them had bet on us, won $200 to $300, which was quite a bit in those days. No kidding, Peggy, I walked the streets like a movie star. Bartenders offered me free drinks. Retail stores, complimentary clothes. Businessmen, jobs. Girls, dates."

I couldn't imagine superstardom status for a high school player. I also couldn't imagine how basketball was played in those days. Dad said Glencoe won the state tournament by absolutely annihilating Buffalo, 22-14! Dad led the game with nine points. He said, "The players of today are bigger and stronger, but we played in four tournaments that year and made three mechanical errors. You get that many in a minute now." But he did admit, "Of course they go a lot faster now. They shoot

MINNESOTA HIGH SCHOOL
BASKETBALL CHAMPIONSHIP TEAM
1931---GLENCOE

Waldron Rogers, Henry Thoene, Glenn Barnum, LeRoy Karsnens, Robert Lindner, Capt. Walter Kruger, James Baker, Arvid Braunsten, Mehlor Leetns

Waldron Patrick Rogers, first on the left

the ball a lot more. If we had a one-point lead on a team, they were in trouble. A three-point lead in those days and the game was practically over."

Winning the tournament was remarkable for Dad, but "Hell, I wasn't a basketball player. I was 6'3"—that was tall then—so they put me on the basketball team. I really was a football player, and Glencoe, wild about sports, was a football town. A big crowd came to the practices every day from four o'clock to eight." Dad captained the team through undefeated seasons.

Scouts from Notre Dame recruited him. All his life, Dad reverently mentioned meeting Knute Rockne, "the greatest coach in college football history." Both Rockne and Dad had played as ends for Notre Dame. Dad's idea of team play and unselfish sacrifice was an echo of Rockne's philosophy. I hear my dad through him: "Every play. Under control. Every play. Today is the day. Win or lose, do it fairly."

When Dad went to college, he reversed his names, becoming Patrick Waldron Rogers. During his second year at Notre Dame, Pat Rogers injured his back and lost his scholarship. He didn't know what caused his bad back. Disintegrating discs? Arthritis? Scoliosis? He told me once that he had back pain even as a kid. He could remember crying at night on the front porch of his house, where he slept—his mother put heated bricks under the mattress in the winter. He would suffer from his bad back his whole life, sometimes barely able to walk. He would try all kinds of cures, once almost burning himself up as he experimented with a Mexican hot-wax treatment. He showed a certain naiveté and gullibility for wacky treatments, plus an eternal commitment to a good sales pitch.

After losing his scholarship, Dad returned to Minnesota and enrolled at the University, where he also worked at the bookstore and as a stadium guard. "Some of those games could get rough. We'd have to patrol some heavy drinkers." On weekends, he sold women's shoes at the Dayton's store in downtown

Minneapolis. Because of that experience, he always made me and my sisters buy the best arch-supported shoes. He'd shop with us, asking the salesman on the floor for the steel measuring plate so he could get our exact length and width himself. "It's so important, girls. You need great arches," he'd say. He picked awful shoes.

For free room and board, he supervised athletics at Margaret Berry House, a settlement home for delinquent boys on the east side of Minneapolis. "They really weren't tough, just so goddamn poor. It was the Depression. Everybody was so poor, you couldn't believe it. I was lucky to have any job at all. I didn't get very good grades at the U. Barely graduated. I'd cut classes to work for another ten cents an hour at the employment office on campus."

Jenny Waldron Rogers

While Dad was at the University, his mother, Jenny, only fifty-three years old, developed throat cancer. Dad adored his mother—Mom said Dad probably never would have married her if Jenny hadn't died; he would have done anything to make his mother's life easier. He helped get her into an experimental program at the University Hospital. Mom said, "Jenny had worked so hard and then died after a tough, lingering battle."

Devastated by his mother's death, Dad finished his studies, graduating in accounting from the business school in 1935. He heard about an insurance agency for sale in southwestern Minnesota; moved to Marshall; met and married Mom, "the most wonderful gal in the world"; and started his own business "with this beautiful woman by my side keeping the books."

When World War II started, Dad was exempt because he and Mom already had three children. His brother John died protecting the field radio, the soldiers' lifeline, at the Battle of Anzio in Italy. He was awarded a Purple Heart from the Army and a Silver Star Medal from the Armed Forces for gallantry in action. When I asked Dad about John, who was a clothier in Glencoe and a bartender in Minneapolis, Dad smiled and exclaimed, "Everybody loved him! A winning personality."

When I set out for Europe after my first year of teaching, Dad asked me to please visit the American Cemetery in Nettuno, Italy, about thirty miles south of Rome, to find his brother John's grave—I'd be the first in the family to pay respects. Because I didn't speak Italian, and it was difficult to figure out how to get to Nettuno on the train, and I was too busy with my own agenda—I had met a handsome Italian architect, who was squiring me around Rome—I didn't get there. I didn't think much about it. But when I got back home, the first thing Dad said to me at the airport, his face one big expectation, was: "Did you see Johnny's grave?" When I said no, his face collapsed. He turned away, excusing himself. Suddenly I realized how much I had let him down. I didn't know what to say or do. I let Mom chatter away. Soon Dad re-entered the conversation, but he didn't mention his brother or Nettuno again.

Years later, I visited Nettuno with my husband. We drove on an interminable road by the sea in a rented car without air-conditioning on an extremely hot day. It took us sweaty hour after hour to get there. Once there we were overwhelmed. The World War II Sicily-Rome American Cemetery and Memorial site in Italy covered seventy-seven acres. There was a broad pool with an island and a monument flanked by Italian cypress trees and beyond the pool an enormous field of headstones of 7,861 American military war dead arranged on green lawns beneath rows of Roman pines. As far as you could see in any direction: simple white crosses and whole acres of land set aside for unknown soldiers. We found Johnny's grave. I couldn't stop crying, not only over his death and all these dead men and the futility of war but also remembering my father's buckled face. I had so let him down.

Six months after Dad's brother John was killed, his father, Merton, died of a heart attack. He was sixty-four. Dad said his father's heart was broken over John's death. Dad's eyes showed he was broken by both their deaths. His whole family gone so quickly.

I can't imagine losing my family. I'm sure the pain of his loss was why Dad didn't want to look into the past and why he retained so few memorabilia of his family. There are few pictures: Jenny's boarding house; Merton's work trailer and road crew; one of my great-uncle Patrick (Pat) and great-aunt Bridget (Bea); a baby picture of Dad and John; a graduation picture of Dad and a military picture of John.

One item Dad did save and treasure was his family's framed copy of the "1916 Proclamation of the Irish Republic": "Poblacht Na H Eireann. The Provisional Government Of The Irish Republic To The People Of Ireland. Irishmen and Irishwomen: In the name of God and of the dead generations from which she receives her old tradition of nationhood, Ireland, through us, summons her children, to her flag and strikes for her freedom." (A proud tradition. Feminist, too: the heritage of free Irishwomen.)

Taped to the back of this proclamation was a census dated 1851 in Templecrone, County Donegal: "Michael and Peggey Rodgers, married; farmer and wool spinner; neither can read or write, speak only Gaelic. Son, Patrick, age thirteen, reads, writes."

Driven out of Ireland—generally by poverty and unproductivity caused by centuries of colonial rule and particularly by the Famine—Patrick, my great-grandfather, was one of the millions of *victim diasporas*. A collective memory of an overwhelming sadness. No wonder my father, his father, and his grandfather didn't want to look back but only forward in time.

My great-grandfather emigrated to Coaldale, Pennsylvania; eventually Patrick Rogers (the *d* was dropped, nobody knew where or how) and his wife, Sarah, left the coal mines and pushed west to the Scottish settlement of Glencoe, where they raised their family, barely eking out a living farming. Merton Daniel Rogers was born on the Glencoe farm in 1880, one of eleven children, nine of whom lived into adulthood.

We kids grew up knowing only Dad's Uncle Pat and Aunt Bea in Glencoe. We'd visit them at Christmas. Sometimes I'd get to stay with them in the summer for a week. Uncle Pat had once been married to a schoolteacher, but she died very young, and from that time on, he had lived with his sister. Aunt Bea wouldn't let me make any noise early in the morning because "Uncle Pat is sleeping." He was a kind, gentle man, who liked to drink too much. He had taken the Pledge to stop, but it hadn't worked. Dad said he himself had stopped drinking because of Uncle Pat and because of what he had heard about his Grandpa Waldron, who could turn mean and ugly after drinking.

Aunt Bea let me walk downtown by myself—only two or three blocks—to go window-shopping. Sometimes she came along with me, stopping at her friends' dress and millinery store. Aunt Bea, a big woman, seemed like a ship next to these friends, the paddle-thin Shamla sisters. I loved their hats, made right on the spot, with all sorts of ribbons, netting, silk flowers, and plastic fruit.

From the front porch of Aunt Bea's duplex, I could sneak looks at the television set of her downstairs tenants—a real treat because we didn't own a TV. I also played canasta with Aunt Bea and her live-in helper friend, Mrs. Levens, on a card table they'd set up every night in the living room. They would let me win sometimes, melding and melding.

On the other side of the kitchen, opposite Uncle Pat's room, tucked in the eave, was the pantry—low ceilinged, you couldn't stand up straight in it—with a brown cookie jar beyond its white door. The jar was always full, and Aunt Bea let me reach in and help myself, anytime. But best of all, she sewed for me: a white towel with a black lamb, embroidered on the bottom with "MARG." (there wasn't room for my full name), and clothes for my dolls—a whole wardrobe of panties and slips, dresses, skirts and blouses, summer and winter coats, and hats. Some she knitted or crocheted. She even designed a little suitcase to keep them all in. My children and grandchildren have all slept under the pink quilt Aunt Bea made for me and my sisters.

I loved Aunt Bea. I wished I had known the other great-uncles and aunts. I think they settled in the Twin Cities. We didn't know any of them. Maybe it was simply distance that divided us or maybe a sophisticated-city / country-bumpkin kind of thing, but Dad once mentioned something about an uncle coming back from the War with a social disease and something about a will being swindled by another. Dad's father refused to have anything to do with these brothers, and Dad apparently followed suit. When Aunt Bea was dying, I overheard Mom telling Dad to remove the special things they wanted from Aunt Bea's house before the *others* descended on the helpless woman. I didn't know exactly who these *others* were, but I do know they were folks like my dad, like me. Family.

The Waldrons, from Roscommon County, immigrated during the Potato Famine sometime in the 1840s and moved to a farm near Green Isle, Minnesota, about fifteen miles from Glencoe. Jane (Jenny) Waldron was the last of twelve children. As with the Rogers, I knew only two Waldron families while I was growing up. Two out of twelve. Mom speculated the falling-out must have happened when Dad's mother died. Dad wanted her body studied at the University of Minnesota to determine the effect of the experimental drug they used to treat her throat cancer. Jenny's brothers and sisters removed her body from the hospital and had her buried in the Glencoe cemetery. Dad never forgave them.

What a loss. I can't imagine not speaking to aunts or uncles or cousins. But I also can't imagine so many to speak to—twenty-three aunts and uncles, not counting their spouses or children. Such a clan!

My mother displayed Jenny's dishes on the shelves of the white corner cabinets in our dining room. She cherished the white, semiporcelain pieces in a royal Brooklyn pattern, dark-and-light-blue scrolls and flowers etched with gold. Well preserved, sturdy and serviceable, unlike the ones from Aunt Bea, which were orange-and-white Japanese hand-painted dishes with an opalescent swirl of color, fragile, with tiny cracked veins. Just a salvaged assortment. I love both sets of remnant dishes, the only tangible connection to my Irish relatives.

I like to be connected. It's important for me to think of my relatives in the countries they left. Some part of me carries the characteristics of those folks living in those native lands. I also like knowing about their immigrant lives in the States. What they did. Who they became. From grilling my dad, I knew Jenny was a great cook, ran a boarding house for teachers, almost died

Grandfather Merton Rogers and Great-Uncle Patrick Rogers on the far right

in childbirth, had fun with Dad and John, and was loved by the whole town of Glencoe. I think she must have been an elegant lady. I know I'd have liked her. And my grandfather, too: Merton, who built roads, logged trees, sold horses and cars, watched his boys play ball, served on the school board, worked for his son. A rugged, easygoing gentleman.

Searching for roots and stems, wondering *Who am I? Where am I going?* I once wrote these lines:

> Beginning goes back,
> back through the genetic line,
> back to the crossing over,
> back to Ireland.
>
> Leaving behind their potatoes and their peat,
> their poverty, ignorance, and oppression,
> they came, risking all,
> for their children
> and a more nurturing land.

THE ENTREPRENEUR

Marshall is a town of challenge...its people are constantly looking for the best. In its public and parochial schools, Marshall has attained its goal.

PAT ROGERS

from Pat Rogers' "Marshall . . . the Agricultural Emerald of Bountiful Minnesota"

D ad always had ideas. In the 1940s, he organized newspaper boys to sell the morning *Minneapolis Tribune* in Marshall. He wanted to connect his small town with the Twin Cities, to bridge the distance of 150 miles, four driving hours. He believed in a larger city, a larger state, a larger world. It was important to him that people knew what was happening, that they developed ideas of their own concerning national and international issues. He believed in education and personal initiative. In a guest editorial for the *Marshall Messenger* in 1945, he wrote: "I wonder how many of the readers of this newspaper really appreciate the heritage that is theirs living in the southwestern part of Minnesota where the soil is black, where many religious denominations are represented and where education has its proper place in the lives of our young folks."

Sixty-nine years later, in 2014, Marshall was recognized

as a land of opportunity in a major study of income mobility by economists from Harvard University and University of California, Berkeley. "The rate at which kids born there move from the bottom 20 percent of household income into the top 20 percent is about 18.4 percent . . . It's about community, and where you grow up really does matter." Just as Dad would have said: "It takes integrated housing that doesn't sprawl; *social capital*, meaning a lot of adults working together in voluntary organizations like churches and community organizations; good schools and higher local tax rates which fund them; the rate of two-parent families."

A civic leader in the 1950s, Dad helped build the grain elevator on Main Street and five houses in the new Soucy neighborhood near Calvary Catholic Cemetery, the first suburb of a town of less than six thousand. The elevator was necessary for the booming farming community, and the new houses were needed for the new families coming into Marshall. Its population was growing because of several large production companies, the food-processing plant and the Schwan Food Company, which eventually became the largest branded frozen-food company in the United States and the second-largest privately held firm in Minnesota. The yellow truck delivering ice cream and Red Baron, Tony's, and Freschetta pizzas to neighborhoods across the United States for more than fifty years—with annual sales currently about $3 billion—is still managed from Marshall.

In the late 1950s, Dad set up a tower on the hills of Lynd to receive better TV reception for low-lying Marshall. He negotiated bringing a cable in from Sioux Falls, South Dakota. As part of that deal, he sold black and white Zeniths. He sold some sets right out of our house, which meant we finally got a TV of our own, something we'd wanted for a long time. Of course Mom and Dad always maintained that we liked listening to the radio. Which we did. My favorite feature shows were *The Romance of Helen Trent*—"Can a girl from a mining town in Montana find happiness as the wife of a rich, titled English lord?"—

and *The Shadow*—"The Shadow . . . knows . . . "—and *Your Hit Parade*. But nothing on radio compared to watching Elvis Presley on the *Ed Sullivan Show*. That was monumental change. I remember sitting next to Dad on the couch. "What the hell?" he said. Exhilarated, I answered back, "What the hell!"

Dad always enthusiastically supported salespeople and their products. He made money that way. His main job, which he conceived, designed, and developed, was to run one of the first low-cost health-insurance programs for individual and small-group employers. Realizing small employers could not receive as good a health package as the larger corporations, he merged small groups to make one big group and then sought a company to insure it. He founded the Employers Group Agency in 1947. In 1961, it became the Upper Midwest Employers Association and then in 1970, Pat Rogers Associates. All my brothers worked in Dad's business for a period of time. Jim and John continue to manage the company, now called Rogers' Benefit Group, which employs over 350 people.

Wildly successful, Dad's insurance company expanded from Marshall to the rest of Minnesota; to neighboring states South Dakota, North Dakota, Iowa, and Wisconsin; then to the whole country. With his tremendous energy, Dad traveled to all of these states, selling his product. It was a grueling life, demanding stamina, concentration, and heart. I wonder if Dad ever found himself lonely, weary-tired, tempted to stray from mission and home, a Willy Loman on the road. As Charley in *Death of a Salesman* says, "A salesman . . . [is] a man way out there in the blue, riding on a smile and a shoeshine." Along the way, like Willy, Dad denied troubles and woe; unlike Willy, Dad achieved; his formula of hard work and earnest intentions pushed him forward into financial success. The American Dream played out in Dad's field.

But I remember him sometimes nervous and anxious, trying to unwind after a long day at the office, or after he'd gotten back from a business trip, staying up late at night, eating bowls of saltine crackers with milk. Sometimes he'd get up very early in the morning, smoke cigarette after cigarette, drink cup after cup of coffee.

He didn't get angry often, but when he did, he could be explosive. He punished me once, when I was about twelve and angry with Mom. She was cleaning in the living room, and I yelled at her from the kitchen, "I hate you, I really hate you," as Dad walked in the back door.

"What did you say?" he asked.

"Well, *she* said . . . "

"Who said?"

"*She* said."

He slapped me across the face. "Who said?"

I shook, utterly shocked, then realized he wanted me to speak of Mom respectfully. But I was hurt and stubborn. "*She* said."

He slapped me again. "Who said?"

Mom came running into the kitchen. "Pat. Stop. Not in the face."

Hating both of my parents, I ran upstairs to cry in my bedroom. I don't remember if any of us said we were sorry later, but we must have. Or maybe we didn't and just pretended it hadn't happened. Frightening thoughts. But perhaps *frightened* is the wrong word—*heightened* might be better—memories recalled so vividly. Me: preteen, pushing limits. Dad: indeed pushed beyond his limits emotionally. Still, I hope we said we were sorry.

Always the optimist, Dad expressed an endless enthusiasm for life. He never lost his fascination with something different and new, especially the latest in technology and gadgets. After teaching in various high schools, Mary worked for a summer in one of Dad's affiliated Chicago offices. She became very excited about the Black Box, an instrument developed by a research friend of Management Programs Inc. Dad believed it was a brilliant idea—measuring people's activity levels, their degrees of introversion or extraversion, by reading their hands in a box.

Dad thought he could use it as a hiring tool. He brought it home to show us. It was a sort of Ouija board, a simple two-paddle device into which you placed your hands. I don't remember how it scored, but I registered equally outgoing and reclusive, which I must admit matched up with my later Myers-Briggs personality-test scores. As with so many of Dad's ideas, I never knew what happened to the Black Box, if it ever was used.

In 1959, when I was fourteen years old, Dad created the CASS plan. It may well have been the first driver's-training program in Minnesota; it was surely a precursor of good-grade deductions. Dad sold insurance companies on giving cheaper premiums to high-school students taught to drive by trained college students. Our whole family got involved with the project. We all chatted with the college students who came over to pick up the huge driving manuals we had collated, section by section, on our kitchen, dining room, and den tables. At first I was shy with the students—they were so sophisticated—but they were also nice and told me about their schools and majors, even their parties.

CASS was so much more fun than PEP, the last product I'd sold for Dad, when I was ten years old. Dad had invested in a Christmas tree-preserving product concocted by a young man he met somewhere, perhaps at the Toastmaster's Club. Wanting to encourage my selling ability, he'd paid me five cents for each bottle of PEP I sold. I trudged door to door in the cold and snow, fingers freezing, carrying a cardboard box of bottles, grateful if the neighbors let me inside. "PEP will keep your Christmas tree greener longer and your houseplants, too. Just mix a few tablespoons in with your water," I pitched. Inspired by Dad's PEP rally—"Go get 'em, honey!"—I sold a lot of bottles.

CASS was a huge step up: I could take phone messages from parents and enroll their children. I impressed them with my witty talk and proficiency in filling out forms. I'd rattle off the meaning of the acronym, the program's Four Point Philosophy: **C**ompeting for the honor of being a good driver; **A**ppreciating law, order, and discipline; **S**elf-asserting the best always; **S**erving others and yourself.

An article about CASS was printed in the *Minneapolis Sunday Tribune* on July 16, 1961. There was a picture of Dad, the father of the National Merit Drivers association. *Founder* is the title under his picture. He was quoted as saying, "We've recognized the negative long enough . . . It's high time we recognized the positive . . . We have faith in young people. It's as simple as that."

But suddenly, it was over. All we knew: Dad paid off the promised salaries—$400 a month and expenses—to the college students from St. John's, Gustavus Adolphus, Hamline, Macalester, St. Thomas, and Augsburg; he paid off the insurance companies; we had to pay back all those who bought policies. Some policyholders even marched over to our house demanding their money back. It distressed Mom, who reacted as she usually did to Dad's investments: pursed lips, jutting jaw. "I can't believe it. Another fiasco. When will you learn?"

When I asked Dad what went wrong with CASS, he shrugged. "Well . . . we were ahead of our time . . . " But I overheard him telling Mom about another investor who had run off with the CASS funds. Dad ended up having to bail out the business with his own money. Presenting themselves as a united front, my parents didn't fight often—but Mom was furious over CASS. Her pursed lips busted open as she scolded Dad. Eventually she regained her equilibrium. "Oh well, it's over. Just don't get involved again." My mother only rebuked my father at home; in public, such as when the CASS clients reclaimed their money or clucked their tongues, she defended Dad: "It was a good idea. Pat always has good ideas."

Dad told us that when he and Mom were first married, he'd join a hot poker game every Friday night: five-card stud, seven-card stud, five-card draw, baseball, blackjack. He told us he didn't leave the game until he had enough money to support them for the coming week. That could be at the beginning of the night or early in the morning. Mom said she made him quit by locking him out of the house. Dad said he quit because he realized how destructive gambling could get, some of his best friends losing everything they owned. They probably both were right.

I wondered if Dad ever lost big. Or had won big and had come to see himself as the destroyer of his friends. Or had he always known it was shady to gamble with friends he knew he could beat—but was a necessary evil, because he needed the money, and would bet only until he could afford to stop? Whatever the case, it struck me how poor Mom and Dad were when newly married and how scary it must have been to bet their scarce money. And terrifying, too, that Dad invested in iffy proposals. Mom continually braced herself for disaster. That would be a pattern in their relationship: Dad investing, Mom worrying.

Some of Dad's other investments, a few more successful than others: a flax company; a city well in central Mexico; water vacuum cleaners in New Hope, Minnesota; a hotel in New Jersey; Auto World in Flint, Michigan; land by Minnesota freeways; jewelry; the biggest RV ever built; the shell of a racing boat.

"Damn." The boat stopped, the motor sputtering dead. "Damn it."

On the first trips out, we kids used to ask, "What's wrong, Dad?" On succeeding ones, we only rolled our eyes and leaned back into the cushions.

"Guess they'll be around pretty soon," Dad would say. *They* meant the Coast Guard. Dad wouldn't even try to putter with the motor; he knew he couldn't get it going, and besides, the fellows didn't mind helping a lame boat out. "Just relax, kids. Alice, what's to eat?"

So went our summer boating trips when we *kids* were in our twenties and Mom and Dad lived in St. Paul. Dad docked his old who-knew-where-he-bought-it cabin cruiser at the Watergate Marina on the Mississippi, down a few miles from the giant Ford Plant in Highland Park. We'd go for a ride on Saturdays or Sundays, through locks heading north to Minneapolis or south to Prescott and Hastings, once all the way to Red Wing. Mom always packed a picnic lunch.

The boat's upholstery and carpeting were worn; its clever gadgets, meant to be tucked in, up, out of the way, hung loose; the little sink's knobs had disappeared, and no water flowed from the faucet. I don't remember ever cleaning the exterior, washing its creamy white shell or shining its silver trim. The boat—no one bothered to name it—bordered on true trash. Dad understood boating protocol and would've liked it to look respectable. "Hell, Alice, let's get these kids to clean up this boat." When we'd groan, "We're working, Dad," he'd say, "Alice, do you know anybody who'd come down here and clean up this boat?" and she'd say, "Well, Pat, we could bring some rags and a bucket next time," and then Dad would groan.

I don't think he really minded; he would climb onboard wearing a white T-shirt rather than his usual starched dress shirt. His shorts, pulled tight over his big belly, showed off his skinny pale legs. His white hair blew in the breeze. He would pop on his pilot's cap—navy blue with gold cording, a red nautical insignia—and plop down in his captain's chair, gifts from all of us on Father's Days. He'd shout over the sound of the failing motor, "What a day. What a beautiful day. Boy, isn't this something? Isn't this grand? What a river. What an amazing river. Alice, what's to eat?"

Mom and Dad only had the boat for a few summers. I don't remember if the Coast Guard couldn't save it anymore or if Mom and Dad just got tired of it.

Or maybe it was the RV that distracted them. Dad bought it as an investment; he and a partner intended to rent it out. But Mom wanted to *give it a whirl*. One steamy Fourth of July weekend, Mary; her husband, Pete; my brother Dan; and I drove to northern Wisconsin in the shiny yellow Chinook. We all rode in the back, sitting around the table, each taking a turn riding with Dad up front. Unlike the speedboat, this recreational vehicle was immaculate, every fancy contraption—for storing, unfolding, containing—in splendid working order. This immense automobile, the biggest I've ever seen, maybe thirty-six feet long, had a shower; a toilet; a changing room; beds to sleep us all; a radio-stereo system; a TV; and a kitchen complete with refrigerator, stove, sink, and cupboards with pots and pans and glass and ceramic dishware.

Dad loved to drive it. When it was my turn up front, I settled into the enormous tan leather seat with all kinds of black built-ins: the cigarette holder—Dad and I smoked away, our windows open a crack (it was too hot to drive without the air-conditioning on at full blast); the drink holder—both Dad and I sipped from our Coke bottles; and the magazine rack with his *America, The Catholic Digest*, insurance periodicals, and *Life* stuffed in, sticking out. He played some Irish tunes on the radio, the lilting melodies perfect for the landscape.

"Peggy, isn't this the best? Look at that old farmhouse! What a plight these farmers have got themselves into. Look at those poor Guernseys. Bunched up like that. Poor cows. Look at the sky; it even looks hot. Boy, are we lucky to have air-conditioning. I'd hate to be driving anywhere today without it. Good to be off the beaten track. Restores your spirit, doesn't it?"

He sped through the countryside. The RV was so wide it didn't fit on the narrow lanes. Soon we felt a bump and heard a scratchy sound. I looked back. A large, silver tin mailbox, with its red flag flopping, tumbled to the ground.

"Dad, did you hit that mailbox?"

He grimaced. "Maybe."

"Well, stop, Dad. We have to go back and fix it."

He frowned. "Can't, honey, we don't have any tools."

"Dad, you can't go around knocking off mailboxes."

"I know, but this thing is just too wide. I can't do anything about it."

I couldn't do anything about it, either, but it certainly

made me feel guilty.

We continued driving up north with no definite destination in mind. In the back, everybody grew a bit testy. Mom complained about the heat, saying her usual, "I've never been any good with it. I'm not good for anything." She finally stretched out for a nap. Dad kept driving.

Eventually we stopped at a park. It had been advertised on highway billboards some ways back as a campground. We pulled into it, motor and air-conditioning squalling, the only RV surrounded by hundreds of tents. Campers stared at us from the logs where they sat. They didn't deter Dad. He found a site to back our behemoth into. The park was near a lake so we all put on swimsuits in the changing room and set off down the trail marked *BEACH*, except for Dad, who said he'd stay in the Chinook. "Too damn hot to go outside."

On the beach, Mary got faint from the heat, and Mom started sweating profusely, so we trudged back up the trail quite quickly. Later Dan complained of an earache and we drove him to an emergency clinic in town. Campers sullenly watched us drive out and then return to our saved spot—we had moved some gear outside on the ground so folks would know it was taken.

As the campers cooked hot dogs and hamburgers and s'mores over their campfires, we ate inside what Mom had packed: fried chicken, green-bean casserole, and a Jell-O salad, a bright red soup with blackened pieces of banana half afloat in it. The whole time the air-conditioner ran at maximum capacity, the condenser on top roaring. The Chinook had its own generator. As night came on, the campground turned quiet. When I made a trip to the joint outhouses down the road, I could still hear the metallic sound from our hooked-up spot.

I rushed back. "Dad, you've got to turn the AC off. People hate us for the sound. It's not fair; they've tried to get away from the city and its noise."

"Can't, Peggy, it's too damn hot."

"Dad, you've got to. At least turn it down."

In his T-shirt and underwear, he replied, "Can't, Peggy. It's too damn hot. We'd bake in here."

I consider it a tribute to my parents that I never thought of myself as poor or rich. I never knew what we were. We lived frugally but not stingily. Generous would be the adjective to describe Dad and penny-wise Mom. My parents set the standard for what I'd always envision the vow of poverty to be: living simply, with necessities and a few luxuries (books, music lessons, trips) paid for in the most economical way.

Big heart and mind. Tremendous enthusiasm and drive. A winning spirit. Thrilled with "making a sale." The money Dad made? He and Mom gave it away—to the Church and its institutions, to charities, to the needy of many lands. When their giving amounts grew larger and they initiated a charitable foundation, I finally realized my parents had become wealthy.

I picture my dad in various settings: on church steps, in school auditoriums, by neighborhood streets, at offices, across dinner tables. I focus on him, zooming in, noticing his dark suit, his white shirt and tie, his polished shoes—he would make my brothers shine theirs every Saturday night. He can be standing, or sitting, or walking, or smoking, but what he's always doing is looking directly at others in the scene, leaning in toward them. Paying attention to them. He had a genuine interest in everybody he met. He asked questions about their lives. His intellectual curiosity was fed by all the ideas he learned through communicating with them. Listen. That's what he did. Not out of politeness. He really wanted to hear what they had to say. People loved him for it. I wanted to be like him.

DROWNING IN LOVE

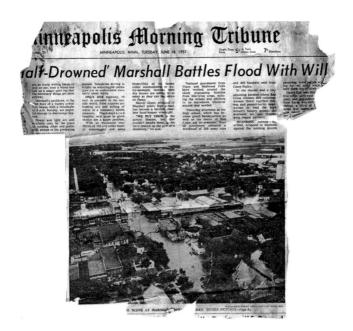

On Father's Day, the sky spilled out. Rain poured down for two days, until the Redwood River overflowed, gushing over banks, soaking every corner of our town. Local radio stations and papers reported the flood. It was even covered in the *Minneapolis Morning Tribune*. A huge headline, "'Half-Drowned' Marshall Battles Flood with Will," ran on the front page, under the date, Tuesday, June 18, 1957. There were photos of our downtown buildings buried underwater.

We got the paper because we were lucky—Jim and John,

on their newspaper routes, could only deliver to the houses in our hilltop neighborhood.

I tried to picture the *roaring* river about a mile from our house but could only imagine the sleepy stream that ran through Liberty Park. In the summer, we hopped across it or stepped over its rocks on picnics at the park or on Wednesday nights when the Marshall Band got boring. We skated on the Redwood in the winter. Hemmed in by trees, their frozen branches stretching above us, we pumped along on its narrow ice. But now the river boomed and brimmed over its banks, and Mom and all seven of us kids were reading about it in the paper spread out on the kitchen table. Mom muttered as she read, "Oh, my. How are we going to get to the anniversary?"

We were supposed to be in Rochester the next day for my grandparents' fiftieth wedding anniversary. Mom worried we wouldn't make it. She also worried about my dad. He was a volunteer assistant civil defense director, but he had assumed command when the flood marooned the chief at his house. Dad had not been home for three days. Mom hadn't even talked to him because telephone lines were down. She fretted, "Does he have dry clothes? What are they doing for food?"

Reading the flood story in the paper, she recited out loud, "Three-fifths of Marshall's homes were either uninhabitable or water-damaged." She shook her head. "I can't believe it." Suddenly she shouted, "Look, here's your father."

And there he was, in the middle of page ten, under another big headline: "Marshall: They Still Can Laugh in Disaster." "Sleep is the rarest commodity of all in Marshall. Pat Rogers, head of local civil defense, is gaunt and haggard as he works at his makeshift headquarters in the half-flooded police station. To him come trouble calls; from him flow orders to the guardsmen, police, firemen and volunteers."

Besides Dad and the anniversary, Mom worried about the flooding around us. Our house was dry, but below the hospital's hill toward our school, Holy Redeemer, we caught glimpses of the most amazing boats. Strange, amphibious—duck boats— they rolled on wheels down to the edge of the water and then sucked up their wheels and floated out. People waved from their roofs: "Over here." The amphibians cruised over to pick them up.

Mary and I, at thirteen and twelve, figured we were old enough to help the firemen with Operation Rescue, but Mom insisted we help her. "Go get groceries before Lloyd's floods out." She handed us a list. "Make it quick." I didn't know if she meant *quick*, before all the store goods swam in the aisles—that would be fun, just grabbing whatever you wished for off a float- ing conveyor belt—or *quick* as in don't dawdle. I could spend hours at the grocery store because it had a rack of comic books and love-story magazines. I'd read as fast as I could standing in front of the rack, hoping neither of the Lloyds would spot me. I never had any money to buy anything.

As we hurried down the street in the opposite direction from our school, Mary and I passed little white bungalows. My best friend Mary Ann's former house next to Mom's best friend Grace Lee's house were decorated with gingerbread red trim. Grace loved to invite us to her house for treats. Mr. Lee worked for the Sunshine Snacks company and brought home free sam- ples. Because she had only sons, Grace also *adored* seeing Mary and me in fancy clothes. Whenever I dressed up for a special event, I'd race down the hill and perform a style show.

Across from Grace's house, at the bottom of Minnesota Hill, our skating rink appeared, swamped with flood water. In the winter, neighbors deliberately flooded it, and we kids spent hours playing Crack the Whip, everybody taking a turn, twisting and twirling at the end of the line. Sometimes I'd sneak off to the rink by myself, skates swinging at my shoulder. I practiced swan glides and pirouettes along with hockey swipes and karate chops with a beat-up stick. My favorite challenge: to skim the entire rink on one leg. I fell a lot, but quit only when my fingers or toes felt as if they'd been shot with Novocain.

Today my wet toes squished inside my rubber boots. Mary and I waded across Highway 19, avoiding the old house with peeling paint and a sinking porch next to Lloyd's. Willy lived there. He could be mean. Once when we were playing ball in the vacant lot next to our house, he snuck up and threw a huge rock at me. Mom wrapped my head with gauze to stop the bleeding and checked the dilation of my eyes for a concussion. I always kept a lookout for Willy.

We entered Lloyd's to buy the emergency supplies. We couldn't believe the quiet. Often Mr. and Mrs. Lloyd sponsored noisy contests and drawings. One time we almost won the largest-family award. We hadn't really expected to win; seven kids was only medium sized in Marshall. Large families had fifteen, sixteen, seventeen kids. But Mom had tried her hardest, sending each of us to the Free-Trip-to-the-Shrine-Circus man in front of the store. "Tell him you're another Rogers," she said.

We always met people we knew at Lloyd's. Mom knew everybody. Everywhere it was "Alice, good to see you," or "Mrs. Rogers, my, how these children are growing." If Mom was in a hurry, she pretended not to see anybody, ducking into the next aisle, mumbling her list under her breath . . . *sugar . . . flour . . . .* She raced down the rows with Patty in the cart, the rest of us shouting after her, "Mom, don't forget the marshmallows." "Cheerios." "Hershey's."

Today only one or two people besides us were hurriedly picking up supplies. Mary and I puddled through the empty aisles, standing on tiptoes to reach milk bottles placed high in a cooler and bread saved on upper shelves. We checked out with Mrs. Lloyd. "Charge to Rogers, please."

Tucking the grocery bags under our raincoats and curving our backs to lug the weight up front, like two large ladies, we staggered back out into the rain that shelled us sideways, in sheets, forcing us to maneuver like crooked crabs. We crossed back over the highway, not even looking for cars. Nothing moved.

Except back home. *Helicopters* circled the hospital. We begged Mom to *pleeease* let us go out to watch the choppers carrying people from their flooded homes to a special wing in Weiner Memorial. Mom eventually caved, granting permission, but told us to take the younger kids, too. We grabbed our ponchos, dashed over, and stood at the edge of the grounds, thrilled by the rescue missions, the deafening landings, unloadings, and takeoffs. I told Tommy, Danny, and Patty to plug their ears. We watched *the saved* crouch out of the helicopters, quickly cover their ears, bend under the blades, and run to the edges of the parking lot.

We watched Jim and John play chicken on their bikes, riding as close as possible to the helicopters. We often played chicken at night under the Charles streetlight. Jim was always my partner. We had added up our ages; he and I equaled John and Mary. Jim was a good partner, protecting me. We usually won. The mighty wind now pushed the boys so close to the spinning blades of the helicopters the wheels of their bikes shimmied. It made me sick to my stomach. I turned towards the rescued crowd who yelled at the armory guards stationed at the hospital.

"It's something, isn't it, water like this?" a lady said.

"Hard to believe the damage it can do," a guard answered back. "Houses gone. People lost."

"You boys are doing a helluva job," a man said, placing his arm around another guard.

"Wish I had your hat, keep the wet out . . ."

Some people wandered around, watching, like us. Because you couldn't help noticing the large wood-and-wire cages attached to our garage or hearing and smelling the fluttering pigeons inside, some of the onlookers strolled over to our backyard. I followed them and proudly showed off the coop Jim and John had built: comfy cages filled with straw inside the garage, with latched doors leading to the outside cages. I even let the people stroke the rare birds. That's what Jim and John called them. *Rare.* They believed these pigeons were smart; they had ordered them from a magazine.

The boys knew pigeons. I told the visitors what the boys had taught me: there are 365 varieties of pigeons in the world, same as the number of days in the year; some pigeons can somersault in the sky; some can roll on the ground for over two hundred feet. "Our brothers set these pigeons free sometimes to practice message-taking or homing instincts," I instructed, but I knew the birds didn't really come back when the boys sent them off. I gestured at our neighbor's house, where the pigeons liked to land. Mr. Marcotte once threatened to shoot the pigeons off his roof, but the boys rescued them in time, climbing up and blanketing them down.

I wondered if I should tie a flood SOS message around the birds' skinny legs, but the droning of the helicopters' blades grew even louder, as noisy as a million, hungry, buzzing mosquitoes in your ears under summer bedcovers.

Mary mouthed, "Let's . . . go . . . in," pointing a finger at our house.

The younger kids refused to leave. "Stay and watch the whirlybirds," they said. We promised food. We threatened punches. We finally dragged them in.

We found Mom banging pots and pans around in the kitchen. She was a wreck with the flood and the golden wedding anniversary. Muzzy and Papa had asked her to sing at the Mass. For days she had been practicing *Panis Angelicus* and *Ave Maria*. Now she sang a new tune: "What if we can't get to Rochester? What are we going to do?" Since the anniversary meant getting dressed up and going to church, I didn't really care if we made it, but I knew Mom was determined to go.

Her two good outfits hung over the ironing board: a pleated navy dress with a white belt and collar and a black skirt and shawl with bright embroidery bought on a Canadian business trip with Dad. Mom mumbled to herself, "Oh, which one? I should have bought a new one. I can't get downtown now."

I imagined going downtown, crossing the bridge over

the Redwood, where lilacs sweetened the river smell, and walking three blocks further to the wide and tall post office. Inside we'd study the FBI's most-wanted criminals hanging high on the walls. As I examined their faces, adding up their scars, my friend Kathy's dad, Mr. Culhane, the postmaster, always called out loudly from his office, "And how's my little Margie?" The people waiting in line would turn and stare at me. I'd blush red. Then they'd say, "Look at all those freckles."

I was afraid the flood would leave its marks. Dirt and sand from the river bottom could freckle and scar even the giant steps of the post office. Granite could be altered. Nothing would ever be the same. In my mind's eye, I saw the soaked merchandise of Ben Franklin's, Addison's Hardware, and Ekberg's Clothing, everything in free fall: a red sequined dress from Millie's Attic sailing next to a bobbing green Prell from Bulowski's; a crumbling yellow cardboard box of Wetherbee's nails sinking behind them.

At my very favorite place, the Carnegie Library, the stories of the Chinese pigtailed girls on the bottom shelves would be ruined, the water rising to Louisa May Alcott. Jo would be destroyed. I wondered if the whole library would have to close down; we'd miss story hour on Saturday. I went to the library twice a week. On Tuesdays or Wednesdays, I'd pick up the books the main librarian set aside for me, and then after Saturday story hour, she'd hand me a new stack. "Margie, I know you'll enjoy these."

She's nice, but if the library doesn't get destroyed, I'm going to tell her I want to choose my own books. She might be shocked.

At fancy Stone's Clothing, people might really be shocked—to death. Whenever we shopped there, a fashionable salesperson put Mom's charge slip in a metal tube, attached the tube to overhead wires, then pushed a button to drive the tube up and away to an upper-level office. The well-dressed upstairs clerk tore off the white copy and sent the yellow carbon copy back to us on the floor. I loved watching the flying rockets. I loved everyone complimenting Mom: "Oh, Mrs. Rogers, it's perfect." "Oh, Alice, it's you." And I loved when they noticed me: "And who is this one, not Margie, oh, how they grow." But now: what would happen if someone stood in water and touched the electrical wires?

And what about the Marshall Theater, across from the post office, kitty-corner from the library? We never missed the Saturday matinee. Every week Dad divvied out a dime to each of us, nine cents for the movie and an extra penny for ten pieces of candy. A few times, Mom took just me, or just Mary, to a movie; she said it was our special night. Coming home, she sang from the Doris Day or Nelson Eddy or Jeanette MacDonald musical we'd just seen. Owls whoooed, stars flickered, and Mom crooned, "I'll be calling youuu . . . I'm headin' for blue horizon, where the mountains meet the sky . . . I'm gonna' ride, ride, ride, ride down that dusty trail . . . " I imagined Mom in the moonlight on top of a tall white horse, riding the Canadian Rockies. So airy and romantic—adventuresome—so unlike being stuck in a real flood. I had lost the safe feeling I usually had walking home along Highway 19, turning right on Minnesota, climbing to our white house with its green shutters, surrounded by bridal wreath, peony, wild rose, and lilac bushes.

Marshall used to have two movie theaters plus the Starlight drive-in. The Barrymore got shut down and the Roxie followed suit after fat rats scrambled onto the stage floor, casting shadows on the screen. We kids shrieked, but serials of *The Perils of the Wilderness* played so everyone shut up and stayed alert. For the last few movies, we sat with our legs tucked tight under us.

Mom told us to be on the lookout for river rats; she said they try to escape to higher ground just as people do. Jim and John bragged they scrambled like rats, riding downed telephone poles. They said they floated on them from our neighborhood, along Church Street, the whole mile to downtown.

John told me that his friend Paul Rehkamp, whose dad owned the mortuary, had needed help hauling caskets from the basement of the funeral home to higher ground. Paul and John and five other boys moved the caskets to safety, but kept one for a little fun. John hopped into it. The boys floated it down flooded streets. On dry corners, they banged it down. John stayed inside, while the other boys ran away to hide behind bushes or buildings. Whenever someone approached the coffin, the boys whistled a birdcall—and out jumped John. They tricked some high-school girls and really scared two old guys. The last time John popped out he found himself staring at the gun holster of a policeman, who said, with a very low voice, "Son, don't ever do that again."

"Or what?" I demanded.

John shrugged.

I promised not to tell, but I knew Mom and Dad would eventually find out.

Mom finally decided to wear the Canadian outfit to the anniversary. She began whipping us into shape. "Boys, put out your shirts, suits, and ties. Get socks and underwear without holes. Shine your shoes. Girls, lay out everything on your beds. I'll be up."

I quickly spread out my socks, slip and panties, black patents, and a hand-me-down dress from Mary, light blue with raised white flowers. Then I snuck outside to the garage. Our fort, my favorite place, was a whole upper story of the garage. Uncle Pat and Jim and John had built it. The flood had me remembering Aunt Bea, who had died three years before, when I was nine and she was eighty-two. I harked back to what she said when we came to say goodbye to her.

Her head had rested on a yellowed pillowcase. On the eyelet sham underneath, her yellow hair had fallen out in clumps, like straw. Her eyes, black as the rosary beads clutched in her hands, seemed on fire in the darkened room. Her own lacy cloths were draped over the dresser, nightstand, rocking chair, and footstool—Aunt Bea took care of the linen for St. George's Church. She had told me that for $15 a month she'd

Aunt Bea

wash, starch, and press all the cloths. Her log-cabin quilt covered her; all of her other quilts hung over the end of her brass bed. Her knitted afghan dangled from the arm of the rocking chair, smelling, like her house, of cinnamon and ginger.

As I leaned over her papery cheek and smelled her homemade soap, she whispered, in a strange, breathy voice, that she could see at the end of a long tunnel a *flood* of bright, bright light. Angels waited to lead her into it. She smiled at me. "I am *drowning* in love." I looked into her black eyes and imagined I could see the angels welcoming her into a long, splendid hall, sort of like King Arthur's—I was reading about him and the Knights of the Round Table. I also imagined saints in medieval dress offering Aunt Bea the Holy Grail. Glints of light beamed from the bowl. I found it difficult to return from my daydream to Aunt Bea's dim room, to her shadowy form in bed. I, too, was drowning in love light. Years later, I thought in that moment I'd glimpsed for the first time what the vow of chastity might mean. Never marrying, Aunt Bea took care of her family and friends and church with ultimate love. I'd also learned of love's companions: obligation, sacrifice, loss.

In our garage fort, which had a swinging ladder, a dormer window, and old carpets covering the rough boards, Mary and I used to carry up our Aunt Bea dolls, dishes, pots and pans, bottles and blankets, and play house for hours. The boys played cops and robbers. Lately, I brought up books to read or snuggled under the dormer and thought about things. Things like what kind of summer starts out with a flood?

I was used to scary weather. Marshall absorbs wind. The previous year, I barely made it home from a friend's house in a dust storm; whirling sand from the road pitted my skin, but I had squinted my eyes and felt my way home. We suffered many hailstorms, too, with hail as big as softballs, ruining crops. Marshall, located in a tornado belt, always had whistles blowing; every single day for two weeks one July we had to stay in the basement for whole afternoons and even eat supper there. Each night, though, I'd slip upstairs to peek out at the sky—pale reddish yellow or dense gray black. I listened for the strangely silent crickets and birds. I waited until the wind began to holler before I headed back to the basement.

But a flood. Who knew how things would turn out? If Dad would get home? If we'd get to the anniversary? Even if I didn't care much about going, others would be so disappointed if we didn't make it. I could see Muzzy's and Papa's faces wrinkled and sad.

And our town. In the newspaper pictures, water rose over the doorways of buildings. It would take forever for all the stuff in the stores to dry out, forever for the water to recede. I didn't want to wait forever. I wanted to ride my bike to the swimming pool, to my friends' houses.

I missed talking to my friends on the phone and swimming and hiking with them in Camden, a state park about five miles from Marshall. The newspaper reported people stranded there. I hoped the people climbed to Tarzan's Peak, Camden's tallest hill, the highest place around. Its top supported railroad tracks. Whenever I climbed there, I put my ear on the rails to listen. If a train barreled down the tracks, I'd move away, plug my ears, hug the ground, and shake with the dirt while that enormous sound raced by. Further down the track, near Lynd, the train blew its whistle. Toooot. Tooooooot. A lonesome sound, just an echo around the bend.

Camden was magical and mysterious. I knew Native Americans, fur traders, and explorers had been in the region for years and years. I found it a bit eerie that those ancient people experienced, just as I did, Camden's spring-fed pools; its rivers containing trout, bass, and bluegills; its maples, basswood, oak, and cottonwood trees; its woodland and prairie wildflowers (trillium, trout lilies, bloodroot, violets, coneflowers, blazing stars). I sensed the ancients at the park. I felt their *presence* as I hiked the trails.

I moved away from the window of the fort because I didn't want to hear the rain bouncing and splashing off the dormer anymore or see the pigeons fluttering in their cages outside, frightened by the racket from the hospital. I didn't want to think about the flood. I wanted to think about our usual Sunday summer trips to Camden when Mom loaded up the old wicker picnic basket with fried chicken in the black frying pan, baked beans in the brown casserole with the silver holder, carrots and celery covered in ice chips in a plastic bag tied with a rubber band, fresh peaches and brownies dusted with powdered sugar, and lemonade and coffee in thermos bottles. In another basket, Mom would pack paper plates and real silverware, paper napkins and the red-checked cotton tablecloth, a blanket, newspapers and matches, swimsuits and towels, mosquito spray, suntan lotion, and always the wet washrag in an old plastic bread bag for cleaning roasted-marshmallow faces.

"Hell, Alice, why all this?" Dad would grumble. "I don't know why you like picnics, anyway; it's so much easier to stay at home."

Once we got to the park, though, Dad had fun, throwing a football or softball around to us kids. He preferred us playing ball or hiking the trails and hills, but we raced to Camden's swimming hole, with its bubbly fountain tumbling over rocky boulders. Dad, as usual, worried about us drowning. He worried even when we swam on the shallow side of the buoys with a lifeguard on duty.

"Margaret, where are you?" Mom called from the back door. "Margaret, come down. I know you're in the fort. Come on. It's time to go to Mrs. Schmidt's."

Thoughts of Camden were wiped away. I couldn't believe it! Mom was going to traipse us across town to get our hair done. Usually, I liked going to Mrs. Schmidt's, lounging in her kitchen under the dryer, listening to the buzzing blower and her loud gossip, and smelling fresh coffee and hairspray. I also liked her styling my short hair—I was grown up, no more baby braids. But going there *in a flood*?! Nothing was going to keep Mom from the anniversary. Ordering the boys to stay home, out of trouble, Mom, like a stubborn Mother Goose with wide slicker wings, marched off with Mary, Patty, and me waddling after. She led us through a half hour of soggy streets.

Mrs. Schmidt dunked our heads, one after another, into the sink. Wrapped up in thin towels, we waited our turns, shivering on chipped cherry metal chairs. We hunkered down with our legs stretched out in front of us, not wanting our pants to touch the rusty legs. Mom paced around the kitchen sipping steamy coffee.

"Poor Verva, as if she didn't have enough trouble," Mom said. "I heard from Jamie that her basement is full, but she can't find anyone to pump it out. Irv's too tired helping others."

"Can you believe that?" Mrs. Schmidt said.

"As if we're not all dead tired . . . " Mom trailed off.

"What do you hear from Pat?"

"Nothing. I'm worried. He's in the middle of it."

While she cut hair, Mrs. Schmidt's remarks tapered to hmmms and uhhhs. She needed to pay attention, make sure the sides of our heads were even. Finishing up in record time, with barely enough minutes under the dryers, she handed us plastic scarves to wear home. "I don't want a little rain to spoil my great works of art."

That night, after a wild supper with us kids picking fights and Mom yelling every few minutes, "I'll have to tell your father when he comes home," Dad finally staggered in the back door. Unshaven, bristling with heavy black whiskers and with dark bags under his bloodshot eyes, he could hardly hug or kiss Mom or put his arms around us. He just wanted to go to bed, but

Mom said, "Pat, we've got to go to the anniversary."

He shook his head. "We can't. There are roadblocks, bridges out. We can't get through."

Mom persisted, "We can do it. By tomorrow, it'll be different. And we don't have to go to Tracy. We can detour through Redwood Falls. We've got to make it. They're all counting on us. I won't miss it."

"Well, hell, Alice, you'll have to." He stormed up to bed.

I heard them arguing that night. I thought I could make out their conversation.

"It can't be done," Dad said, rolling over in bed.

"You won't even try," Mom said.

"Let me sleep," Dad answered, again rolling over in bed.

"Not until we talk this over," Mom said, her voice rising.

"I'm exhausted," Dad said.

"So am I," Mom said.

Their voices eventually softened to a murmur that lulled me to sleep.

Early in the morning, Mom gently shook us awake and told us to get dressed in our good clothes. Still spread out on the floor of our room so they wouldn't get wrinkled, they looked weird, as if we were laid out, without our heads or feet, as if we were dead. Our best burial clothes. I thought of John in the casket, real dead people in coffins in the cemetery, rats rooting around in dugout plots, Aunt Bea floating overhead, her yellow hair streaming down over somersaulting pigeons in metal rocket urns, ghosts of Sioux Indians and French voyageurs waving from Camden's lookout on the Dakota Valley Trail. Scared, spinning these images out of my head, I yanked my dress over my head and my hips, and raced downstairs—alive.

We crammed into the car. All nine of us. I tried to seat myself carefully to protect my dress and my hairdo. I had worn a stupid hairnet all night so my curls wouldn't flatten.

Dad drove the car, his hands tight on the steering wheel. At the bottom of Minnesota Hill, water splashed up to the

Dodge's windows. On Highway 19, Dad slammed us against one another as he checked the car's brakes. We didn't say anything. No one spoke. Not one word. We just looked out. And watched. Watched the soppy countryside go by. Watched for washouts, amazed at fields full of water, sometimes two to three feet high, and highway ditches filled with water, overflowing the road.

The bridge had collapsed in Redwood Falls, and Dad turned around to find a different way. Several times the road just disappeared underwater, and he had to circle back to follow other routes. We'd be traveling to Rochester certainly more than the usual five to six hours.

But Dad finally loosened up, telling Mom what Marshall would have to do to prevent flooding again, something about trenching a new channel, creating a new bed for the Redwood.

Mom started to sing, "I've been working on the railroad . . ."

We kids joined in, "All the livelong day . . ."

Soon our old sedan was full of sound, clicking rhythms on the windows, bouncing butts on the backseat, and finally Dad's deep voice joining in, "Oomph pa, oomph pa, oomph pa pa, my pa's better than your pa paaaa. Ooma, ooma, oo, ma, maaaa, strummin' on the old banjo."

Dad and city officials did make sure Marshall wouldn't flood again, successfully convincing the United States Corps of Engineers to build a diversion channel around the city. Years later, I would look back at the flood and realize my parents got us through that crisis by working together, not panicking or overreacting but compromising and accepting each other's strengths—a diversion channel for us kids, keeping fear and sadness and loss at bay. We might have felt inklings of these emotional states during the flood, but living through a natural disaster superseded them. We entered into Marshall's atmosphere of cooperation and helpfulness, a small town that rallied together. We were learning valuable lessons of communal life:

how to make the best of things, how to get along in good times and bad.

And we made it to Rochester. Just in time for Mass, which carried a new surprise. While Mom sang from the choir loft, and the rest of us were not paying attention, Patty walked up with all of us for Communion, knelt at the rail, and opened her mouth. Out of the corner of my eye, I saw the priest place the wafer on her tongue. I quickly grabbed her, pulling her back to our pew.

"Patty," I hissed, "did you swallow It?"

Taking a big gulp, she smiled wide. "I did, Marge."

"Ah, geez. You haven't gone to classes for making your First Communion."

This was a serious mistake. Everyone spent a lot of time preparing for First Communion. You couldn't just do it; you had to know your soul was clean of sins; you had to have fasted; you had to know how to reverently walk up and back from the communion rail, and how to put out your tongue and swallow the host. Patty didn't know any of this. I looked at her. She was wearing the red dress Muzzy had originally made for me, the one I liked until I realized it was old-fashioned. Patty fidgeted with the rhinestone buttons on its bodice. The taffeta crinkled. Licking her lips, Patty seemed pleased with herself.

"I'll tell Mom after Mass," I said.

When I did, Mom immediately ordered, "Don't tell Muzzy."

But I knew Muzzy wouldn't get upset. She only got upset when Mom called Patty *special*.

I was right. When Muzzy found out—almost immediately, from Danny—about Patty's First Communion, she simply asked her, "Do you know Who you received, Patty?"

"I do, Muzzy."

"Who was It?"

Pulling at the red taffeta sash, Patty answered, "It was God, Muzzy."

"Exactly, Patty." Turning to the rest of us, Muzzy adjusted the lacy collar of her beautiful blue silk dress; patted her sparse, white, curled hair; and exclaimed, "Fine, then. What a wonderful day for Patty. She can celebrate with Papa and me."

The day after the anniversary we made our way back to Marshall. The town looked like a scary movie set of the end of the world: dirty and disheveled people with shovels digging out mud from ruined buildings and stacking trash smelling strongly of mold and mildew. Powerful winds blew that putrid smell along with fine particles of dirt up, down, and around. The sound of wet-dry vacuum cleaners and sump pumps competed with the sound of the wind. A mess. But we were glad to be back home.

DON'T TELL MUZZY

*P**oor robin is dead and he lay in his grave, lay in his grave, lay in his grave. Poor robin is dead and he lay in his grave, oh, oh, oh.*

Muzzy sang the robin song to me when I was little. I always begged for the robin song. She sang and I played with her hands, tracing her bones and veins, pulling apart her fingers, smoothing out her knuckles, measuring my hand against hers.

I was close to Muzzy even though she wasn't the hugging kind of grandma, didn't bake cookies or ask about school or friends. Even though she had a warm, fuzzy nickname, she was distant, aloof, old-fashioned, with definite ideas of conduct and behavior. One rule she tried to force on me: to not freckle in the sun. She tried to keep me from playing outdoors in direct sunlight; she enforced a hat rule. Failing these, she smeared different creams on my face, attempting to erase or at least lighten the freckles.

Yet Muzzy could be modern. From 1885 to 1981, her life spanned almost a century of changes. She hired a *girl* to clean and cook and care for her children while she kept the books for Papa's business. She updated from horses and buggies to horseless carriages to automobiles; from scrub board to wringer to automatic washers; from wood to coal to gas burners. She always called the refrigerator the "icebox."

Muzzy and Papa didn't visit us often. When they did, before they arrived, Mom cleaned with a frenzy, even closets and drawers. "Muzzy might look," she said. In Muzzy's home, everything was neat and impeccably clean. Mom was more casual and freewheeling.

I'll never forget one time when Muzzy and Papa *were* visiting, a summer day in 1951, when I was six, playing at Mary Ann's house. I loved playing there; Mary Ann had tons of toys. On this particular day, she and I had paper-doll outfits spread all over the living-room floor. Suddenly we heard a loud crashing sound; the Eves lived close to Highway 19. I stood up and began walking carefully through the paper clothes to look out the window, but Mrs. Eve, who had already bolted out the front door and dashed back in again, caught me and said, "Margie, why don't you and Mary Ann go play in the bedroom."

I thought that was a strange request, but I didn't argue. We were taught not to speak back to adults. In a little while, Mary Ann and I heard a shrieking siren. Looking out Mary Ann's bedroom window, we watched Weiner Memorial's ambulance speed past. I hoped whoever crashed was all right. About a half hour later, Mrs. Eve found us and said maybe I should go home. As I walked out the door, I saw Jim's blue jacket at the bottom of Minnesota Hill, where it joined Highway 19.

I turned back to Mrs. Eve. "That's Jim's jacket."

"No, honey, I'm sure it's not," she replied.

"Yes, it is," I yelled, running and picking it up. I knew, even before I saw the blood, that it had been Jim who crashed. Mrs. Eve was crying at the door.

I raced home.

Muzzy met me at our front door. "*You. You.* It's all *your* fault."

"Muzzy, what's wrong?"

"*You're* always playing over at that Eve house. If *you'd* been home, none of this would've happened." Muzzy looked wild, rocking back and forth, wringing her hands.

"Muzzy, what happened?" I asked.

Papa walked up to Muzzy. "Julia, Julia," he said, putting

his arms around her, leading her upstairs.

I found Mom at the kitchen table, staring out the back window at Weiner Memorial. I sat down beside her.

"Mom, is Jim at the hospital?"

She didn't look at me. "He's only eleven years old."

"Mom?"

"'Like a sandwich,' they said, 'his bike between two cars.' Your dad ran out of here without even telling me, so scared by the telephone call from Pat Eve. I ran after him. 'Pat, Pat, what is it?' I couldn't run fast because of the baby." (Mom was very pregnant at the time.)

"Mom, where is Jim?"

She saw me then, recognized me. "Margaret, Jim's hurt. So badly the Marshall doctors sent him immediately to Northwestern Hospital in Minneapolis. Dad rode along in the ambulance. It's a four-hour drive. Your father and the doctors made me stay home and take care of the rest of you."

We waited for Dad's call, sitting at the kitchen table, looking out the back windows, watching people come and go from Weiner Memorial. As soon as the telephone rang, and Mom answered and sighed, we knew Jim would be all right.

We helped Mom fix up the sunporch on the first floor because Jim would be sleeping downstairs for a long time when he came home. To mend his broken femur, the specialists put a long rod through his hip and leg and a cast over it. Doc Murphy and our next-door neighbor, Doc Hedenstrom, made house calls to check in. We peeked at the instruments in their black bags. Sometimes they let us use the stethoscope to listen to the beating of our hearts. Lub dub. Lub dub. Lub dub.

Friends and neighbors stopped by. They signed their names on Jim's cast and gave him gifts. Usually tough and independent, Jim became soft and spoiled. But as he got better and bored, he let us play with his presents, and at night, when we thought Mom and Dad were asleep, we sneaked past their bedroom and crept downstairs. Raiding the refrigerator for milk and the cupboards for crackers and cookies, we set up feasts on Jim's bed. Then we dealt out cards. We had quiet, flashlit canasta parties. Until Dad discovered us one night and swatted us upstairs.

Eventually I told Mom that Muzzy thought I caused Jim's accident. She hugged and kissed me. "It wasn't your fault. It wasn't anyone's fault. Muzzy was just afraid for Jim."

About once a year, Muzzy and Papa stayed at our house for a week while Mom and Dad went on vacation. One time Mary frightened us all. She was allergic to fish. She could break out in hives and have trouble breathing if she even smelled it cooking. Muzzy and Papa were babysitting us during Lent. They made Mary eat some bullheads fixed in beer batter. "Don't be silly. Allergies are all in your head. We always eat fish on Fridays."

Mary's face instantly turned chalky white with bright splotches of red. Her mouth and tongue ballooned up like a blowfish. Deep purplish hives rose on her arms and legs. She gasped for air. Luckily, right then Mom and Dad came home. Dad took one look at Mary, then grabbed her, shouting, "What the hell!" throwing a look to kill at Muzzy and Papa. Cradling Mary in his arms, he dashed out across the alley to Weiner. Mom laid down the law to Muzzy and Papa: "You will *never ever* make her eat fish again."

As we grew older, we had to change our behavior when Muzzy and Papa babysat us. I often stayed late at school for play practices and piano lessons. Muzzy didn't believe in these activities. "Your mother is overworked looking after all you kids. You don't have any time to help her. What's important is helping your parents." Muzzy didn't make me skip anything, but she made me feel guilty. I'd listen to her complain and then I'd play gin rummy with her and Papa, which was fun, but I worried about getting my homework done.

Jim and John sometimes came home from college on weekends with a couple of their friends. They all stayed out late and slept in. That stunned Muzzy: "Mornings are for getting up, getting a start on the day. You waste the good part of the day sleeping. And who are these other boys? And what are they doing out all hours of the night?" Muzzy didn't say any of this to the boys but to my sister and me and to my mom when she returned home. Which was strange—why didn't she complain to the boys?

For several summers, I stayed with Muzzy and Papa in Rochester for a week. Muzzy made sure each visit had a purpose. The summer I was seven she resolved to teach me to sew. "Girls need to sew. I couldn't teach your mother. If she sewed, she could be saving money. You can sew. Anyone can sew. For that matter, you can do anything you set your mind on doing," she said, busily pulling open the top of her Singer sewing machine. She patted the bottom of her cane sewing chair for me and pulled over an upholstered dining-room chair for herself.

Every day Muzzy and I labored with the thread and the cloth. I pumped the foot treadle too fast or too slow, Muzzy impatiently grabbing my hands or pushing my feet or tapping a rhythm on my thigh. "Steady. Steady," she'd say. Muzzy smelled like baby powder, and her skin had a silky feel. I tried to relax, but always the needle zipped, ziipped, ziiipped, ziiiiiipped. Stuffed with too much material, it would break. Each time it did, Muzzy's spirits sank, her head dropping to her chest.

Finally giving up on the machine—but not on me—Muzzy resorted to hand sewing. I concentrated on sewing buttons of different sizes and colors on remnants of cloth, cutting the buttons off, and then sewing them back on again. For hours, I sat on the settee next to the tea cart in the sunporch, eyeing through its French doors the dining room with its multicolored, flowered and leafed oriental rug; heavy, scrolled wood table and chairs; and Muzzy's little writing desk in the corner. Muzzy checked on me periodically, usually coming in from the kitchen, wiping her hands on her apron. "Practice makes perfect," she'd say. That summer, I learned to sew on a button, sew around a buttonhole, and fix a hem.

The next summer Muzzy promised to make me a dress. We walked, hand in hand, down to the store and picked out a pattern from what seemed to me an overwhelming display. I had never shopped for patterns before, wasn't aware of measurements, didn't even know my dress size because I usually wore Mary's hand-me-downs.

Muzzy and I bought a pattern on sale: simple straight lines, sleeveless with a low square-cut neckline. The cloth on sale was blazing red taffeta. Muzzy said she liked the price and the feel of it. She immediately began sewing the dress, gathering it in at the waist. She saved enough material for a large sash to be tied in back. On either side of the bodice flap, Muzzy decided to add buttons, which I would sew on myself.

She sent me downtown, one of many such trips, to window-shop for buttons. "Look and see what other dresses have buttons on the front." On other days, she sent me for thread or bias tape or a zipper. It was only a three- or four-block walk to the stores, but I understood I was supposed to take my time. Muzzy wanted to call my Aunt Grace—they talked every day—or to take a nap, or she simply wanted me out of her hair.

The buttons I chose were huge rhinestone nuggets, on sale, two for a quarter. Muzzy liked the price. I hand sewed them on. With movement, they flashed, shimmering light across the shiny, crinkly taffeta. I loved that dress. When my week with Muzzy and Papa was over, I carefully packed the dress to take home with me. I hung it in my closet on a special silk hanger and raced up to my bedroom several times a day to look at it. I wore it for a piano recital, smoothing it over the bench. It was one of my own dresses—and red, always my favorite color. A few years later, embarrassed by its homemade and gaudy quality, I handed it down to Patty.

Muzzy hunted for bargains. She endlessly discussed prices. "Don't buy that; it's cheaper at Piggly Wiggly's or Massey's or Lawler's." We trudged from store to store. Big sales, like holidays, were anticipated, planned for; we rose early, arrived first in line, and stayed until we dropped. But we always took time to treat ourselves to lunch or a soda or at least an ice cream cone. Over the food, we hashed and rehashed our good fortune. "Can you believe it?" Muzzy would say.

"Let's look at it again," I'd say. "Only five dollars."

Or we justified our misfortune. "Asking that kind of money," she'd say. "You wouldn't have wanted it anyway, sewn so flimsy."

As Muzzy aged, her white, curly hair thinned, but she was still pretty. She always looked very handsome for our shopping expeditions. She armed herself: good dress; good coat; good purse, hat, and gloves. She settled for sturdy shoes so her bunions wouldn't act up. Straightening her hat and pulling on her gloves, she'd step out the door. "Hurry up," she'd say, her favorite phrase. The white-laced hand waved in the air. "Hurry up." Tucking her purse under her arm, she strode down the walk. Even if she was barely 5'1", she commanded attention.

She was as tough as her leather pocketbook. At eighty-four, she had surgery at Mayo Clinic for uterine cancer. After the operation, the doctors informed the family they had done all they could; Muzzy might have a few months left, maybe the summer. She lived to enjoy *twelve* more summers.

She never spoke of her illnesses or her sons' deaths or other bad times. I never really understood the Muzzy sparing, the *not telling Muzzy*. I thought she took things in stride. I always told her whatever I wanted to.

I remember telling her I was divorcing my first husband. We'd been married less than a year. I guess I knew from the beginning it wouldn't work. I hadn't told anyone about any marriage problems though. Mom and Dad were shocked, very quiet. Dad asked if I had to do it. When I said, "Yes," he said, "I'm sorry, honey. You'll be OK." Mom said my divorce would be the first in the family as far as she knew and not to tell Muzzy.

Of course I needed to tell Muzzy. Being a strong Catholic, like my parents, she wouldn't believe in divorce. She, too, was

Muzzy on her 90th birthday

quiet. Then she offered me a glass of wine (whenever I'd visit, she'd open her compact pantry cupboard and pull out a bottle of Mogen David wine and a tin of shortbread cookies), but she didn't say anything. Simply sipped her wine.

Muzzy eventually buried all the men in her life. Papa died when he was eighty-five years old, thirteen years before she did. At ninety-two, Muzzy still played bridge, sang songs from her choir days, and recited her prayers out loud, her famous memory and humor fully intact. She pulled out her dentures for her great-grandchildren. "Here's something you can't do." She looked up at her grandchildren, her eyes twinkling behind wire-rimmed glasses as she alluded to a male friend who had just stopped by: "He's after my money."

After visiting, she'd ask me to whisker tweeze. "I can't see close up anymore to get these things off my face." She pulled at one with her liver-spotted hands. "This one's an inch long. Don't worry. It doesn't hurt."

At the end, she was moved to the nursing-care wing, where she shared a small room. There was no space for her big pink leather chair with oak claws or her dainty writing desk. Without wine and cookies, no hospitality to offer. When I brought my young children to see her, she received us in the TV room. In her wheelchair, Muzzy reached out to touch the kids' arms and legs, stroke their hair and faces. She asked other residents if they wanted to feel the kids' softness, their plumpness. They gathered around, touching gingerly, smiling: "How sweet." "How pretty." "So healthy." "So young."

Muzzy died in 1981, at ninety-six. Her family—three daughters and their husbands, fifteen grandchildren, and seventeen great-grandchildren—circled the gravesite. It was raining, with a wicked north wind. A cold, dark, dreary day. The incense and words of the burial rite seemed to blow away with the wind. My four-year-old shared her daddy's umbrella, my three-year-old, his grandfather's. The baby was tucked under my coat. The robin song kept running through my mind, the song my mom now sang to my children in Muzzy's rocking chair that creaked and groaned in time: "If you want any more, you can sing it yourself, sing it yourself, sing it yourself. If you want any more, you can sing it yourself. Oh, oh, oh."

Muzzy gave me a small *Autographs* book on my ninth birthday. She wrote the first entry:

> *Rochester Minn.*
> *Feb 7 – 1954*
>
> *Dear Margaret Ann.*
>
> *When rocks and hills divide us*
> *And you no more I see*
> *Remember it was Grandmother*
> *That wrote these lines to thee.*
> *Sincerely,*
> *Mrs. E. Schreiber.*

A loving, formal statement from my loving, formal grandmother.

THE QUIET MAN

I heard Dad speaking loudly, "Papa, get back in bed. You can't go now. Papa, come back here."

I peeked out my bedroom door and in the hall light made out their forms: my mom, looking frightened; my dad, torn between anger and pity, shoving yet holding Papa; Muzzy, crying softly into her handkerchief, repeating, "I can't do it anymore. He's too strong. I can't take care of him anymore. Now you know. I can't do it anymore."

Papa stared straight ahead, stubborn, determined.

The next day Papa packed Muzzy in their car and drove to Rochester. He couldn't be stopped. My mom drove to Rochester a month later to help her parents move out of their little house, bought only a few years before, and into the high-rise, institutional Madonna Towers. Eventually, as his "hardening of the arteries" got worse, my grandfather had to go to the State Hospital in Rochester.

In the two years Papa lived there, I don't believe he ever said a word. But Papa never did talk much. He never told stories about Muzzy or my mom or her sisters. He never mentioned his sons, never explained how they lived or how they died. He never chitchatted about his store or spoke of God or Church or politics. A man of few words, he'd mutter expletives under his breath, oftentimes when he read his papers: "Hell" he'd say about a prediction in the *Wall Street Journal*, "Gosh all fishhooks" to a story in the *Rochester Post*, "Damn" to a headline of the *Min-*

neapolis Star.

Only once did I witness an outburst from him. I was staying in Rochester, along with my brother Jim. Goofing around behind Papa's store, the Olmsted County Implement Company, we climbed boxes and old machines, scaling the walls. Jim reached the roof first. King of the Mountain. Suddenly he fell through some loose shingles. Inside the store, Papa looked up at Jim dangling from the rafters, ready to drop to the floor, and me peering through the hole in the ceiling. Papa yelled and swore, shaking his fists, "God almighty, what the hell, you damn kids," as he ran for a ladder. Once Jim was retrieved and I was dragged down, Papa packed us off. "You kids go back to your grandmother—and stay there."

I remembered Papa listening to the radio's stock-market report, playing golf and bridge and game after game of solitaire. He cheated at solitaire, but, until he became senile, he executed a mean hand of bridge, always knowing who held what cards after the first trick was played. Papa also loved baseball. For years he had managed and played on the Ghent baseball team. The family had followed the team to all his games in Granite Falls, Canby, and Marshall every Sunday in the spring, summer, and fall.

When I was young and stayed with Papa and Muzzy in the summers, I helped Papa weed and water his garden. Papa grew everything, vegetables and flowers and all kinds of berries: strawberries, gooseberries, raspberries, blueberries. In the early morning, "before it got hot," we grabbed our pails, walked out the sunporch door, through the backyard, down the stone path, past the garage, and up the steps to Papa's raised garden.

Papa and one of his cars

After we filled our buckets, we set aside the

best berries for canning; the others we ate right then for break-fast, smothering them with cream and sugar. Worth the pricks of picking, the berries tasted delicious, soft, and sweet.

In the quiet kitchen, though, I worried Muzzy and Papa would hear my tongue swishing against my teeth trying to dis-lodge the tiny trapped seeds. I waited impatiently to be excused from the table so I could pick my teeth, wander around, not be watched over. My grandparents' house was proper, quiet. I could hear clocks tick, floors creak, chairs sigh, toilets gurgle.

The house smelled of tobacco and smoke. Papa loved ci-gars, Havana Cubans the best. Several times a day he would take one, carefully cut off its tip with a small silver jackknife, smell and chew, and then touch it to the flame of his silver lighter. Sit-ting in Muzzy's pink leather chair, he puffed away, occasionally tapping the cigar or dropping pieces of it in the greenish metal ashtray standing ready by his side.

The smoke hovered over the gold-framed pictures above the upright piano and drifted down to the Oriental rug and wood floor. The pleasant-pungent aroma emanating from Papa and his clothes settled in the heavy drapes and Muzzy's needlepointed chairs.

The smell enveloped me when Papa leaned over to peck my cheek or pat my head or take my hand. I didn't dislike the ci-gar smell. It was homey and comfortable, like Papa, and I loved it when he held my hand. He held it just right, not too hard.

I thought of Papa as strong and assured, always in charge. Every morning, as soon as he got up, he did his exer-cises—stretches and jumping jacks. "It's important to keep your body sound," he'd say. Although he was only 5'6", Papa didn't seem short; he was solid, vigorous.

When I first began to write memoir, I asked Mom if there was anything really interesting or scandalous in our family backgrounds. "We're so boring," I said. She looked at me hesi-tantly. "Well, there was the effigy . . . but Margaret, you'd never write about that!" Then I heard about 1933, when Papa was a banker.

Mom told the story this way:

For twenty-five years, Papa successfully managed the hardware store. In 1929, tired of handling such a large enterprise, Papa decided to sell and become a banker in Ghent. Another bank already existed in Ghent, the First Bank, run by Charlie Foulon. Charlie's wife, Clemence, was called "The Queen of the Belgians." I remember a picture of her taken at the Ghent Ball Club in the '20s, wearing a black taffeta dress and big brimmed hat, and holding a lacy umbrella. She and Charlie sent their girls to boarding schools in Europe. But she was also the midwife for Alfred and me.

Papa thought the town could support another bank beside the First. He borrowed money and started the Farmer's State Bank. But then hard times came to America, between the World Wars and the Depression. Papa desperately tried to keep the bank from failing. It suffered one foreclosure. Papa reorganized and managed to keep it operating while hundreds of other banks closed in Minnesota. But two years later, the Farmer's State also had to close its doors.

The furious Belgian townspeople vented their anger at us German Schreibers. Muzzy received the silent treatment; my brother Eddie, in grade school, stones and epithets: "Kaisers." "Krauts." At night people crept up to our house and scattered tacks on our driveway, a special insult to Papa, who loved his cars, the one at that time a particular favorite, a big Buick with blue and red stripes and red-rimmed wheels.

I was in my twenties then, living at home and working at the law firm in Marshall. The others were away: Alfred at the seminary and Grace and Rose at St. Catherine's. I lost a boyfriend over the bank failure. His mother and lots of other people talked behind our backs. Even in Marshall, some people gave me dirty looks. Convinced Papa had done nothing wrong, I'd give them looks right back.

But the final outrage, which I didn't find out about until years later: two nuns from St. Eloi's, Sister Dorinda and the principal of the school, Sister Lamberta—both very good friends of our family—rushed over one night to our house. 'Quick,' they whispered to Papa at the back door, 'get down to the bank. Don't take Julia or the children with you.'

An effigy of Papa hung from the bank's flagpole.

Angry and ashamed, Papa swore his wife and children would never learn anything about the incident. At Bethany Convent, the retirement home for the Sisters of St. Joseph in St. Paul, Sisters Dorinda and Lamberta told me. They said they needed to "clear the books" before they died, to tell me how tough it was for Papa in this chapter of his life. They had remained true friends of our family over all those years.

Attempting to satisfy the bank's debt, Muzzy and Papa lost the Schreiber farm and our home in Ghent. Penniless, Papa accepted the loathsome job of a traveling bill collector for John Deere. Forced to leave our family in hate-filled Ghent while he was on the road, Papa saved up until we could move to Sauk Centre. He was also promoted to a regional manager for John Deere. When the family moved, I found a nice boarding house to rent in Marshall. I was glad to be on my own.

Two years later, the company offered Papa a store of his own in Rochester. He did well there and was prosperous once again, like when he had the hardware store in Ghent.

I wondered why Mom never talked about this time in her life. Or why didn't Muzzy or Papa?

"I guess we wanted to remember the happier times. I guess we all just wanted to forget," she said.

At the time she told this story, I had no idea of all that my mother wanted to forget.

Papa "worked his butt off," as he always said, for years at the Olmsted County Implement Company in Rochester, establishing a very successful business. Finally retiring in his seventies, he and Muzzy travelled in the wintertime to St. Petersburg, Florida, where Papa golfed and they both played bridge. In the

Papa's store in Rochester, Minnesota

summers, until he became ill, Papa still planted his garden. When I visited, I would again grab a pail and help him pick berries.

The last time I saw Papa, in 1969, he wasn't working. He wasn't impeccably clean. He wasn't himself. He wore diapers under drab brown overalls and a gray institutional shirt, faded and messy with snot dribbles and bits of dried-up food. Tied to a chair and spoon-fed some awful-looking gruel by a disinterested nurse, Papa grunted occasionally, but mostly his head slumped over his chest.

Papa didn't know me. Earlier on, he had mistaken me for my mom or my aunts. But at the end, he didn't recognize anyone—except Muzzy. Ignoring the rules and regulations of the State Hospital in Rochester, she brought cigars and lit them up. She puffed until Papa's head slowly lifted and his mouth worked, opened. With both of her hands, Muzzy held the Havana Cuban between his lips. Papa puffed his cigar. Soon his old brown-leathered hands with the heavy gold wedding ring reached to cover Muzzy's veiny, white hands on his face. Teeth clamped round the cigar, he smiled.

After writing about my mom and her secrets, and my grandfather and his, I began to understand the Schreiber family in a more significant way. Knowing their stories helped me to understand myself, not only as a member of the human race but also as a descendant of these particular, complex human beings. I'm linked to their history, connected to their struggles and failings, successes and joys. It's been said family stories contribute to the development of confidence and resiliency in children. An ordinary family is special after all. If you know the stories, you belong. It's a fingerprint.

FAITH

As a young girl, my prayers took the form of spiritual bouquets. I presented them to Mom and Dad for their birthdays, for Christmas, and for Mother's and Father's Days. The bouquets didn't cost any money; you made cards, writing down the number of times you said particular prayers for a specific person. I loved that I could offer any number or kind of prayers. I particularly liked writing *big numbers*: fifty Our Fathers, fifty Hail Marys, seventy-five Glory Bes. Ejaculations—short prayers, simple one-liners, "Mary, pray for me," "Jesus, help me"—were the best; I could do hundreds of them. Creative with my cards, I drew sprays of vivid posies on the fronts and smaller, lighter petals inside, next to the listings of prayer names and numbers.

Spiritual bouquets were something like saving Green Stamps. The stamps, printed in one, ten, and fifty points, could be punched out of sheets, licked, and pasted into free S&H collectors' books. Books of stamps could be redeemed for items in a catalog—physical rewards on earth—housewares, games, camping equipment, furniture, even a sporty motorboat for 170 books. But spiritual bouquets promised a higher prize, to reach Heaven.

Both appealed to me for their checking-off qualities, similar to Confession. Once you confessed your list of sins, and Father blessed you, and you performed your penance, your soul was a clean slate, ready for the next stain of wrongdoing, like the erasable drawing pads whose marks were wiped away when you lifted up the plastic sheet. I constantly lifted my soul's cover, never worrying about the deep scratches forming on the black background underneath.

I was a carefree kid, but even I couldn't help being affected by Catholic culture. My sister Mary worried about everything religious. She would spend a lot of time thinking about doing the right thing. I simply performed the rites and rituals without much contemplation.

I saved loved ones on All Souls' Day. You could release a soul serving time in Purgatory if you went to a church and said the right prayers. Visiting a cemetery and devoutly praying for the departed was, of course, better, but our relatives weren't buried at Marshall's Catholic Calvary. I rode my bike to St. Mary's Chapel in Holy Redeemer School or downtown to the big church on Lyon and 5th Streets.

The church visit plus reciting an Our Father and the Creed offered a plenary indulgence to your named soul in Purgatory. A partial indulgence could be obtained for the souls if you only prayed the "Eternal Rest" prayer: *Eternal rest grant to them, O Lord, and let perpetual light shine upon them. May the souls of the faithful departed, through the mercy of God, rest in peace. Amen.* I never really understood indulgences. The sisters or priests tried to explain: "The remission of temporal punishment due for sins which have already been forgiven." What could that possibly mean? Just to be safe, though, I recited all three prayers, guaranteeing my souls Heaven right away.

Actually, "Eternal Rest" was a good prayer for the whole month of November. If you said it with certain other prayers for the full week of November 2–8 (called a novena), the souls in Purgatory racked up release points. I didn't do novenas: too long. I liked to get quick results. On November 2, I'd say prayers for my named soul, leave church, stand on the steps outside for a few minutes, come back in, bless myself with holy water from the baptismal font, and pray again for another soul. I saved Dad's family over and over again. I could feel their souls rushing up to join all the angels and saints in Heaven every time I earned my indulgences. I saved them for years, until I finally questioned the whole thing. Saved was saved. Why did I do the same thing year after year? Why should I doubt the success of my previous prayers?

The Church didn't help with that question. People were just encouraged to keep praying. What was important, I guess, was that even if you weren't actively praying—just counting and crossing off—you still consciously concentrated on these people for a day every year. Not knowing any of them in real life, except for Aunt Bea, and only recalling their faces from the few pictures I'd seen of them, I still wanted to remember and pray for them, as I did in the spiritual bouquets for my parents. I wished them well and asked God to do the same. I felt responsible and connected—and also hoped those souls were looking after me.

We spent a lot of time and attention on being religious. We followed the example of my father. Living by the Golden Rule, he was known for putting belief into practice. One of his practices was to take care of us kids when we were sick. On an old, green metal tray, he'd bring up tomato soup with white crackers and 7-Up. He would serve that combination for every kind of sickness: colds, sore throats, flu. He'd sit on our beds and we'd talk. When I told him stories about my friends I called them by their last names: Jerzak, Culhane, Van Moer, Luchtel. We all did that at school, but Dad didn't like it. He said it didn't show respect. Showing respect was another of his practices.

I remember one time when I was sick and in kindergarten. I asked Dad if what Kathy Culhane, my good friend, bragged about could be true. Could she be more Irish? When Dad explained Kathy was 100 percent Irish, and I was only 50 percent, I cried. Dad got me smiling again by saying that with my blue eyes, dark hair, and hundred freckles, no one would guess I wasn't all Irish. I loved being Irish, treasured the romantic, lyrical country. The words, the songs, the faces; the way my father looked, talked, sang, and smiled.

Irish and Catholic, Dad *believed*. I never understood his deep, constant faith. He lived his religion quietly, steadily, without fanfare, never acting pious or self-righteous. He never made us kids walk his holy path. Because he was so kind and likeable, we willingly hiked along with him, imitating his gait and gestures, trying to live as large and lovingly as he did.

Mom's religiosity took a different form. She prayed with us at church and at home, attended Mass, led the rosary on car trips, but what she really liked was singing in the choir. She was more practical and active than Dad. She had things to do: linen to wash, food to prepare, records to keep. She didn't have time to contemplate or read *The Catholic Digest* or the Jesuit *America* magazine. Her life contradicted the usual generalization that women tend to be more religious than men.

I was with her. I certainly thought we prayed way too much. In church, before a game, Monsignor Neudecker "beseeched the players to compete as Christians." After the game, if our team won, we begged for humility; if it lost, we pleaded for faith. My brothers signed the cross at the free-throw line in basketball, and the whole football team huddled an Our Father before charging onto the field to block and tackle.

In our house, going to a game was like going on a holy pilgrimage. We tried to plan for it ahead of time because Dad always wanted to leave early. "C'mon, Alice, let's go. We can't be late." But no matter how she worked, Mom was always late getting us ready. Like a shepherd, Dad guided us out the door to the car. "Let's go. Let's go. Let's really go," he would chant, patting our rumps as we rushed out. Invariably, someone would try to escape, turning back for something. Dad would hook his arm around the stray, herding him or her toward the car.

He hated to miss even the warm-up sessions of my

brothers' varsity games at Central Catholic High School. While I chatted with friends and bought pop and candy at the concession stand, Dad sat motionless, watching. While I ran underneath the bleachers looking for money and other treasures, Dad never moved. Didn't yell or cheer. Just watched. At the end of the games, he'd immediately head home with us, not waiting to congratulate or sympathize. He was tired from watching so faithfully. Later he would talk about the games, play by play, at the dinner table with the boys. It was sacred time. For us girls, boring. We weren't part of this world. After the boys hashed it all out, we would talk about piano, and dance, and school plays.

It was a sexist era. Girls didn't play competitive sports; we were cheerleaders. Our smart mother was *only a secretary* in a law firm, even though her old boss told us she ran the place. Both Mom and Dad always encouraged Mary and me to be whoever we wanted to be, saying before we'd heard it anywhere else: "Why be a secretary? Be the lawyer." "Why be a nurse? Be the doctor."

They didn't promote gender divisions. When we were young, we all played ball. Dad played football with us on Sundays after Mass. Leading us out to the side of the house, he'd throw the ball, yelling, "Go out for a pass. Go on out. Deep, deeper." He'd run backwards, singing, "Cheer, cheer, for old Notre Dame / Wake up the echoes cheering her name / Send a volley cheer on high . . . " The first songs we learned to sing and the only ones Dad taught us were "The Notre Dame Victory March" and "The University of Minnesota Rouser." "Minnesota, hats off to thee / To thy colors true we shall ever be / Firm and strong, united are we."

Big and strong, over two hundred pounds, when Dad tackled me he set me down nice and easy, saying, "There. I got you, Peggy, my fine halfback." Dad called me *Peggy* or *My Little Colleen*, Irish nicknames. Sometimes he called me *Sarah Bernhardt* because I liked to put on little plays and dances for him and Mom—or maybe because he thought I was a big ham.

Dad loved to coach, saying he was teaching us team play: "No one should stand out—no prima donnas—but no one should stand alone either. Everyone supports one another, gives 100 percent. Win or lose, it doesn't matter. It's trying that counts." Team play: the Golden Rule for Dad.

A friend of coaches, Dad gave advice if they asked, and he hired a number of them to sell insurance. He often sent me to babysit their kids but didn't like me accepting money for the job. "Consider yourself lucky to have the honor, Peggy." I didn't think I was so lucky or honored, but I still did it. I always wanted to please him. All of us kids did.

In Marshall, on Sunday nights, after we cleaned up from football and had supper, we walked over with Mom and Dad to another Catholic home and prayed the neighborhood rosary. Mom and Dad knelt down in whatever living room we were visiting and loudly recited the Our Fathers, Hail Marys, and Glory Bes. They gave us kids dirty looks if we weren't attentive. And we never were. We knelt next to our friends and goofed around with our eyes, and, if we could get away with it, our feet and elbows. "Holy Mary, (kick) Mother of God, (kick) . . . "

Just like at church, someone would giggle and the sound would spread. Titters. Snickers. It couldn't be stopped. Struggling to keep it in, the snort burst through shaking shoulders, through tears running down faces. Then a hoot or holler—which brought parental intervention. "Stop. Behave. Shame on you." The parents frowned, their father and mother eyes piercing in disapproval. Everything settled down. We prayed, faces cast downward, hands together. Then a sideways look, and it started again. "Holy Mary, (kick) Mother of God, (kick) . . . ."

Every Friday afternoon in May, Holy Redeemer, both elementary and high school, *processed* from asphalt parking lot to asphalt parking lot, winding around a couple of times and finally ending up at Our Lady's Grotto in front of the convent chapel. Instead of the usual 50 Hail Marys, 5 Our Fathers and Glory Bes of one set of mysteries, in the procession we prayed all 15 mysteries, the joyful, the sorrowful, and the glorious: 15 Our Fathers, 150 Hail Marys, 15 Glory Bes. While we prayed, we were to remember Mary from the Annunciation, when the Archangel Gabriel announced she would be the Mother of God, through the sad days of the Crucifixion, to her glorious Assumption, when her dead body was taken to Heaven and she was crowned Queen of Heaven and Earth. Marching and praying our rosary beads, we crooned Marian songs between the mysteries: "Hail, Holy Queen, enthroned above, O, Mar—ri—a; "Immaculate Mary, our hearts are on fire . . . A-ve, A-ve, A-ve Ma-ri-a. A-ve, A-ve, Mar—ri—i—i—a."

I marched, fingering my rosary beads, mechanically reciting without considering the Virgin Mary's blessings and challenges. I kept trying to find friends to walk beside, to whisper with between the rote prayers and songs. I'd turn my white stone rosary this way and that. I'd hold it up over my head. The stones snared the sun, sending out colorful sparks of light. That light, not the light of faith, is what I remember.

After we moved to St. Paul, our family never missed the Catholic May Day Family Rosary Procession. We joined thousands of other people barely moving as we progressed, answering the Our Fathers, Hail Marys, and Glory Bes led by a monsignor, riding in a truck at the front of the line. He used a thunderous loudspeaker. The prayers echoed above us as we *processed* for miles, from Nativity Church to the Cathedral, past police barriers blocking off streets. We marched along Summit Avenue on that first day of May, the same day the Communists goose-stepped in the Red Square of Moscow. Spiritual might defying military power. I was almost embarrassed by the public spectacle of religious fervor.

But religious fervor is what Dad possessed. When he lost his football scholarship to Notre Dame because of his back injury, he carried no resentment. He just shrugged and said, "That's just how it was done in those days. It wasn't anybody's fault." Playing for the "Fighting Irish" was a highlight of his life—Our Lady, Irish, and football all tied together. He was so proud when Dan and a number of grandchildren graduated from Notre Dame.

When we were young, Dad sometimes got tickets for Notre Dame games and we drove to South Bend, a thirteen-hour car trip. Mom packed lunches and demanded bathroom stops. We kids took turns throwing money into the Illinois toll-booths. We gawked through Chicago. We pinched our noses through Gary. We cheered at the Knute Rocke travel plaza on the Indiana Toll Road. We were as excited as Dad.

I watched him watching the game. Standing very straight, hand across his chest, Dad devoutly sang the national anthem. At the kickoff, he raised his arm. "Let's go get 'em!" At the end of the game, I sang heartily, "What though the odds be great or small / Old Notre Dame will win over all / While her loyal sons are marching onward to victory," but noticed Dad just smiling at the college kids linking their arms, swaying to the Alma Mater. "Notre Dame our mother / Tender, strong and true / Proudly in the heavens gleams thy gold and blue." As at my brothers' high-school games, Dad didn't join the spectators; he stood tall but apart. The believer.

In his mind, sports and faith entwined. He believed in a life where players skirmished and fought, lost and won, sinned and were saved. This happened of course on an individual basis—sort of an honorable warrior—but it was quintessentially a communal expression. Team support and love. We scheduled holiday dinners around Notre Dame, the Big Ten, the NFL, and the NBA. When I grew up and roasted the turkey at my house, Dad would say, "Peggy, why don't you put that bird on really early in the morning? We could eat at halftime." Watching games on TV, he would situate himself in his big leather chair long before the kickoff and then stand for the national anthem, hand across his chest. By then I had grown tired of professional sports—and of watching them—but I loved my dad and let him have his way.

His team support stretched into politics as well: love of our country, the Big Team. In 1960, the Catholic community of Marshall prayed for one of its own, asking God to bless the candidacy of John F. Kennedy, the first Catholic since Al Smith to run for president. Holy Redeemer Grade School and Central Catholic High School stood solidly behind JFK.

Our family, however, supported Richard Milhous Nixon. During the primaries, nuns and priests pulled me aside in school halls and on the playground to ask if my father had reassessed his position. They couldn't believe Pat Rogers wasn't supporting Kennedy. They only asked us about Dad; I don't remember who Mom supported or how we kids felt about it. My guess is that we stood behind Dad out of family loyalty. But why Dad stood behind Tricky Dicky is hard to understand. Politics trumped religion.

We all knew Dad was a Republican and believed in states' rights and responsibilities. Still, if he thought the Republicans were going to win a landslide in a national election, he'd vote Democratic. "No one should have too much power. That's not good for our country." At least that's what he told me, always a Democrat. For a time, he was the chairman of the Lyon County Republican Party. He told me he resigned from his position because of *the heat.* "No kidding, honey. Folks get really angry. And I don't want to fight. I just want to talk."

At the time of the Kennedy-Nixon election, Mary supported Dad and represented Nixon in an official town debate held in the high-school gymnasium; her opponent was the fellow who would also compete with her for valedictorian of their class. Before the debate, Mary worked through tons of research, cataloguing hundreds of notes. She stored them by category in index-size cardboard boxes. She'd talk to me in bed at night about domestic and foreign policy until I shouted, "Stop! Turn off the light." Mary and I still shared a bedroom and a double bed. Too old now to draw the middle line down the mattress— "Get over. You're over!"—we had learned how to protect our individual rights.

It was a packed house the night of the debate. Mary sat behind a long cafeteria table full of her boxes. The American flag and a large bouquet of flowers stood next to her on the shiny hardwood floor. Everyone stood, sang "The Star-Spangled Banner" and recited the Pledge of Allegiance, hands across chests. Then a coin toss. Mary won heads, and, as Dad said, "proceeded to beat the pants off her worthy opponent." The Catholic community filed out, fiercely disappointed. The nuns and priests eventually forgave the Rogers family their political sin only because the country voted Kennedy in as president.

Dad didn't miss any of the football or basketball games Tom and Dan played for Cretin High School when we moved to St. Paul. Or many of Cretin's games from then on. After Dad retired in 1988, the coach of the football team, a friend of Dad's, asked him to speak to the players. It looked as if Cretin had a chance to win the state championship and Dad, an inspirational speaker, could motivate the players. Dad met with the team twice, each time stopping over at my house in St. Paul for coffee beforehand. Nervous about what he was going to say, he had his notes and wanted to go over them with me.

GOALS

1. Name your goals.
2. Write them down.
3. Look at them frequently.
4. Remember God has given each of us the right to choose.

AMBITION

1. Desire to be your best self.
2. Give everything your best shot.
3. Copy from winners.

4. Deeds are more important than words.

ENTHUSIASM

1. Go for broke.
2. Help others to get excited.
3. Look for positive rather than negative thoughts.
4. Spread it around your friends and family.

COOPERATION

1. Try to get along with everyone.
2. Rely on your teachers and coaches for advice.
3. Helping others is your best way to help yourself.
4. Listen to the adults you respect and like. Role models.

DISCIPLINE

1. Do what you say you are going to do.
2. Be on time.
3. Take responsibility.
4. Put all things in their order.

LOYALTY

1. Be loyal to your friends and to the team.
2. Be who you say you are.
3. The team is more important than you (a member).
4. To make your school the best by going first class at all times.

THREE THINGS EVERYONE WANTS:

1. Trust.
2. Commitment to excellence.
3. The Golden Rule.

Dad told me his talks went well. "The young lads even

seemed interested."

Sports—and faith—to the end. In the summer of 1991, Mary, Dan, and I left our families to accompany our parents on a trip to visit their grandchildren, our nephews, studying abroad. We were to meet our folks in Madrid. They had been pilgrimaging in Medjugore, a Catholic miracle place in what used to be Yugoslavia, with a group from their parish in Minnesota. My flight from Minneapolis and Mary and Dan's from Chicago landed earlier in Madrid and we waited together for Mom and Dad's flight to arrive. It took some time. Many groups jostled through the arrival gates but not our folks. We began to worry that they had missed the plane, that something was wrong. We were already worried about Dad's ability to travel. He recently had undergone surgery for prostate cancer.

And then I spotted him in the crowd. Always so tall and with his shock of white hair, Dad stood out like St. Christopher, a sort of a giant who carried the baby Christ across raging waters. Dad helped petite Mom through the gate, pushing through the current of hugging, exclaiming folks.

"Is it good to see you kids," Dad said. He was very tired but ecstatic about the holiness of Medjugorje. He and Mom had stayed with a poor lady who offered hard pallets for beds and basically only bread to eat. Dad watched crippled people climb the steep and rocky hills of the village up to the grotto of Our Lady to pray, and even though he was suffering from his surgery, he figured if they could do it, he could, too.

Mom affirmed, "He did."

He believed in the miracles of Medjugorje. He believed he saw one. He spoke to me about it, sort of sheepishly, in their hotel room. "I know, Peggy, you're going to say *Don't be silly*. But, honey, I did, I swear I saw the sky change. The clouds rolled over the blue, then off again." He smiled at me.

Mom smiled. "He did."

I smiled back at them. "C'mon, you're sounding like Aunt Bea with the visions. You're scaring me."

What they practiced—what they were so enthused about—was the scripture rosary, a new concept, the traditional rosary broken up by meditations on biblical passages. We *kids* thought it was a great idea, leaving behind simple, mindless recitation.

Our little group stayed in Madrid for a few days, and we saw the sights. Dad especially liked to visit churches. The great Prado Museum couldn't compare. He was moved by every mosaic, statue, painting; by every Mass celebrated. He was particularly enthusiastic about the Valley of the Fallen. Inaugurated by Francisco Franco in 1959 outside of Madrid, the Valley boasts a cross 150 meters high, a crypt 262 meters into the mountain, and a dome 33 meters in diameter. So enormous, so pretentious, it hardly feels prayerful, and indeed Franco is buried in the crypt along with Republican and Nationalist soldiers. Dad still loved it. He was willing to overlook a Fascist regime, or at least to not question it, because it constructed a magnificent structure to honor God.

We thought it was good for Dad to get exercise on the trip. We had no idea his cancer had already spread to his bones. We made him walk to the nearest plaza each night. His leg was already bothering him, angling out when he walked. I'm sure it pained him, but he never complained. He said the only thing that troubled him was not being able to communicate. Or to do business. One morning walking near our hotel he asked us what the word *seguros* meant, saying he kept seeing the sign over buildings. When we said insurance, his face lit up; he bolted down the block, his leg hobbling. When he got to the door of the building, his shoulders slumped as he remembered he couldn't speak in Spanish. He turned around and walked back to us. "Shit," we heard him mumble.

We traveled through Spain in the largest car we could rent, a Citroën, but Dad still barely fit in the front seat. Listening to a tape of Irish music he had brought along, we sped through the countryside, spring-gorgeous with wild red poppies, magnolias, and mimosa. From the middle of the backseat, between Mary and me, Mom, the smallest of us all, sang Dad's favorite songs: "Danny Boy" and "I'll Take You Home Again, Kathleen."

Tending to just yell louder in English if he wasn't being understood, in Cordoba, Dad shouted out the car window, "The mosquito, where's the mosquito?" We were trying to find the mosque—in Spanish, the *mesquita*. Mom tried to speak Spanish—she had studied in community-education classes, preparing for the trip—and preceded and followed Dad's bark with *Por favor* and *Gracias*.

They were eager travelers, willing to go anywhere and do anything. When we visited my nephews in Seville, they took us to a premier matador training school. Enthralled, Dad proclaimed to me, "Can you believe it, Peggy? Such courage. Such strength. Beauty. Ballet. Like football." To him, the bullring was like a stadium: a community of believers assembled for worship.

From their spring Medjugorje trip to at-home hospice the fall of that year, Dad prayed the scripture rosary. A few weeks before he died, Mary flew home from Chicago to spend time with him. Mom bustled in and out of the den doing various tasks. She wasn't so keen on saying rosaries. In fact, she complained about having to say several a day. "Girls, he's getting too holy here at the end." As I myself was becoming more unreligious at this time, I agreed with her, but I respected my dad's belief.

Mary and I prayed with him. Once as we sat together by his hospital bed, Mary began, "Glory be to the Father," and I automatically answered, "As it was in the beginning, is now, and ever shall be, world without end. Amen." Mary shook her head and giggled, "No, it's not that prayer; it's from the Bible." She giggled again. I giggled. She snorted. I hooted. Our shoulders shook. Tears ran down our faces. Dad, barely able to move or speak, looked at us with those blue father eyes, and suddenly we weren't middle-aged women sitting next to our dying father; we were young again at the neighborhood rosaries and at church, where once a giggle started it passed down the row and couldn't be stopped.

Minutes before Dad died, we were again praying to Our Lady. "Hail Mary, full of grace, the Lord is with thee." Dad's labored breathing changed. The death rattle stopped. His face smoothed, his eyes focused out, beyond. "Blessed art thou among women and blessed is the fruit of Thy womb, Jesus." His hands, which had been knitting the air, relaxed. Mom took one in hers. I took the other. "Holy Mary, Mother of God, pray for us sinners . . . " — Dad took a long, peaceful breath and then let it out— ". . . now, and at the hour of our death. Amen." A perfect ending for this man of faith.

FROM THE HALLS

I was in the air, hanging onto the sides of my desk. The ink bottle tipped over, pen and notebooks rolled to the floor. Randy Bartles, who sat behind me, was at it again. Sister St. Edmund, our eighth-grade teacher, had assigned these seats, figuring I could handle him.

"Put me down, Randy," I hissed, *"right now."*

Pulling his hands through his long, greasy hair and jerking his big feet out from under the rails connecting our desks, he banged the section of track down. Boooom. No one noticed; it was just an ordinary classroom sound.

We'd been listening to *masterpiece music*—it wasn't cool to like it, but secretly, I looked forward to music-appreciation. That day "Bolero" blasted away, a great Spanish-sounding song, the same tune played over and over, rising higher and higher, louder and louder. The rhythm built steadily. I had been daydreaming of matadors and ladies with castanets, until Randy started in.

He had poked me in the back with an old spark plug. Wacky about engines, he stored car and cycle parts in his jacket. And he must have been crazy about that rotten old leather jacket, too, because he never took it off. As "Bolero" crescendoed and Sister wrote on the blackboard, he stuck the spark plug into his inkwell, grabbed the sides of the desk, jabbed his feet under the tracks, and hoisted us up. He was strong; he could raise the whole row.

"Time for the ride," he'd whispered loudly. "Here we go. Whirrrr. Whirrrr. Holy cow, I forgot, we need some gas. Here it comes, look out, here comes the biggest fart I've ever let fly."

"Oh, man," everybody groaned. "Randy again."

"God, Randy, that's disgusting," I croaked, desperately wanting to throw open a window, to let some air in.

It was fall, my favorite season. I loved getting my sweaters out of the cedar chest—brand-new again even if they smelled like mothballs. I loved watching leaves change color and fall off the trees. We raked them up into huge piles to jump into and helped Dad burn them in little piles on the side of the road. Dad let us use his lighter to start the fires sometimes. The teeny flame caught the dry, crackling leaves, flickered, then flamed, then blazed up. The leaf smoke joined the wood smoke of fireplaces and that smell followed you everywhere.

The fall air could also cool off the classroom. Holy Redeemer had just turned on its furnace, and the dusty, clanking radiators poured out heat. Sister said it'd take a while to regulate the second floor. It was stuffy and stinky—over forty of us jammed into this room, and a lot of kids didn't wash much or use deodorant.

I was feeling sick anyway. Cramps. Again. My period had come early, at the end of fifth grade. My mom hadn't believed me when I told her.

"I've got what Mary just got," I told her.

"No, you don't," she said.

"I do."

"You can't. You're too young."

"I do."

"I'm sure you don't."

"I do."

"Then go talk to your sister."

Mary confirmed my diagnosis. Upset and embarrassed, I went back to Mom.

"I do too, Mom, and you should have believed me."

Mom said she was sorry, brought me up to her bedroom, handed over the strange sanitary belt, and offered me those bleached-white but still-stained cloths she stashed in her dresser drawer. "These are what I wear during the *special time*."

"Ick. No thanks." I squirmed. "I'll use Mary's Kotex. And I don't think it's special at all."

Mom was old-fashioned and always saved by doing without. *Waste not* was her motto. She even made her own laundry soap, frying up lard and straining the fat though a net, then adding lye and boiling water, and stirring all this up in a tub with a big wooden stick. At a sleepover my friends told me *their* mothers used tampons—in fact, ancient Egyptians had invented the first disposable tampons, made from softened papyrus. My friends wouldn't quit until I tried one. Ordering me into the bathroom armed with a jar of Vaseline and a box of Tampax, they waited in the hallway, whispering through the locked keyhole.

"Did ya get it in?"

"What's taking you so long?"

I finally emerged. We celebrated, storming the grocery store to buy two Fudgsicles apiece.

I'd never shared my cramps with anybody—too embarrassing—but once they hurt so bad, I asked Sister if I could stay in at recess. She gave me that questioning-mother look, but thank God only answered, "All right, dear, you *may*."

I should have been out for recess, for push-up-against-the-building, our new game. The girls huddled together in a pack, trying to keep the boys from singling any of us out to shove up against the bricks. Of course we all wanted to be caught, to feel the boys' bodies pushed up against ours, but we pretended it was the worst thing and ran around screaming, "Don't let them get me!" When one of the girls did get cornered, the rest of us had to break through the boys' pack to rescue her. I was tough. The girls probably missed me out there.

I rummaged in my desk for the *Baltimore Catechism,* the book of questions and answers for anyone who wanted to grow in their knowledge of the Catholic Church. Sister wanted us to study it whenever we had free time. Our class was to be confirmed, and Sister wanted us totally prepared. I could already spout most of the questions and answers. We had been practicing them forever.

"Who made you?"

"God made me."

"Why did God make you?"

"God made me to know, love, and serve Him in this world, and to be happy with Him forever in the next."

I didn't care what any of it meant. I just wanted to be ready for the bishop's questions. Confirmation I would do right—not like the other sacraments.

In Penance, I had made a fool of myself. A few weeks before First Confession Day, our second-grade class marched to the chapel for a rehearsal. Immediately after we lined up in the pews, Sister was called away on an emergency. She instructed us to stay in our seats. "Boys and girls, be very quiet. Pray. Pray for forgiveness."

But I quickly grew tired of being good and feeling guilty. I stood up and announced, "C'mon. Let's practice ourselves. I'll be Father. You guys come in and out." Plopping down on the bench in the priest's stall, I started to hear confessions.

I slid open the little door on my right side: my first sinner. "In the name of the Father, and of the Son, and of the Holy Ghost. Bless me, Father, for I have sinned. This is my First Confession. I was mean to my brother or sister seventy-five times; I talked back to my mother or father ten times; I stole twenty-five times."

"And what did you steal, my child?" I asked.

"Cookies, umm, Father."

We had debated cookie snitching in the classroom. Sister had concluded that a forbidden hand in the jar wasn't serious stealing, but if it bothered us, we should confess it.

"What kind were they? And are you sorry for stealing

them, my child?" I asked.

"Chocolate chip. They were really good," said the sinner, "and my mother spanked me for taking so many of them. Should I tell you that, umm, Father?"

My second sinner had the same list as the first. Sister had drilled us for days on sins, even writing a sample list on the board, which we all copied down. Since each kid told me the same vices, no grievous offenses, no mortal sins, just boring venials, I assigned the same penance to everybody: "Five Our Fathers, five Hail Marys."

I slid the little door back and forth between stalls, signed magnificent crosses over my penitents, and pronounced, "You are forgiven, go in peace, and sin no more."

Suddenly, the big confessional door flung open. There was Sister, her glasses bouncing up and down on her blotchy red face. "Margie, what are you doing in here? Oh, terrible. Terrible," she muttered. "A sacrilege. Boys and girls. Children. Up to our room. We'll practice later."

As a punishment, Sister sent me to the cloakroom, full of boots, jackets, mittens, hats, and scarves. I tried to breathe through my mouth; the rubber and wool were still wet and drying, a putrid smell.

So different from the sweet smell of my First Communion Day, when I was in third grade. Early in the morning, I put on white: lacy slip and dress, stockings, shoes, satin bows at the ends of my braids, and the beautiful long veil. I clutched a brand-new, white rosary and missal, the book that contained the words and music to be used in Mass every day of the year. I was ready to receive the Holy Eucharist for the first time and then be accepted forever as one of the faithful, allowed to go up to the altar with Mom and Dad and my older brothers and sister.

My soul was white, too, made spotless by Confession the day before. I worked to keep it that way over the hours that followed, creeping through the house, avoiding everybody and staying out of the kitchen, away from temptation. It'd be awful if I broke my fast and couldn't receive with the class. I perched on the edge of the wing chair in the living room, my eyes and ears fixed on the mantel clock ticking slowly to the hour we'd leave for Holy Redeemer Church.

"Receive the Body of Christ," Monsignor said, and he laid the Host on my tongue.

Thank the Lord, I thought, It hadn't fallen on the paten or, horrors, onto the marble railing or floor, but cripes, It had stuck on the roof of my mouth. Sister had warned us about this possibility. I strained with my tongue, finally got It loose, and swallowed It, but, Holy Mary, It had touched my teeth. I was a sinner, not worthy to receive your Son. I faked happiness through the whole reception party.

By nighttime, I had come up with an idea to end my agony. I planned to confess first thing in the morning, tell Father about *teething* the Host, and then receive, for real, my First Communion. But it got all fouled up.

My younger brother Tommy, serving Mass for his first time that day, was doing fine, not forgetting his Latin, bowing, carrying the cruets without spilling, but at the holiest and quietest part of Mass, when I was deep in prayer, Tommy tripped over his cassock and tumbled down the altar steps, the consecration bell along with him. "Ding a ling . . . a ling . . . a ling . . . a ling."

I couldn't help it. I giggled along with the rest of the congregation after Tommy looked out at us with a shrug and the famous *What, me worry?* look of Alfred E. Neuman. So. For the second time in my life, I received God irreverently.

Not so good on the sacraments. That was why I wanted to do Confirmation perfectly. I had already decided who my sponsors would be, but I couldn't decide what name to take. In Confirmation, you added another name to your first and second names. While the kids filed in from recess, I was thinking maybe I'd take Julia, Muzzy's name, or Alice or Rose, one of Mom's. Hard to decide.

I hadn't really chosen a patron saint for my first name yet. Sometimes I took Margaret Mary Alacoque, the nun who started the devotion to the Sacred Heart, but I hated the picture on the cloth scapulars and the scapular medals—Jesus, His robes pulled back, His finger pointing to His exposed beating heart, red fire above it, a sword through it. I'd never wear those scapulars around my neck. I considered Margaret Mary only because her feast day took place during the school year, so my name would be mentioned in morning announcements. St. Margaret of Scotland's day, June 10, came a week late, but she was a queen and a widow who brought up, all by herself, eight holy children and at the same time helped the kingdom's poor. Another Margaret appeared in some of the saint books, but she was a lesser saint, just another virgin martyr.

Tap. Tap. Tap. Sister's pointer chased away thoughts of names and saints. "I think that I shall never see / A poem lovely as a tree," she recited. Time for poetry. Everybody was tired after recess; heads slowly nodded in meter. We'd already done scary Poe with his rapping, rapping nevermores, and Robert Frost with his promises to keep. Sister made us act out "Sea Fever," but let us beat drums straight through "The Congo": "Boomlay, boomlay, boomlay, BOOM . . . "

Gerard Manley Hopkins, my favorite, wrote about my name and my freckles: "Márgarét, are you grieving / Over Goldengrove unleaving?" "Glory be to God for dappled things . . . whatever is fickle, freckled (who knows how?)" Hopkins was Sister's favorite, too, because he was a priest poet and wrote about God.

We all chanted: "A tree whose hungry mouth is prest / Against the earth's sweet flowing breast." The class snickered. Randy snorted. Sister scowled. Timmy Leahy twisted backwards in his chair and smiled at me. I smiled back. He winked at me. I blushed and covered up the pimple on my chin. Timmy scribbled a note and handed it back. Whoops. Sister eyed it. Leaping up from her desk, she bounded over and snatched it.

She read aloud, "Meet you on the steps after school." Everyone laughed.

Sister scowled and demanded, "*Who* wrote this? For *whom* is this note meant?" We shifted in our seats.

Sister's black shoe tapped the floor. "I'm *wait-ing,* class." Silence.

"All right. Kathy, Sharon, Terry, Dorothy, Margaret, Joanne, you stay after school."

I would miss Timmy today, miss meeting him on the chapel steps. He was short—if he stood on the second one up, we could talk face-to-face. I was hoping he'd kiss me soon. It was important to have a boy kiss you; it made you popular. Like being a cheerleader.

In history, we studied Roman times, the construction of roads and amphitheaters. I had my own gladiators stabbing away in my stomach. Like swords and daggers, these cramps really hurt, and now it was time for math. I wasn't dumb in it. I got good enough grades, but it didn't come easy so Dad helped me with my homework. He started out OK but usually ended up yelling, "Why can't you get this? The other kids did. It's easy. Think. Think." It made me think I was stupid, made me think about Sister making only me stay after school one day to take a test. I supposed Sister told Mom and Dad. I guessed it was some kind of IQ test, and no one wanted to tell me how I'd done.

Diagramming—a relief—dealt with simple, compound, or complex sentences. We sorted objects, complements, phrases, and clauses. The challenge sentence depicted autumn. When it looked like this in my notebook:

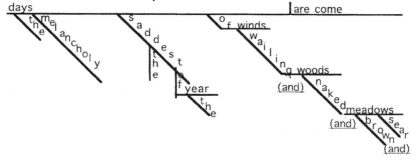

we moved on to spelling.

It was Friday, so we had a bee. Standing made the pain worse, but Sister named me a captain. I had to pick a team. I chose the best spellers even though I felt sorry for the crummy ones— not too sorry, though, because a lot of them would be first for football or basketball or baseball. Still, some kids—like Randy— were always last. Nuts. I misspelled *principal*—forgot to think she was a *pal*—but got to sit down. Not for long. Sister put last week's *masterpiece*, the "Peer Gynt Suite," on the record player, and we circled the classroom to its music. Each time we passed Sister's desk we dropped a penny into a metal cup. Every week we brought money for the overseas missions to help priests and nuns convert pagans and unbelievers to believing Catholics.

I slowly followed in the parade, wishing I was light, airy, a prancing troll from Edvard Grieg's "Hall of the Mountain King." I'd dance, twirling around and round and round the room. I'd swirl and whirl and spin on top of the desks.

Instead, I trudged back to my seat. I had only brought ten cents; my ten turns were up. We waited. Leroy marched and marched, dropping in twenty-five pennies. He was going to make it another *bles-sed* day. Already in October we had saved two pagan babies, five bucks each. Sister was so proud of us. We named our babies, voting on good Christian choices. In fancy calligraphy, Sister wrote the winning names, David Joseph and Elizabeth Mary, underneath their pictures on the bulletin board.

These African babies were pinned next to Vincent Van Gogh's *The Starry Night*, October 1959's Picture of the Month. It made me sad—the children looked so serious, and Van Gogh was so crazy he cut off his ear. I loved the stars of the painting, though, like headlights in the darkness. The babies made me think of Limbo, the place where unbaptized children who die in infancy go, because they're too young to have committed personal sins, but weren't freed from original sin. Even though I knew it was silly, sometimes when I passed by the bulletin board, I whispered, "Hi, Davey, Hi, Lizzie, I'm happy you'll never be in

Limbo, and I hope you're happier now that you're baptized." I thought they were better off because they weren't hungry. That made me happier.

Briiing. Briiing. Briiing. The last bell. Everyone rushed, pushed out the door. Sister slowed them all down before the stairs. Tall and wide, she was a good one to block traffic. My friends and I looked out the windows, watching the farm kids load the buses and the city kids scatter from the asphalt parking lot. Nervous about being told to stay after, we dashed for our desks when Sister pounded back into the room.

Heading straight for the blackboard, she grabbed a piece of chalk and wrote, with a wide sweep of her black arm, her white plastic bib crackling, **B O Y S**. The enormous white letters screamed at us from the blackboard. Sister towered over us.

"There. That's all you girls want. That's all you girls think about. You're only interested in one thing," and she sprang back to the board, her rosary smacking her hip, to furiously underline each letter. **B O Y S**.

No one dared look at each other. We stared at the awful word.

"Why, girls?" she demanded. "Why only boys on your minds? You all have talent; you all have such promise. Why?"

She went on, forcing tears from some. I saw them wiping their eyes on their sleeves. Not me. I wasn't going to cry.

Sister finally finished: "Remember, girls, you are made in the image and likeness of God. Never desecrate your body with pen or pencil marks. Remember, you are temples of the Holy Spirit. Never let anyone touch you. Remember Maria Goretti. Remember Saint Agnes and Saint Cecilia. Remember the Blessed Virgin. All right, girls, you are dismissed."

We packed up our books and raced out. Beyond the school door, we shouted, jumped, punched each other. "Maria Goretti." "**B—O—Y—S**."

Laughing hysterically, I threw my head back—and spotted Sister staring down at us from the second-floor window.

"Shh. Hey, quiet, guys. Shh, hey, stop. She's watching us."

Quickly we said our good-byes. "See ya tomorrow." "Call ya later."

Kathy and Sharon walked off to different ends of town. The others waited for parents or older brothers and sisters who drove them to their farms or nearby towns. I walked home alone, shortcutting through the hospital field. It was only a three-block walk to my house, but I felt cold. The wind was strong, blowing dust into my eyes and nose. It blew weeds around, scratching my ankles. It blew up my plaid wool skirt and over my bare legs. I noticed the fall trees. The poem I'd just memorized, "A tree that looks at God all day / And lifts her leafy arms to pray," wasn't about now. As I shuffled through the leaves circling on the ground, faded browns, yellows, dark oranges, I thought about the sun bursting awake in music, the orange crescent moon glowing in the starry night, Randy's ride, Timmy's smile, Sister's words. I kicked up a bright-red oak leaf to carry home with me. The wind blew it back and forth in my hand.

I grew up in the heyday of Catholic education: the 1950s and early 1960s. There were plenty of sisters teaching, all highly educated and trained in their disciplines and in religion. I can attest to a quality education. My eighth-grade teacher, Sister St. Edmund, opened my world to music, poetry, and art. A little nutty about the threat of BOYS, she was an early feminist: she wanted more for us than marrying very young and having baby after baby; she wanted us to be more than second-class citizens to the boys.

Sister St. Edmund entered an essay of mine in a state Catholic writing contest. I found the piece in my mom's saved folder. Written in cursive, the front cover includes my name, Margaret Rogers, and my home address; Holy Redeemer School and its address; the pastor, Rev. R. A. Neudecker, and the principal, Sister Elaine. The title: "What Would I Like To Do Most If I Had A Religious Vocation?"

What would I like to do most if I had a religious vocation? I knew the answer to that question five years ago. A little baby was brought home to the Rogers' family. She was cute and fat and sweet but over a period of weeks we noticed that she didn't comprehend many things. Mother and Father took her to a doctor who told them that Patty was a mentally retarded child. Since the first day I saw Patty I have felt a desire to be a Sister so I could teach her and the many other retarded children. One might ask, "Well, couldn't you teach retarded children without becoming a sister?" I think back to early childhood when I first saw a black-garbed sister. I asked Mother what it was? I will always remember her answer, "Margaret, these wonderful women have given up their Mommy and Daddy, their brothers and sisters, and many worldly pleasures to become daughters of Jesus and to teach you and other youngsters. They are very kind and I am sure that all Sisters will go to heaven." Heaven for sure! I knew then that I was to be a Sister so that I too could go to heaven.

Although the retarded child is intellectually slower, he has many stable qualities such as humility, unselfishness, and a love for all people. To build up these qualities so that they may have self-confidence, that they may become respectful citizens, that they may know that God's ever-loving arms are opened to them, that they may become good Catholics, is my great desire.

Some retarded children are still in their baptismal innocence and we might say they are saints on earth though they know nothing of the God who dwells in their hearts. Patty can not talk fluently but she can say "Jesus" and make the sign of the cross. I wish you could hear her say the sacred name, Jesus. She whispers it with profound reverence. I'd love to teach other subnormal children to say "Jesus" with equal devotion . . . I'd love to give friendship, guidance, love, and kindness to these special children.

After a hard day of work at the school I would love to find Jesus waiting for me at home. The chapel is the center of the convent. Here I can pray for success in my work and an increase of holiness and grace. Here I can pray for the mentally retarded people as well as the spiritually retarded. But again the theme of the paper is What would I like to do if I had a religious vocation? As I said before my sister made up my mind. This is Patty.

I was amazed by the content of this piece—not only by the use of the words *subnormal* and *mentally retarded* (although those were the terms at the time) but by the very Catholic quality of it all. I don't remember ever thinking about entering the convent until high school. And yet here's this young Margaret Rogers's piece. Did I write it just for the contest? Or to please Sister? Did she help me with it? Extensively? I do find the focus interesting. I wanted to do something to help others. That rings true. The message resonating from family and school: you've been given much; you need to give back.

I received some commendation for this essay. I think Sister was disappointed I hadn't won. When she told me, she had a sad-angry look on her face, eyes flinty, mouth pursed. She encouraged me to continue on in writing and in my vocation as a sister. She would be one of my first visitors in the postulancy when I entered. Beaming, with bright eyes and open mouth, she announced how happy and proud she was of me.

There were other teachers to remember at Holy Redeemer. Sister Consuella, in fourth grade, rapped our knuckles with a ruler for inattentiveness or loquaciousness, but she let me write and direct a play about honest George Washington. We put it on for another classroom.

The summer before fifth grade I wrote a memoir, pages tied together with colorful yarn. I proudly presented it to my parents as a gift. My mom saved *My Life* along with the vocation essay. In the first section, "My Family," I introduced my mom and dad and brothers and sisters with names and ages and taped-on pictures, concluding with "We are a very very happy family." "My Vacations," the next section, ended with "On every vacation I went on I had the most fun. It's hard to explain it." "Days Of School"—"I had a very nice school year"—offered notes about piano lessons and dancing classes and included school pictures of myself and favorite friends, along with some math flash cards and spelling and vocabulary sheets. The last section, "My Relatives," contained random pictures and the repeated sentences "I couldn't find a picture of him (or her)" and "They are now dead."

In seventh grade, Sister Mary Robert, a friend of Sister St. Edmund—both from Prince Edward Island—moved rapidly up and down the aisles of our classroom, indicating with a pointer who should answer the questions from our textbooks. We'd start counting ahead to see which question might be ours, hoping she wouldn't switch rows. The first day of class, when I whispered an answer to one of my friends, Sister's booming voice echoed in the classroom: "Miss Rogers, what do you have to say? Come up to my desk. You are silly, Miss Rogers. I will call you silly Miss Rogers." Sister had probably heard from my kind sixth-grade teacher, Sister Amatus, that I was the most vocal girl in the class, and wanted to show me immediately who was the boss. It worked. I was humiliated by being singled out. I didn't talk out of turn for the rest of the year. Sister Mary Robert probably gave some kids ulcers, but we all learned a lot.

At Central High School, I loved French and biology and

English. I would have loved history, but the teacher, one of only two lay teachers, lacked classroom control and seemed enamored with the boys. She seated them up front and leaned over her lectern asking what they had done the night before. I think she wanted to hear about drinking and sex. She paid little attention to the girls. I told my parents about her, but as usual, their allegiance was with the teacher—and the fact that she was the daughter of some friends didn't help either. "Always give her and all teachers your respect. Try to get something out of the class. Don't mouth off." At first, I did mouth off and ended up in detention with the boys (the teacher would continue to flirt with them there).

I decided to teach the course to the girls in the back of the room. The teacher didn't like that either and continued to send me to detention. Even though I got all As on her difficult tests—and my students scored high as well—she gave me a C- for the course. Perhaps my parents came forward after that, because the principal of the school called me into her office and inquired about my history teacher. I told her everything. Miss Sexpot was gone the next year, but the C- stayed on my report card. At the time, it didn't matter. I didn't blame my parents and never asked them if they had talked to the principal, but this mark would be part of the reason I didn't graduate in the top ten of my class. That did matter to me. I was competitive, especially with my brothers and Mary—and with myself. I wanted to be the best I could be.

TO SERVE

C'mon, gang, next table! Up and over," Verva Wiltrout shouted, her voice deep and throaty in our living room. When we were young, my brothers and sisters and I used to sneak out of our bedrooms, squat on the upstairs step, and peek through the railings to spy on the bridge group our parents entertained every other month. We couldn't sleep on those nights because Verva's irresistible laugh echoed through the house.

As we grew older, we helped set the tables for the bridge dinner parties. Mary and I ironed the linen tablecloths and napkins, spread them over the card tables, set up chairs, laid out the dishes and silverware, and arranged the flower centerpieces. The boys helped serve, and we all took turns cleaning up. It was a lot of work, but we liked Mom and Dad's friends. They were friendly and kind. We even liked hearing their remarks about what great helpers we were, how we had grown. "My, Margie, what a big girl you are now. What fun watching you kids grow up."

Besides the bridge group, Mom and Dad often entertained young assistant priests from Holy Redeemer. They would sometimes walk the mile from church to visit us. Without their stiff white collars and silky black vests, they seemed very different. In cardigan sweaters, they acted different, too—jokier, jollier. Sometimes they would cook at our house. Father Dolan once steamed huge pots of spaghetti on every burner of our stove, madly, badly, seasoning the sauce with lots of garlic and orangey spices. There was a large crowd that night, lots of friends of Mom and Dad's, everybody, even the ladies, dressed casually in pants and shirts, smoking—ashtrays all over the house—and drinking Mogen David wine, but no one ate much spaghetti. Everybody would take a bite and concentrate on swallowing, trying not to make a face. After Father left, Mom seemed to search her soul. Wasting food was a sin in her eyes, but she figured God would forgive her this transgression. "Throw it out, kids," she ordered as we cleared the table.

Mom and Dad welcomed everybody into our house: their friends, our friends, Jehovah's Witnesses, Mormons, Fuller Brush salesmen, encyclopedia salesmen, homeless drifters. Whoever stopped at our house around dinnertime was invited to stay and eat with us. Mom wasn't the best or most organized cook in the world, and we didn't have an abundance of food, but my parents believed in calling people in, making them feel comfortable. Our home was a hospitable place.

If we had guests, we ate in the dining room instead of the kitchen. With our best manners, we perched on chairs with tied-on, blue-pinstriped slipcovers and sat at the dark-cherry, French-provincial table. We used the good dishes, the set Mom and Dad bought on their honeymoon in Canada, hand-painted with maroon and gold flowers on a white background with delicate fluted edges, and the heavy sterling, gifts from their wedding, all stored in the scrolled white corner cupboards of the dining room, the hollowware separate in its scratched mahogany box on the bottom shelf.

Conversations zoomed around the dinner table. Everything was discussed—several topics at once. Dad asked questions, added responses, told jokes, kept everything lively. When unexpected guests stayed for dinner, Mom worried if there would be enough food to go around. She would eye the plates and bowls being passed. If she signaled any of us from the table, we'd excuse ourselves and follow her through the swinging door into the kitchen. She'd whisper, "Go light on the beef," or "Easy on the squash." We ate carefully, properly, and lightly in the dining room.

Not so in the kitchen, around the old oak table. Big and heavy, round with extra legs that supported the weight of three leaves, the table had been left in the basement of Dad's first rented office on Second Street. Since no one claimed it, Dad brought it home, and Mom took it to Walter Freese, the wood finisher, to get it sanded and shellacked. We did our homework and projects on it. It stood in the eating nook by the back door so outdoor things got dropped on it—balls and gloves, coats and hats. Whenever it was time to eat, Mary and I would have to clear it off and wipe its gritty or gummy or greasy top before we could set it. It was something we did every day; we *knew* that table.

We seldom went out to eat—once or twice a year at the Atlantic Hotel—so except for guest meals and our Sunday supper, as soon as Mom called, "Ready!" we scrambled to the built-in benches of the kitchen nook, and with elbows touching, recited grace: "BlessusOhLordandtheseYourgiftswhichweareabout toreceivefromYourbountythroughChristOurLordAmen."

My brother John's best friend, Rich Chalmers, ate with us a fair amount in high school, and John often stayed at the Chalmers family's farm. I did, too, since Rich's sister Joanne was one of my best friends. She and I played in the hayloft, sliding down a hay chute from the windows at the very top. John always tried to ride the pigs in the sty. He'd fall off, and as Rich said, "be full of shit from head to toe." The grand parlor of the Chalmers house stretched forever. We played hide-and-seek and board games and gossiped there. The bathroom on the second floor was enormous—you could put a bed in it—and the kitchen table was the longest I'd ever seen. The Chalmers family had ten children. Mrs. Chalmers fed them and a number of field hands at that table. Whenever I stayed for dinner, hot, aromatic, delicious food was calmly served all together at the same time. Not at our house.

As soon as we had said grace, we'd reach across the table, stab into the vegetable bowl, fighting over who got more peas on their forks. Dad would yell, "Where are your manners?" Mom would jump up, hover at the stove, and then dash over with roast beef, setting it down in front of Dad, who'd divide it into nine semiequal pieces, his head shaking as he sawed at it with the *why-is-this-so-dull* knife. We would try to spear the biggest pieces without his noticing. Patty would bang on the table, leaving embedded spoon marks in its golden finish. Danny might slip her some of his saved peas. Dad would shout, "Alice, these kids are starving." Mom would dash to the refrigerator, reach in, and pull out a Jell-O salad with a slimy red bottom. On top would be brownish-yellow bananas and cut-up white marshmallows. Everybody would scoop some of the slippery stuff onto plates. When John began cutting his into shapes, Dad would reach across the table and jerk the knife out of his hand. "No playing with food."

Then he'd lean back in his chair, adjust his glasses, and ask, "OK, boys, what'd you think of the game? Jim, should that backer have been able to take you down on the twenty-yard line?"

Jim, his oiled, slicked-back hair not moving, would say, "Naaa, I guess not . . . I'm really hungry."

Then Dad, noticing the lull in food delivery, would say, "Mary, Peggy, go help your mother."

"No, sit down, girls. I'm coming. Coming." Mom would plunk down a basket of dinner rolls. "John, do you want to rice the potatoes?" She bustled between the stove and the sink, draining the white potatoes as John hurried over. We'd watch him jam the potatoes into the rusty potato ricer. Red in the face, he'd squeeze until those spuds came stringing out, long, thin white ropes into the cracked Fiesta bowl he carefully carried to the table. Pale and lanky, John resembled the riced potatoes he loved so much.

At the stove, Mom would pour hot gravy into the chipped

pitcher and bring it to the table. She would wipe the cooking moisture from her glasses onto her cobbler apron and finally sit down. Then she'd jump up again. "Does anyone want pickles?"

Like the beef, the gravy smelled rich and greasy. It pooled at the bottom of the lukewarm, spaghetti-like mounds on our plates, brown lakes under white mountains.

"OK, let's hear about the day," Dad would say.

"The singers aren't getting their lines down," Mary would say. She played the piano accompaniment for Central's musicals. She was a great pianist. Her long, strong fingers could stretch more than an octave. Very tall, Mary bent over the piano, her arms and hands bouncing along, pounding the notes, her legs jerking, feet pedaling, keeping time.

"It'll be OK, Mary," Dad would say.

Mom would nod as she helped Patty with her food.

"Sister Mary Ruth wants me to try out for a role in the play," I would say. I loved acting. Once I played a scatterbrained mother so in character I knocked over live plants on the stage at curtain call. The water from the planters sprinkled the front-row seats. The audience just laughed, wiped themselves off, and clapped harder.

"Good, Peggy. Go for it," Dad would say, giving his thumbs-up sign.

If Danny said, "I didn't like school today," then Tommy might have nudged him: "When do you ever like school?"

Tommy's freckle-faced grin would broaden, his big ears wiggling. I didn't like to see Tommy's ears stick out; I'd tape them to his head at night to try to train them to lie small and flat. It didn't work.

Danny would push Tommy. They'd start to fool around.

"Boys, not at the table. Why didn't you like school?" Dad would ask. Danny would just lower his head.

Dad would give him a look. "So . . . let's talk about that later . . ." He knew—Danny had trouble with reading and Dad would help him after supper with his homework.

Then Dad would turn to the older boys. "So, let's go back to the game . . . " He would tilt toward the old oak table, beat a rhythm on it with his fingers. He would reach in his shirt pocket and pull out a pack of cigarettes. Slowly lighting one, he'd bend back again. With one yellow-stained hand, he'd wave his Salem Menthol, balancing on his chair, straining it with his tall body. He'd lean back so far we expected him to fall. Mom was already busy clearing the table.

After we had finished eating, everybody scrambled from the table. I would be left washing it, scrubbing over its chips and dents, its beaten leaves stained with various spillings, rubbing the dishrag over its cracked pedestal, its spindly supporting legs. I would spot a black mark where Dad's cigarette had scorched a hole. The table held history.

When Dad and Mom moved to Edina Towers, they brought the table to the cabin in Wisconsin. Up there, Dad and Mom played cards on it, teaching our children gin rummy, Oh Hell, Widow, and Norwegian whist, even some bridge. Now the old oak table is at our cabin on the St. Croix River. Cards are stacked on it to play with our grandchildren. I've refinished it, sanding and applying three coats of polyurethane. The pedestal is still cracked, the top full of chips and dents. There's still the scorched hole at the table's edge. Deeply embedded, the mark

is ingrained forever. The table, too, is fixed in my mind, a symbol of hospitality and communal meals. I would practice both—in and out of the convent—inviting people to share food and to check in over the dinner table.

The Rogers children around the old oak table

A BIGGER WORLD BECKONED

In grade school, Mary and I both won a state piano contest. The prize: a performance at Northrop Auditorium at the University of Minnesota. Dad drove us to the Cities for the first rehearsal. We left Marshall early, about five o'clock in the morning. While we practiced, Dad met with his business partner and worked at his Minneapolis office at the huge, white First National Bank building on Fifth Street.

Northrup, too, was enormous. Dad dropped us off at the stage door. I nervously walked up the steps and out on the stage and then gaped at the rows and rows of seats in the orchestra section, the balconies, and the boxes. Awed by the huge chandeliers hanging from the ceiling, I whispered a *cripes*. I had never seen such an impressive building. I couldn't believe I was going to play in it. I became more nervous, feeling flutters in my stomach.

I was supposed to play a duet with nine other kids, five playing one part, five the other. There were ten grand pianos on stage. My piano teacher had warned me about the keys, which would jump when you put your foot on the pedal. I was frightened by that and by the booming voice of the conductor. "Take your seat, Number Five," he said, after calling out my name. My group was assigned Handel's "Water Music." The piece sounded like hornpipes. The other kids all knew their parts. They looked happy and confident. Their parents, in the front rows, did, too. Their heads nodded in rhythm as we started to play.

Not totally prepared—I never seemed to find time to practice—I watched the parents' heads move and faked my piece. I figured the other four would do fine with our half. I silently promised myself I'd get the notes down before the next practice session. I was so focused on how I would do that—setting up practice times, crossing them off, rewarding myself when I accomplished my goal—I didn't notice the music director staring at me. Suddenly he shouted, "I don't hear Piano Number Five. Play, Number Five."

Everyone looked at me. All the kids. All the parents. I was so embarrassed. My face felt hot; I knew it had turned cherry red. I wanted to drop though the trapdoor of the stage. It was impossible to play not knowing the notes, but I couldn't stand the director yelling at me again. I kept faking it, hoping for the practice to end, but the minutes crept by interminably. When the director finally announced our group time was up, I beelined out to find Mary.

Dad met us on the steps of Northrop. We walked through the campus, Dad pointing out where he had attended business classes when he was a student. I could only think of telling him about practice. We walked over to Bridgeman's ice-cream parlor in Dinkytown for hamburgers and malts. We loved going there, almost as much as we did Mike's Truck Stop in Marshall. Dad knew everybody at Mike's. We'd watch him talk, basking in the gasoline and bacon-frying smells.

Dad said, "What's wrong, Peggy?"

I hesitantly told him what happened at rehearsal, trying to keep my voice from wavering. "I didn't know my piece. The music director yelled at me. It was—horrible."

Dad put his arm around me. "Don't worry, honey. Today is over. You now have to promise to practice and be ready to give 100 percent. Can you do that?"

All the way home I resolved to change, to give piano my all, but in the succeeding weeks, there was always something more interesting to do—talk on the phone, go shopping, read, watch TV. Still, before each of the next two practice sessions, I did *apply myself, buckled down* and practiced. Each time I went to Northrup I had more of the piece under my belt, and by the final performance, I played like a horn trumpeting water music. I was proud of my accomplishment.

Sometimes we all went to the Cities when Dad had business there. A long trip—four fighting hours. Dad would do his arm thing, throwing it across the backseat about every half hour, catching whoever was sitting up or goofing around. Whomever the hand caught would cry for a bit, settle back for a while, and then tentatively begin poking, picking, and pinching again.

We'd stay at the Curtis Hotel in Minneapolis, a ten-story building with a swimming pool. As soon as Dad, Jim, and John lugged our suitcases into the big family suite where we all slept, we started pitching clothes out of the grips, digging out our bathing suits. Then, racing for the elevator, we fought over who got to punch the lobby-level button—unless we shared the elevator with strangers—and pushed one another through the long, light-brown lobby with its elegant blue sofas and gold-braided lamps.

There the guests, much fancier than the best dressed in Marshall—the men in fine suits and ladies with hats, gloves, and high-heeled shoes—used crystal ashtrays and glasses, smoking and drinking, discussing the weather, languishing on the sofa. "It is *so* humid I think I'll *die.*"

When we arrived at the pool, we stamped our handprints all over the steamy glass doors before we dove in. When Mom finally got us out, we each took a wonderful warm shower, not worrying about using too much water. "It's OK, kids," she said. "There's plenty of hot water here." She told us to turn out the lights, though, and not to use too much toilet paper or to flush the toilet too often, just like at home.

We dressed up in our Sunday best and Mom and Dad took us out *on the town*, strolling along the crowded, busy sidewalks, passing all the stylish people. We craned our necks to find the tops of buildings. From the observation deck on the thirty-first floor of the tallest, the Foshay Tower, we stared down over the city. We saw tiny barges and a paddleboat winding through the city on a little stream called the Mississippi River. The great flour mills on the west side of the city looked smaller than Marshall's grain elevator. The many tracks of the Burlington Northern Railroad looked like a play train set. All of the streets and cars were miniatures, like on a board game, the people just bits of color.

We shopped at Dayton's, opening and closing brass doors, riding up elevators with operators, using plush women's lounges, staring up into crystal chandeliers. We went out to eat, peeking into Nankin's Chinese lanterns.

Herding us, Mom tried to keep us quiet, with good manners. "Shh. Keep it down. Shh. Don't touch," she'd whisper.

Danny once sat on—and broke—a fancy little table at Anderson's, an expensive furniture store. He tumbled to the floor. We kids looked upon the scene with trepidation. "Oh, Danny, wait until Mom sees this."

Danny brought the pieces to Mom, at the front of the store. We all crowded around.

"Danny," she murmured. "How did this happen?"

"I don't know," he said. "I just sat on it."

She took the pieces to the clerk, who looked down his nose at us. "These children should not be playing in the store."

Mom looked up at him. "Sir, we'll buy this table." She dug into her purse, pulling out her worn leather billfold.

On her way out of the store, she turned to Danny, who carried the broken parts of the table in his hands. "Don't worry, honey, we'll make use of it."

Although she'd go without something to make up for the cost, Mom didn't yell at Danny. Dad didn't either. We didn't get punished, unless we deliberately did something wrong.

At home, we stood the expensive, glued table next to

Dad's chair in front of the fireplace.

The whole family set off for St. Paul when Central Catholic won basketball regionals. We watched the state tournament games in the huge auditorium and heard Jim and John's names called over the PA system. That week their names appeared in the *St. Paul Pioneer Press* and the *Minneapolis Tribune*. I watched them play but also bought hot dogs, cokes, and candy at the concession stands, and discovered kids from all over Minnesota.

I was a teenager, in junior high. My girlfriends and I tried to get cute boys to notice us, walking back and forth in front of the stands. Sometimes they'd talk to us. We'd be excited—and a little scared—if they followed us.

We stayed in St. Paul's Lowry Hotel with other Marshall families. Until late at night, we ran around like crazy in the hallways, getting ice and pop, or anything we could think of for an excuse, until parents poked their heads out of rooms and demanded peace and quiet.

Between the games, we toured the Capitol and shopped for clothes and shoes at Schueneman's and The Golden Rule. It was all gold and glittery to me, from the horses on top of the Capitol to the perfume counters and thick carpets in the stores. The salesclerks spoke in hushed, cultured voices, not chitchatty or gossipy.

No one knew us in the Cities, and I think Mom liked that. She got tired of "everybody knowing your business." The Cities offered us all a chance to try out new personas. We could be anyone we wanted to be. I didn't have to be a *little Rogers*. No one had to know I went to a Catholic school. I could try out a behavior—like flirting with boys—and see what happened.

Marshall could be stifling. All the adults seemed to know us, and everything would get back to our parents. Once John drove me past the country club on Highway 23 on a joyride. He floored the gas; I watched the speedometer rise to ninety, ninety-five. "We're on our way to a hundred," John yelped.

Sirens bellowed behind us. When we stopped, the police officer took a good look at us. "You're Pat Rogers's kids, right?"

Uneasily, John nodded.

I nodded, too, frightened.

"Listen, son, don't ever try this trick again, OK? I won't give you a ticket this time, but we'll be watching you. Know we'll be watching you."

My reaction was twofold: at first relieved—no one had to find out—and then angry. The officer probably would have issued a ticket to some teenager whose family he didn't know. He should have given one to John. The double standard rankled. The twofoldness would stay with me: grateful for being treated well and judgmental as hell about my privilege. I'd advocate for fairness and equality in my personal and professional life.

Twofoldness in another capacity would also stay with me: I'd reach out to a larger world—reading, traveling, working—and equally be attracted to the safe, small circle of loved ones. I'd break out of a parochial atmosphere to end up cocooned in the even smaller world of the convent.

EXODUS

Je suis enchantée de faire votre connaissance."

His head popped up, his body jerked to face me across the aisle. His beady black eyes bored into mine. He nudged his sleeping wife. "She speaks French." He turned back to me and let loose French *plus rapide* than any I'd ever heard.

"Oh, Monsieur, *lentement, s'il vous plât*. Slowly, please. I speak French only a little. *Un peu*."

He stared, then turned back, grimacing, sinking into

his seat. "Oh," he mumbled, and then swore in French.

I was disappointed. I had wanted to make this strange French couple a part of our group—she was so blowzy, lots of makeup and low-cut dresses, theatrical with wide gestures, garrulous. The day we monitored a squall outside the windows of our bus, she had called out, "An electrical storm!"

"Lightning," I had said. "It's called lightning." Mary had muttered, "Be quiet. She can't understand you."

Now Mary jabbed my arm. "Look, you've made him mad. Why'd you do that? You can't speak French. I can speak it better than you."

I didn't think he was mad. He was lonely. An outsider. There was no one but his wife he could talk to on this whole bus. We were on a round-trip Greyhound charter to Los Angeles, in the summer of 1961. Many of our fellow travelers had boarded on the East Coast. Mary and I got on in St. Paul. Mary had just graduated from Central Catholic and intended to enter the convent of the Sisters of St. Joseph of Carondelet in St. Paul in September. This trip was my parents' graduation gift and send-off for her. That summer our parents had also announced our family's move from Marshall to St. Paul. Because Mary didn't want to go on the trip alone, and because I was going to be leaving my school and friends, I got to accompany her. Mom and Dad signed us up with a Greyhound agent who offered an itinerary and a promise to be responsible for us.

I was happy to go. Sophomore year had finished with a number of firsts: the first time I got a C in any class; the first time I was assigned detention; the first time I was recognized as an actress (I had played the mother in *Don't Take My Penny*, the ingénue in *The Mystery of the Masked Girl*, and a young girl in the operetta *The Mikado*); the first time I had to admit I might need to change—become more flirty, possibly with kids from Marshall High, in order to get a boyfriend. I didn't know anybody but Central kids. When my parents told us we were moving to

St. Paul, I remember thinking that maybe it was time, since I didn't know anyone from the public school. I was such a typical Catholic girl.

On our trip, we stayed in some quaint, quiet towns in Iowa and Nebraska. We found the mountains in Colorado and Utah and swimming in the *you can't sink!* Great Salt Lake astonishing. We started a snowball fight on top of Humphrey's Peak in Flagstaff, Arizona, and rode the first mules in line down into the Grand Canyon. In California, we bought souvenirs in San Francisco's Chinatown and Fisherman's Wharf, at Disneyland and Knott's Berry Farm. We loved it all: hilly climbs, ocean breezes, desert sands.

Mary and I mostly got along OK, but at every new hotel, she would immediately go to the check-in counter and inspect the cardboard box of free pamphlets. She'd then embarrass me by asking the person behind the desk if the time for the Catholic services the next morning was the same as she had found in the materials. Mary would touch her glasses, then point to the pamphlet. "It's still eight o'clock? Good. We can go before the bus leaves at nine. Could you give us directions to the church, please?"

We fought over attending. "Mary," I'd say, "I'm not going. *I'm* not entering the convent."

She'd beg, "Please come with me."

"No. This is daily Mass, not even Sunday. No. I'm not going."

"You have to."

"I do not."

Sometimes I did. Sometimes I didn't.

During the trip—with a whole lot of time on the bus—I read. Constantly. It was the summer of Leon Uris's novel *Exodus*. Everyone was reading it. Well, everybody under forty. Those of us with the wonderful, dreadful blue-covered book nodded at each other. I could not put it down.

I was Kitty Fremont, madly in love with Ari Ben Canaan, from Palestine. I could die for him. I could be courageous and save children for him. I could lead three hundred of them out of detention camp onto the ship *Promised Land*. I was Dov Landau, seventeen, angry and bitter, a survivor of the Warsaw Ghetto Uprising and Auschwitz concentration camp, able to remember only barbed wire, guns, soldiers. I was Karen Hansen Clement, sixteen, who fell in love with Dov on the *Star of David*. I was Jordana Ben Canaan, Ari's fiery younger sister, a "sabra," and David Ben Ami, her lover, a young, passionate soldier of the Army. Involved with Operation Gideon against the British, I sailed on the *Exodus*. I was helping to build Israel, the bridge between darkness and light.

I had discovered the Holocaust. After *Exodus*, I read Anne Frank's *Diary of a Young Girl*. I became Anne, too: kind, generous, funny, jealous, petty, a young teenager like myself. I couldn't believe she could love and hope and believe in a better world. And then Elie Wiesel's *Night* affected me just as powerfully. I will always remember learning from these three seminal books of the horrendous evil operating in our world, a knowledge that darkened my spirit.

In real life, I wanted lightness surrounding me. My instinct was to take care of the French couple. I smiled at Camille and Pierre, spoke poor French, gestured, spoke baby English, smiled. Pierre eventually came around. Whenever we got off the bus, he'd follow me, pointing, clapping; his short, round body bobbing; his heavy black moustache pulling into a grin. He and Camille became part of the group. We all belonged together.

I wouldn't forget the dichotomies of this trip: Mary desiring worship; Ari, Anne, Eli desiring life. It would take many more years of reading and discovery for me to rail at my Church, realizing the extent to which Pope Pius XII disregarded the pleas of European Jews. My country had turned a deaf ear as well. I blamed my parents, demanding to know why they hadn't voiced their objections.

"To refuse Jews into our country: horrific. To have remained silent: outrageous," I said.

"You're right, but at the time we just didn't know much," my mom said.

"Well, that's a fault, too," I shot back.

I was shocked by institutions I had believed in. I brooded over the lack of action by the Catholic Church. How could a spiritual, moral entity choose not to help millions of innocent, suffering people? How could it not witness their deaths?

I was on my way: to challenge this institution while becoming a nun—involving myself by doing right by it—and much later, by becoming a *none*—belonging to no established church.

II. HABITS AND MOTIVES

*I*ntelligence, the ability to get along with others, a sense of humor, generosity and a desire to consecrate oneself to the service of God and neighbor are the qualities the sisters would like to find in the postulates.

– Consensus from a national meeting of women religious in St. Paul, 1964

IN ST. PAUL

Our family moved to St. Paul in 1961 so Dad could be closer to the Minneapolis-St. Paul Airport and his business partner in the Cities. Even though his office was in Minneapolis, he and Mom looked for a home in St. Paul, which was Catholic and had cheaper real estate; and while its largest ethnic group is German, it's always been considered an Irish city.

Both cities seemed the same to me: tall downtown buildings; dense neighborhoods; cars, buses, and trains on streets, roads, and tracks; cities easy to get lost in; difficult to get to know. Later, I could discern physical distinctions: flatter Minneapolis with its beautiful parks and lakes, hillier St. Paul with its intriguing bluffs and caves, and the same mighty Mississippi flowing between them.

From their beginnings, a civic rivalry existed between the Cities. Minneapolis, the Mill City, demonstrated industrial might, and St. Paul, the capital, dominance in trade and transportation, but they competed rather than connected to form one major city. My first fall at Our Lady of Peace High School (OLP), I was shocked to discover my classmates' insularity, how content they were to stay in *their* city.

In homeroom—which also served as our religion class—Sister, who usually had us prove over and over the existence of God by St. Thomas Aquinas's definition, broached a recent news story. A man who had hired a high-school girl to babysit his children murdered her at Minnehaha Park—not far from my family's home in Highland Park. Sister said this murder clearly proved two things: one, we shouldn't babysit; two, we should never go to Minneapolis. Even though I was shy and new in school, I couldn't keep my hand from shooting up (although, to be honest, it shot up to dispute St. Thomas Aquinas as well). "Sister, you can't mean that. We all need to babysit to make money; it's about the only thing we can do. And besides, not to go to Minneapolis—it's a twin city."

Sister stared at me and then asked how many girls in the class had *ever* been to Minneapolis. Out of fifty in the room, I was one of three who raised a hand. I slowly brought it down, not believing what I was seeing, thinking, *how provincial, how parochial.*

The move to St. Paul and this very large school, over one thousand girls, was difficult; it was tough enough being a junior in high school and sixteen years old, but Catholic St. Paul proved especially challenging. Everybody was known by parishes, St. Luke's or St. Mark's or Holy Spirit or Nativity; everybody's parents seemed to know each other from childhood; everybody knew everyone's children; and everybody knew kids from the other Catholic high schools, the all-boys Cretin and St. Thomas Academy, the all-girls Visitation, St. Joseph's Academy, and Derham Hall.

My mother had wanted me to go to Derham Hall, her alma mater, but it was a tiny school, only about two hundred students, and the principal told us there would be no room when we first inquired. My mother had mumbled, "Imagine that!" and "They could add one more student . . . " The nuns at Central Catholic in Marshall, in the same order of nuns as Derham Hall—Sisters of St. Joseph of Carondelet—were furious. They must have lobbied Derham—maybe saying how supportive Mom and Dad were to Central Catholic, how Mary was entering their order, and maybe I would too—because the principal called in August to offer me a spot. It provoked another discussion with Mom.

"I'd like you to go to Derham, Margaret."

"Mom, are you kidding? They turned me down. I'm registered at OLP. I already have my schedule."

"But OLP's so big. Derham's about the same size as Central. We could call Derham and get your materials right away."

"Mom, they said no even after pressure from their own nuns. I don't think so."

A long pause from Mom. "OK, honey."

So I carpooled to Our Lady of Peace with a neighbor, a freshman with big blond hair, whose father, a business executive, drove us. There was little sharing in the car. I couldn't think of a single thing to say to them—and apparently they couldn't to me either. I would have preferred taking city buses to school but that meant a circuitous route with transfers and a long ride. I could never figure out the bus routes. The first time I tried to take a bus home from school, I waited on Summit Avenue. I wore the OLP uniform—white blouse; navy-blue, collarless jacket; matching, flared skirt, rolled up after school to show some knee; navy-blue saddle shoes—but no one talked to me or even smiled at me. No one asked what I was doing there. No one told me that buses didn't run on that avenue, to walk over to Grand. I waited and waited for a bus that never came and finally walked the three and a half miles home.

The high school maintained a huge front lawn facing Summit, which was known for its large historic houses, stately Victorian mansions, churches, synagogues, and schools. The Sisters of Charity of the Blessed Virgin Mary (BVMs) whose motherhouse was in Dubuque, Iowa, ran OLP. The sisters offered either a college-preparatory program—math, biology, chemistry, physics, Latin—an Ivy League prep-school curriculum, with the later options of teaching or nursing; or a basic education for those who would work as hairdressers, stenographers, seamstresses, or cooks until they left the workforce to stay home with children. Motherhood: an option for all. Except, of course, for the few called especially by God. We viewed the nuns as feminists, Jesuit educated and widely traveled, free from the demands of husbands and children.

I was placed in regular classes my junior year. I didn't realize this for a while, not until I figured out I wasn't in the top English class, which included the yearbook and newspaper staff. My teachers must have recommended I move up because I was assigned the college-prep classes my senior year—too late, though, to be involved in literary pursuits. That I missed.

I never let on I had a hard time with the move, but I cried into my pillow almost every night for weeks. I promised myself I'd become popular. I forced myself to go to parties. Even after a disastrous one where I sat for an entire night on a sofa right in front of everyone dancing. The wallflower. There was no place to hide in my friend's little house so I'd get up for snacks or go to the bathroom or talk to her parents so I wouldn't cry. When the lights got turned down low and every-one slow-danced to Johnny Mathis's "The Twelfth of Never" and the Righteous Brothers' "Unchained Melody"—two of my favorite songs—I wanted to die. But I had to stay, waiting for a ride home from one of my girlfriends.

Dad thought he helped my adjustment by insisting that an all-girls' school wasn't that different from a co-ed school. He shrugged off the fact that Our Lady of Peace was at least four times larger than Central Catholic. He preached the old "Go for it. Give 100 percent." I'm sure he meant it to imply enthusiasm, to care deeply about something, but it also worked as an inner push, a competitive drive. It was hard to live up to his stan-dards—not because he made you, but because you wanted to. You wanted to make him proud. I felt it now as a subtle, forceful pressure.

Eventually life did get easier. I did well in my classes— especially American history, with a lay teacher I truly admired. During the course, she served on jury duty and missed classes for several weeks. When she returned, she looked like she had aged—a few white hairs, lines around her mouth, a deep furrow between her brows. In a low, sad voice, she told us she had been the one responsible for the murder trial taking so long. She ended up being the sole dissenter, believing the defendant guilty. She couldn't persuade the others; stalemated, she finally voted with them. With tears in her eyes, she said, "On his way out of the courtroom, the defendant mouthed to me, *I did it.*" My heart dropped. I couldn't imagine living for the rest of my life with that on my conscience. And my favorite teacher—was she safe from this guy? I've never forgotten that moment.

     Sister Mary Ruth, who had directed plays at Central Catholic, made me promise to try out for parts at OLP, but you had to take drama as a class if you wanted to participate. It wasn't like at Central, where you could do everything—paper, yearbook, band, glee club, choir—just by signing up. I had done it all. Even dance band. Recruited to play piano by Central's conductor, he kept me on even after I once totally froze on a solo for "Ball and Chain." With my lapsed sixteen measures, everybody on the gym floor stopped dancing, staring at the band. Everybody in the band glared at me. The conductor beat the rhythm in the air over my head. I stared at the keys, totally red in the face. I simply couldn't remember my part.

     I did sign up for drama class at OLP and got the role of Annie Sullivan in *The Miracle Worker.* I really needed to remember my lines because we played it *theater in the round* with the audience sitting in a circle around us; no one backstage could help with a forgotten line, and my friend Dieta, the actress playing deaf and speechless Helen Keller, certainly couldn't help either. The staging proved challenging in the use of props as well; everything had to be placed exactly where needed. At the main Saturday night performance, I had to fake hold and cuddle a missing doll. I also tried to speak with a bit of an Irish brogue and to hauntingly sing "Hush, Little Baby." Both proved difficult. And the fight scene with Helen produced real anxiety;

I got smacked in the eye and kicked in the shins. Finally, a guy from Cretin, my friend Tom Barrett, came opening night and sat in the very front row with his eyes glued on me. I didn't think it was my best performance. I dreamed—some nightmares—about *The Miracle Worker* for years.

I sang and danced with Tom and other boys from Cretin and St. Thomas at the St. Patrick's Day show, an annual event at OLP—"I'm Irish, and I'm beautiful, and I'm beautiful 'cause I'm Irish / And if it would improve, the love tale I'd tell, I'd wear a shamrock in my lapel." I acted in several productions at Cretin. I played the mother in *My Three Angels*, enamored with the angels themselves, Tom and another friend, Matt. Cretin's drama coach trusted me with renting costumes for his productions so I'd drive to a huge warehouse in Minneapolis and pick out outfits. I loved acting like a professional.

My brother Jim finished painting my new bedroom before going back to college. It had pink walls with white woodwork and a little alcove with built-in shelves on either side of a window overlooking Fairview Avenue. I could look out on the busy street below and the quiet grounds of the College of St. Catherine beyond. I could put all my books onto my own shelves and clothes into my own closet. Our bedroom in Marshall had been so full with the single bed for Patty and the double one for Mary and me that our short closet under the eaves always overflowed with clothes. But this year Patty was away at school and Mary was across the street in the convent. Now there was just one bed—mine. I had my own room!

My new pink palace even had a second window. I could open it in every season except winter, and see, smell, and hear the side yard with its large flower garden, which included huge peonies around a gurgling fountain. We could play volleyball there. My brothers played pickup ball out back, behind the alley, on the football field of St. Paul Academy, a private boys' school.

Our house was a stone, brick, and wood Tudor, with four bedrooms, one large bath and a tiny half bath on the first floor, a sunporch off the living room, and a screened back porch off the kitchen. It even had a semifinished basement with a built-in oak bar and a stone fireplace. Still, I missed our Marshall house's basement with its ugly, old shower that we all ran under on Saturday nights when we were little and its toilet sitting right out in the open, underneath the steps. Those steps served as *jail* for games of cops and robbers. In the wintertime, Mary and I played jacks on the basement's concrete floor—tough because of its chilly roughness. We'd end up with scratches and cuts on our hands.

I had also practiced balancing on that concrete floor. Feeling alone and bored one day in the basement, I decided to walk on a basketball like lumberjacks walk on logs. Stepping on and falling off the ball, I fell—full body slams—onto my face several times that day. I'd wipe away the blood from my nose and try again.

Like that balancing act, the move to St. Paul had set me against myself. I felt divided into two persons, *twins*, one person in Marshall and another in the Cities. Back and forth I'd vacillate, reminiscing and then forging ahead.

I was lonesome that first winter in St. Paul. I remembered in Marshall when we were little, after the first magical snowfall, going out in that great white space, carving angels and playing foxes and hounds. We called it *Cutting the Pie*. We'd tramp out wedges of the pie, lines leading to safe center. Sometimes if the snow was really deep, it banked up so high deep trenches formed, and you couldn't see the other kids in the runs. We screamed when we met each other and wildly ran so we wouldn't be tagged. I missed *Cutting the Pie*. Getting to safe center.

And Christmas. I loved it in Marshall. About lunchtime on Christmas Eve, Dad always packed all seven of us kids into the car and drove to Bulowski's Drugstore. Dad talked to his good friend, John Bulowski, while we poked around at the bargain table, finding something to buy for Mom, from us. Then we moved to the expensive merchandise and picked out something fancy—perfume or earrings or a scarf—for Mom, from Dad. I don't remember if this was his only gift to her. I don't remember, either, if she knew we had done his shopping for him. I do remember we always had to pull Dad away from his friend after a saleslady had wrapped up all our presents.

Then Dad drove us slowly home—and there was Mom— "You'll never guess, it happened again. Santa Claus dropped off all the gifts while you were gone." We'd peek in. All the presents under the tree: we'd get so excited, jumping up and down, but Mom said we couldn't open them until we had oyster stew with the Halls, her old boss and his wife. It was a tradition for them to arrive at five o'clock, bringing us kids crisp, one-dollar bills.

Dad always got shortchanged in presents. I'd find ties in the attic I'd given him the Christmas before and wrap them up again. Dad never let on, always said, "Peggy, what a great-looking tie. I'll be the best-dressed man in Marshall."

It would never be like that again.

That first winter one of my best friends from Marshall was in St. Paul, staying at the Catholic Infant Home, for unwed mothers. She called to tell me she had gone to the Home only at the end of her pregnancy because so many girls were waiting to get in. I hadn't even known she was pregnant. The first Saturday after her call I drove over to see her. The Home was close to downtown. A massive building of yellow limestone, it had huge windows, heavily draped. It was dark, foreboding, intimidating. I timidly rang the doorbell.

A Sister of St. Joseph answered. "What is it?"

When I asked after my friend, she said, "Who? We don't have anyone here with that name."

Confused, I said, "But she told me she was here."

"Well, her name is Susan."

My parents later told me they probably change the names of the mothers-to-be for security reasons. At the time, it felt so wrong. Secret. Shaming. I hated the place.

Shocked at how large my friend was in her muumuu, I

was aware of how thin I must have looked to her in my black tights, turtleneck, and straight plaid skirt, but we were delighted to see each other. She caught me up on the news of our Marshall friends. We gabbed all the way to my house.

When we walked in, Tom and Dan had to have been surprised to see "Susan," but they asked about her younger brothers and what was happening in Marshall. We all sat down to dinner, then I gave her a ride back to the Home. On the way, she told me she was giving up her child for adoption. She said she wanted to, but I could tell she didn't.

"Isn't there any way you could keep the baby?" I asked.

"No," she said.

I hugged her and told her to let us know when it happened. If she needed anything, my family would help. We heard from her in a few weeks: her baby was born but then died.

I cried. Then I was overwhelmed with a confusing mix of emotions. Anger: how could my friend have let herself get pregnant? How could the sisters be so cruel, enforcing secrecy and work? ("Susan" told me they cleaned and cooked all day long.) Sympathy: for my friend because of the lack of birth-control options. Pity: for my friend, to lose a baby twice, through adoption and then death, and for the sisters who supervised adoption proceedings over and over with so many young girls.

"Susan" and I stayed in touch for a while. She got married, had children—then we grew apart. At our fortieth high-school reunion, I learned she had terminal cancer and that she and her husband had moved away from Marshall. I tried the telephone number and email address I had found in the reunion materials, but no one returned my messages. Right before our fiftieth anniversary, an email arrived from another classmate saying she had died.

I miss her.

After our move to St. Paul, Dad missed his Marshall buddies, too. Of course, it didn't take him long to meet folks, but I wondered if he was glad he moved us. When we arrived in St. Paul, he'd told me, "Peggy, we waited for you. We thought you'd be the one who'd most easily adjust. We wanted the boys to finish up their sports and for Mary to be valedictorian. We figured you'd be fine." When he said it, I was proud, but then I thought, *Hmmm, so I don't have anything special?*

I didn't really know what Mom thought of the move. We never talked about it. As usual, she kept us all going. She did, however, that first winter compare the handwriting on Christmas cards with a note we had received in the summer, shortly after moving in. The note complained about our family's activities, particularly by the garage—basketball games on the driveway, music, cars. The note was signed, "Your Hartford Neighbors." Mom suspected right away the author of the note: a tough, elderly lady who lived next door to us on the Fairview side. Mom encouraged Tom and Dan to help our neighbor with mowing and raking and shoveling. "Uh huh," Mom said when she read that woman's Christmas card, with a personal message thanking us, saying we were the best neighbors.

Probably lonesome, too, Mom liked having me around during the summer. She let me suntan in the backyard and on the shingled roof over the garage, and read in my favorite chair in the living room. I had to plead with her to let me get a job. She wanted me to help her in the house. I wanted a real job. I found one as a soda jerk at Snyder's Drug Store in Highland Park, close to the Mississippi River and the bridge to Minneapolis. In my hairnet and light-blue shirtwaist uniform, I worked the whole counter at the front of the store from 4 to 10 p.m. Showing support for Mom, Dad wouldn't drive me to work, so I walked the mile and a half both ways; at night, I'd run home, frightened by boys honking and whistling at me from their cars.

The job was something! A soda jerk had tremendous responsibilities: the steam table with its warmed vegetables, meat, and potatoes; the sandwich table with tomatoes and lettuce, cold cuts, tuna and chicken, condiments and spreads; the grill for hot dogs, hamburgers, steaks, even fried eggs—you had to set down a metal shape to contain them; the greasy basket for French fries; the shaker for malts; the mixes and fizzes for sodas; the brew station for coffee; and the twelve large cartons of ice cream to scoop. The soda jerk also had to continually clean around the equipment and the counter; set up silverware, napkins, and water for the customers; scrape off the grill; wash the dishes in a mighty hot machine with a handle you had to hold down for three minutes; write out receipts for what was ordered; work the cash register; give back change.

I worked solo on the night shift. Sometimes ten people might be waiting to be served at the counter. I had my regulars, mostly older guys who just stopped by for a cup of coffee. "Hi, doll," they'd say. "Just a cup." My favorite customer was the owner of a nearby liquor store. He once gave me back a lot of money, because he said he didn't want me fired. "Hey, Irish, you'd have been short. You must have thought I gave you a fifty-dollar bill." That was the hardest thing for me to do: figure out change in my head. Several times Tom Barrett came and browsed the paperback and magazine racks. I couldn't do anything but smile at him. I was so busy. But there at Snyder's Drug Store, becoming an independent city girl, I realized I was happy.

MIXING IT UP

Our Lady of Peace May Day Coronation

By the end of junior year, I had been elected a secretary of the class and joined other newly elected officers to crown the statue of Our Lady in May. At the grotto, I proudly presented my bouquet of red tulips, purple lilacs, and yellow daffodils, just as I had done in fifth grade at Holy Redeemer.

By senior year, I had not only made peace with the move to St. Paul but was busy with school and activities. I hadn't forgotten the earlier year. I hadn't forgotten the mixers—the dances—every weekend, walking around and around Cretin's gym, fluffing my hair, oh about every fifteen minutes, so it looked like maybe I'd just finished dancing with someone. When I did dance, though, it was with creepy guys who only wanted to do the Twist, and my big toe always turned into a big, ugly blood blister.

My brothers teased me. "Whoa, watch this," they'd say, grinding the balls of their feet into the floor like they were putting out cigarettes. "I'm so cool, look at my big red toe. You want to dance with me?"

"Excuse me," I'd grumble, "it was so funny, I forgot to laugh."

At the mixers the previous year, my new friends had warned me which guys to avoid—usually ones they were interested in themselves. Tom Barrett, for an example. When I first met him, I thought he was sharp, tall, a good dancer, easy to talk to, but Geri said he was hers. So I became friends with him, nothing more.

I did invite a guy from the College of St. Thomas to go to a Christmas dance with me. Because he was from a small town near Marshall, according to my dad, he did the right thing: picked me up at our house and chatted with Dad in the living room before we left. In St. Paul, boys didn't pick you up at your house except for special dances; instead they asked to drive girls home from the mixers or football or basketball games. Dad would have a royal fit if this happened. When he took me and friends to games, he would wait in the car in the parking lot, tapping on the steering wheel, smoking a cigarette, muttering in between puffs, "I'll . . . take home . . . those . . . I brought." Finally, when he drove off with just me, he'd say, "That's it, and you can't do anything with those kids again." The pits. *Those kids* were my new friends.

But my senior year, I was allowed to drive myself or ride with friends and avoid the whole scene with Dad. By the spring, though, I ran into trouble with Mom. I was invited to two different proms and told Mom I simply had to have three prom dresses, two for the other schools, one for OLP.

"It'd be humiliating to be seen in the same dress."

"That's ridiculous. I've never heard of such a thing. You can get one prom dress."

"I could wear Mary's for a second, but couldn't I please get another?"

"No," she said.

I finally convinced her to let me buy one at a second-hand store. I had my three.

Formal dances were *formal*: gloves, corsages, tuxes, even "bids"—little books girls strung on their wrists. As soon as we arrived at the dance, boys would write their names next to dance numbers to save them. I'd always be happy when Tom Barrett signed up. He and I especially liked to do the Lindy, say to the Crystals' "He's a Rebel"—"See the way he walks down the street / Watch the way he shuffles his feet . . . " or a combination of a Lindy and a slow dance, say to the Teddy Bears: "To know, know, know him / Is to love, love, love him / Just to see him smile / Makes my life worthwhile . . ." Tom and I'd twist to Chubby Checker; we did partner glides and turns and got down almost to the ground.

On OLP prom night, before the dance, we brought our dates to school for a reception in the auditorium. The sisters eyeballed our dresses for modesty. If anyone wore a short dress, the fourteen-inches-from-the-floor hem could be extended by a piece of cloth. If a bodice failed in modesty, cloth could be added there. Ridiculed by other students during the dance, the wearers didn't mind; they knew the rules and were willing to accept the consequences. To rebel was cool. The snickering would be surreptitious anyway. In the OLP auditorium, the best behavior was demanded. Earlier we had spent time in homeroom or with our homeroom in the cafeteria, called the Tea Room, practicing proper introductions. "Sister, this is Kevin. Kevin, this is Sister." We wore our white gloves and ate our cookies daintily.

My dates and I chewed breath mints because we had stopped earlier at Grace Lee's apartment in Highland Park.

When her husband had died, Grace moved from Marshall to St. Paul. Just as when I was young, I stopped by—now with my dates—to show her my dresses. Now instead of Sunshine snacks, she offered us a glass of wine. My boyfriends loved Grace Lee.

Before the proms, letters had gone out. One to parents:

OUR LADY OF PEACE HIGH SCHOOL
880 Portland Avenue
St. Paul, Minnesota

March 22, 1962

Dear Parents:

Prom night, May 4, is an eagerly anticipated social affair for your daughter—and one that should be an occasion of good fun for each girl and her date.

While parents and teachers alike are anxious to share in making Prom night a happy one, we are also concerned that the evening be spent in keeping with Catholic ideals of modesty and behavior. Accordingly, we feel you will want to know the regulations mandatory on O.L.P. girls attending the Prom.

Included with this letter is a mimeographed sheet listing recommendations made by the National Crusade for modesty in dress. Your daughter has been given a copy as well. Since these recommendations are in keeping with the mind of the Church, we have adopted them as our norms and ask that you be vigilant in your daughter's choice of Prom apparel.

We ask you to remind your daughter to be home no later than 3 a.m. and to avoid alcoholic beverages. You are well aware from reading the daily newspaper that excessive fatigue or drinking writes a tragic end to Proms all too often. If your daughter attends a house party after the dance, we urge you to determine whether responsible adult chaperones will be present.

Since observation of these regulations will depend on the integrity of your daughter and your cooperation with the school, we ask that your response be as wholehearted as it has been in the past.

Sincerely in Our Lady,
SISTERS OF CHARITY, B.V.M.

Another letter had gone out to students:

<u>NOTICE</u> — *To All Young Ladies Concerned With Cretin Social Events*
We would like to call your attention to the basic principle laid down by the National Crusade for modesty in dress. This applies particularly to the Cretin High School Junior-Senior Prom, April 20.

<u>GENERAL PRINCIPLE</u>
CHRISTIAN MODESTY DEMANDS, UNDER PAIN OF SIN, THAT DRESS BE SUCH AS TO CONCEAL AND IN NO WAY EMPHASIZE THE PARTS OF THE BODY WHICH, IF REVEALED OR SUGGEST, ARE AN OCCASION OF SIN TO NORMAL INDIVIDUALS.

<u>THEREFORE</u>
1. All strapless and halter style formals are considered objectionable, and are not approved. Formal dresses should have either reasonable broad straps over the shoulders or cap sleeves.
2. Transparent fabrics are NOT considered as coverage. This applies to all sheer nylon fabrics, organdy, net, sheer batiste, etc.
3. The top of all garments must not reveal or be lower in front than the line where the line of cleavage begins. This applies even when bending or stooping. It definitely excludes all plunging necklines and applies to underarm fit in sleeveless dresses.

4. The body of the garment should not be lower, in back, than a horizontal line drawn from midway between each armpit and shoulder.

WE ASK YOUR LOYAL COOPERATION IN THIS CRUSADE FOR CHRISTIAN MODESTY AT ALL OUR SCHOOL FUNCTIONS.

<u>*REMINDER*</u>

1. Drinking should be considered an insult to your status as a respectable Catholic woman. This should not be present on any date.

2. Junior-Senior Prom night is a big night—don't spoil it by sin.

3. If St. Paul stores do not stock proper formals, there is an organization called Marylike Fashions which does. Information concerning this organization is sent with this notice.

We thank you for your fine taste in the past and cooperation in the future.

The Junior-Senior Prom Committee

What a time for Catholics. Today I'd guess parents would laugh at the "National Crusade for modesty in dress," and Cretin-Derham Hall High School (the two schools combined in 1987) would send out a different letter. *Marylike Fashions.* Really? But then I think of conservative religious groups around the world—women putting on veils or chadors or burqas—and we're back to "dress be such as to conceal and in no way emphasize the parts of the body which, if revealed or suggest, are an occasion of sin to normal individuals." An era continues.

After the OLP Prom, I dared a group to climb down to the Mississippi River and party on the beach. We didn't drink, but we shouted and laughed and danced and sang, until security police drove by in a boat, shining powerful lights on us. We raced up the bluffs to our cars. My long white dress's hem was dirty and torn, but I didn't care. We later made out with our dates in their cars, not worrying about whether we were spoiling the big night by sin.

We talked about sin in depth in our religion class, Preparation for Marriage and Family Life. A priest from the St. Paul Seminary lectured us in the auditorium each week about our bodies as temples of the Holy Spirit and the evils of fornication; about adultery; about the sanctity of life and why our Church didn't believe in abortions. Father had a round body and he lisped through missing teeth. He also sweated profusely and periodically wiped his forehead with a limp handkerchief from his pocket. I took notes, but my mind was elsewhere: religion couldn't compete with mixers.

In late spring, we took our senior trip east. Planned by Regina Tours, the invocation on the brochure read: "Regina, Queen of Heaven, May She bless our travels!" We toured by train, sleeping in coach seats. We visited the cracked Liberty Bell in Philadelphia and Kennedy's White House in Washington, D.C. Fascinated by the decorative changes elegant Jackie was creating, we didn't miss peeking into any of the rooms on the tour. We hoped to get a glimpse of Jackie or Jack or Caroline or little John-John. No such luck. The naval officers who greeted us in Annapolis—a handsome sea of whites—stunned us, and in New York, the original musical comedy *Bye Bye Birdie*, on a Broadway stage, blew us starstruck away.

The Cloisters, part of the Metropolitan Museum of Art, wowed me. One of the sister chaperones had pulled me aside and suggested I should go there instead of shopping during free time. She said I'd love it. I convinced a couple of friends to come with me. We figured out the subway system and zipped up north to Fort Tryon Park and the Hudson River. We couldn't believe how quiet and peaceful it was after the bustle of the train and the subway and lower Manhattan and staying up all night talking.

We entered the Cloisters—like a medieval abbey—and discovered the tapestries, particularly the unicorns. I was enthralled by the gardens, with pillars forming open windows looking out to green grass (representing rebirth and life and nature and spring), pomegranate and pear trees, and symbolic white angelica flowers. I've always been mesmerized by windows and doors and the frames they make. I hold Anne Morrow Lindbergh's *Gift from the Sea* in the same enchanted category. Her poem on the seventh tapestry, "The Unicorn in Captivity," captivated me: Confined. Free. Alive again. I had read C. S. Lewis's *Chronicles of Narnia* that year also. An abundance of Christian symbolism. The lion and the unicorn. Dying, rising. I loved it—and the whole Cloisters experience.

The final night of our tour we prayed the rosary together in our cars and on the last day disembarked in Chicago to attend Sunday Mass. A Regina ending.

During the course of senior year, my very likable piano and speech teachers tried to convince me I'd be an ideal candidate for their convent. Convents, they said, didn't want super-devout, introspective young women; they wanted girls who were cheerful and giving. I found that surprising. Mary qualified as a devout, introspective young woman, but she seemed happy, and the Order seemed happy to have her.

The nuns also made it known that they wanted me to join their order, Sisters of Charity of the Blessed Virgin Mary. Aware I had come from Marshall Central, run by the Sisters of St. Joseph, and that Mary had entered that order, they wanted to make sure I knew enough to make a decision between the two.

Sister Mary Eliza and I spent most of my piano-lesson time discussing my future. A good excuse, too, because I never practiced. I simply replayed week after week my senior-recital pieces: MacDowell's "March Wind," Lecuona's "Cordoba," Shostakovitch's "Three Fantastic Dances," Schumann's "Farewell" from his *Forest Scenes*, and Mozart's "Fantasia in D Minor."

Sister Mary Christophil coached me for a state Catholic speech tournament at the College of St. Thomas, which was fun and challenging. So was conferring with her—fun to talk about

Margaret Rogers,
high school graduation

both of us being new to the school (she came in '61, too) and challenging to discuss my plans after graduation. I simply didn't know what to say. I didn't think I would be a nun, but I didn't seem to have any other ideas.

And then I was called. That day in the auditorium at the end of our senior retreat when I couldn't say no to God. He wanted me.

I wasn't going to tell anyone about my *call* right away. I needed to let the idea jell in my mind and heart. I went to a mixer that Friday night after the retreat. I didn't think I acted differently at all, but when I was dancing with Tom Barrett, he leaned down and whispered to me, "You're entering the convent, aren't you?"

I was flabbergasted. "How did you know?" I asked.

"I just did. It's girls like you who do."

"What do you mean?" I said. "Like what?"

"Well, nice, funny, smart."

I was pleased he thought that of me but nervously cut off the conversation. "Please don't tell anyone," I said.

I don't remember when I told Mom and Dad. I don't remember when, or if, I told them about my grades either. Towards the end of senior year, the principal called me into her office to tell me she couldn't give me full credit for my grades at Central. "Your marks are excellent, but a small-town school isn't comparable to our institution. It's not the same caliber. I deducted points from your grades."

It brought back memories of my history teacher at Central Catholic, the one who flirted with the boys. Its unfairness angered me: Central's teachers were certainly as qualified as OLP's. I don't remember Mom and Dad going to talk with the principal, or if Sister's decision was made too late for them to make any difference, or what. I do remember being hurt and embarrassed on graduation day, with my whole family watching, to be the first of the family not to walk across the stage as one of the top ten scholars.

Maybe my parents' concern was totally taken up coping with my convent decision. Mom told me she cried for a week at night in her bedroom. She told Dad that giving two girls to God was too much. She wanted me to go to college, to marry, and to have children. Dad said, "Peggy has to make up her own mind."

Another reason for entering the convent might have been that I was just plain exhausted from the move to St. Paul. I had used up so much energy adapting to my new life there, I couldn't face the process of looking for colleges. In a way, entering the convent was an easy way out; I wouldn't have to prove myself all over again. And, like my brothers before me, following each other to the same college, I probably found shadowing Mary an acceptable choice. I liked what she said about nuns living together not only for their apostolic work but also for mutual support, challenge, and inspiration. I knew from family visits what the convent entailed in some sense. But I never talked to Mary or anyone else about the convent in day-to-day terms. Being called was an individual, private consideration until I announced my intention.

I also believe I entered the convent in some sense because of Dad. Going into the convent would be the way to give 100 percent. I could change the world: bring love and peace and understanding and goodness. Be poor and chaste and obedient for a greater cause—something that would impress him. Or maybe Dad didn't expect or even want me to join the convent. When my family came for their monthly visits at the postulancy, then later at the novitiate, he would ask, "Is this what you want? Are you sure you're happy? You can always come home."

The summer before I entered, Mom again wanted me close. She rented a tiny cabin below the bridge on the St. Croix

River across from Hudson, Wisconsin. Our family filled it to overflowing on the weekends, when Jim and John brought their future wives, Dad brought Patty, and Tom and Dan hitchhiked from the Cities after their jobs. Mom and I stayed at the river weekdays as well. I suntanned and read on the dock, swam, and entertained friends. We didn't have a boat but next door to us was a nice family who did. They also had a son who was a senior in high school. He and I spent a great deal of time together. I thought that if I was entering the convent, this was my last chance for romance. His dad pulled us waterskiing. We took walks and drives in his car. Saw movies. Watched sunsets and moon shinings. Danced in garages with Tom and Dan and other kids who stayed at cabins on the river. Kissed and made out. A glorious summer.

Meanwhile, I received a letter from the assistant priest in Marshall, a handsome, energetic, fun-loving, great guy, who was off to begin a mission in Guatemala—which he very successfully ran for fifty years.

Rev. Gregory T. Schaffer
Holy Redeemer Church
503 West Lyon
Marshall, Minnesota
June 6, 1963

Dear Marge,

May I extend my warmest congratulations to you for your selfless decision. Believe me there is no greater life than one of 100% dedication— and the greatest dedication is to God. Marge you will be happy—more than happy as you know. But most important of all you will be so very badly needed in this special life of leading others to their God and God to his people.

When I know of a young lady going into the Convent, I know she will learn special prayer. May I beg that special prayer for our mission in Guatemala? I am sure I can.

Marge don't change. The one rule you must constantly keep is—stay Marge! When the glorious title of Sister is added to your life—fine—but still be Marge because it is Marge that will make the great nun—not Sister.

My prayers are with you.

In Christ,
Fr. Schaffer

Another letter arrived a month later, July 6, 1963, from St. Joseph's Novitiate, saying my application, physician's report, academic transcripts, and letters of recommendation had been received. A clothing list was included: a blouse pattern, diagrams for a black slip and an apron, and a measurement slip for the uniform jumper. We were supposed to send our measurements in within a week. These items would be made and be ready for us when we arrived.

In September, Mom helped me pack up the black trunk we bought at Sears. We folded in underwear; T-shirts (Strange. Why masculine T-shirts?); handkerchiefs (Also strange. Who used them anymore?); black stockings; two pairs of black oxfords with soft rubber heels; one pair of rubbers and overshoes; one pair of plain black bedroom slippers with soft soles; one six-inch sewing scissors; one stainless-steel nail file; one clothes brush; one hairbrush; one comb; coat, scarf, and mittens; a Bible—Confraternity Edition (I deliberately chose the Protestant Revised Standard Edition because I thought it was a better version, a sign of what I thought the nuns would want, a thoughtful, critical person); a daily missal; a large, loose-leaf binder with fillers; one pen and pencil; an inexpensive rosary and case; and a hundred-dollar dowry (Why so little or so much, depending on what it would be used for?). We could also bring skates and a tennis racket if we planned on using them. Optional items included: hair curlers or rollers, a girdle, a razor with blades.

The day finally arrived. Even though the grounds were

just across the street from our house, we drove over to the novitiate. Getting out, hugging my family, looking back to Fairview Avenue, looking forward to Randolph Avenue, lugging my big black trunk up thirteen steps—my brothers helped me—past four tall pillars, to the huge, double oak doors, I thought how I might be entering a narrow world, but it was one that would give me the opportunity to make a difference in the larger world. A Sister called a *Portress* met me. I looked back and waved to my family, then walked through the doors. I didn't feel trapped or set free, or vulnerable or safe, just excited.

My eighth-grade teacher, Sister St. Edmund, sent my mother a letter on that day. I later found it along with all the other writings Mom had saved.

St. Mark's
Sept. 15, 1963

Dear Mrs. Rogers,

I've been wanting to call you but these precious days were so distracting and busy that I didn't wish to disturb you. Today we had the beginning of Forty Hours and you and Mr. Rogers were indeed in my prayers for I know this day was a glad and sad one for both of you. I know the human side must feel the ache terribly. In the years to come, both girls will become closer and closer to you but right now—the distance seems great. How wonderful that neither of you tried to influence Margaret away from her decision when her going means such a sacrifice to you.

You will continue to be in my prayers—and Margaret and Mary that they persevere and also that Tom or Danny may one day stand at God's altar.

God love and bless a heroic pair of parents!

Sincerely,
Sister St. Edmund

Tom and Danny? How many children is a good family

supposed to give? My brother John had entered the monastery at St. John's but stayed for only a short time. He was called in by the abbot to explain why he missed so many Masses in the mornings. Always a sleep-in guy, John had answered that it was just too early for him. The abbot kindly said that probably was a sign John didn't have a vocation.

Tom also thought of joining the Maryknolls, an organization whose focus is on the overseas mission activity of the Catholic Church. Tom wanted to be a missionary in Africa. He was a friend of a priest who lived his whole life in East Africa. Even though he never became a priest or a lay minister, Tom would contribute financially to the Maryknolls all his life.

At the time, Catholics generally were proud and supportive when a child went off to the seminary or convent. It was a badge of honor, a sign that they were a good family. For many parents, there was an assurance that their child, who would be educated and taken care of financially, was fulfilling the American dream, ascending the social ladder. And producing large families ensured that their other children would marry and have grandchildren. Parents often selected which children should be called, though I don't remember my father or mother ever saying anything to any of us kids about vocations.

AS A POSTULANT

Fifty years ago, I entered the novitiate of the Sisters of St. Joseph of Carondelet at 1890 Randolph Avenue, adjacent to the College of St. Catherine (St. Kate's) in St. Paul, Minnesota. I entered with forty-nine other girls, almost all of us right out of high school.

We *postulants* (applicants for a year) immediately got to know each other and our surroundings. Half of the *reception* (the group who entered together) were already friends from St. Joseph's Academy in St. Paul. Others hailed from rural or suburban areas of Minnesota, mostly from Catholic but a few from public high schools. Some appeared shy and retiring; others, loud and boisterous. All of us: curious and nervous.

We quickly discovered the nooks and crannies of our new home, a stately brick-and-stone beaux-arts landmark, built in 1912 by architect John W. Wheeler. A mammoth building, the basement held the laundry room, the library, lockers, showers, a tub room, a sewing room, a pantry, and an enormous kitchen and *refectory* (dining room). The first floor included visiting rooms, called *parlors*, the office of the Mistress of Novices, two large meeting rooms for receptions of novices, the atrium, and a chapel. The second floor was reserved for postulants and contained our meeting room, our Mistress's office, our dormitory rooms—three or four to a room, with floor-to-ceiling curtains (white sheets) dividing our *cells*, and the infirmary. The third floor held many dormitory rooms, some single, some double, plus a huge room for many novices, called the Holy Family Dormitory—a sea of hanging white sheets.

We never walked out the oak doors we had initially entered except for the very few times we took a bus to a doctor's appointment. The backyard, with a sidewalk path winding around the perimeter of a central grotto of the Blessed Virgin, was huge and inviting. We *recreated* on the outside grounds in all seasons of the year. We would walk and talk with a friend or in a larger group. Sometimes we'd roller skate on the sidewalk. During silence, we would bring books and read on benches or would slowly pace the perimeter by ourselves.

The very far back of the yard housed the laundry facility for the college. Steam continually poured out and over its red bricks. Beyond this were fields of the college. We were invited at times to play on the tennis courts. And the pool and gym were sometimes available for us on Saturdays. We'd wear the same swimming suits and exercise shorts and tops as the college girls. We could also wander farther out among the vast grounds of forests and flowered gardens. During retreats, I liked to stray to the college's Dew Drop Pond with its spraying center fountain. Below the beautiful Our Lady of Victory Chapel, I watched geese and ducks graze on the pond's shore and students and their dates kiss on the bridge. I'd go to the *Back 80* beyond the pond to find private areas for reading or contemplating.

In our classes on the traditions and practices of our order, we heard about its founding in 1650, in Le Puy-en-Velay, France, where a community of women, named the Daughters of St. Joseph, were called to be "entirely lost and absorbed in God and for God" and be everything "for the dear neighbor." Different from other women religious orders at the time, the Sisters of St. Joseph did not seclude themselves in convents (a *cloistered* order) or wear habits but worked with the sick and the poor out in public while wearing inconspicuous widow's garb. The sisters grew in numbers and expanded beyond France, coming to the United States in 1836 to work among the deaf in Carondelet, Missouri.

At the request of Bishop Cretin in the Minnesota Territory, four sisters came to open a school for immigrant children, to live and work among Native Americans, and to establish a hospital. They arrived in St. Paul in 1851, and immediately founded St. Joseph's Academy, for day and boarding school girls. One of the Academy's first graduates, Ellen Ireland (later Sister Seraphine), sister of the famous Archbishop John Ireland, joined the Sisters of St. Joseph. She would go on to found the College of St. Catherine in 1905, despite serious skepticism among other professionals about higher education for women.

We learned about the first president of the college, Sister Antonia McHugh, who sent her sisters off to earn degrees at secular and even Protestant universities all over the world. She required sisters to obtain their doctorates before the age of thirty-five and to travel to Europe and New York City as part of their education. During her tenure, the College of St. Catherine became the first Catholic college in the United States to receive a chapter of Phi Beta Kappa, the oldest and most prestigious honor society in the United States.

I was one of four of our reception who was sent to study on campus during this year of postulancy. We took two classes, Spanish and logic. The Sister who taught Spanish was a quiet woman who didn't worry too much about our speaking proficiency, but we could certainly conjugate verbs. At first, I found logic, in the philosophy department, difficult but eventually discovered its lessons—on the nature of good (correct) reasoning and of bad (incorrect) reasoning—were helpful. The process helped you solve problems; its methods sharpened your ability to discern propaganda and false advertising.

Mary, two years ahead of me in the novitiate, was beginning her studies in the history department of St. Catherine's. She loved her classes and her professors and found them stimulating and demanding. She felt lucky to be part of the great St.

Catherine tradition. She shared the college's belief that women could achieve the same high academic standards as men.

I didn't quite warm up to the college. We postulants were instructed not to speak to other students. Thinking this a stupid rule, I flitted and fluttered, like a butterfly, from the novitiate to see all my old friends from OLP on campus. I'd talk fast and furious between classes. My friends didn't understand why I couldn't talk to them. They knew I was different now, my clothes a constant signal. We wore black blouses, long skirts, capes, stockings, heavy lace-up shoes, and stiff white cuffs and collars—daily reminders that we had detached ourselves from the world. But, of course, I had not detached myself yet.

Our days as postulants were filled with prayer, study, and household chores. We received an orientation to Christian and religious life and to the customs of the community. Instructed in etiquette and grooming, housekeeping duties, sewing, and gardening, we also took college classes in practical and theoretical theology. Our secular courses, taught by faculty sisters from the college who came to the postulate room to teach, included world literature, history of western civilization, and basic design in art. In summer session, we took music fundamentals (Gregorian chant) and physiology.

At the beginning of the school year, we took a qualifying English exam. When Sister handed it out, she instructed, "When you come to the end of the first part, it will say STOP. But don't stop. Go on to the next sections." She repeated this directive again after everyone had her test on top of her desk. Sister pressed a stopwatch to time us.

I worked fast. When I came to the STOP at the end of the first part, I stopped, forgetting what Sister had told us. I looked up, noticed everyone still diligently filling in the bubbles on the answering sheet. Thinking I must have worked quickly, I relaxed and slowly checked over my answers. Suddenly, I realized what I'd done. I flipped through the rest of the pages. Tons of questions left to do. My heart dropped. I stood up, dashed over to Sister.

"Sister," I whispered, "I know you told us . . . "

"You're not to be talking to me," she said. "Finish the test."

"But I stopped when I shouldn't have, Sister. I won't have enough time."

"Finish the test," she said.

I returned to my desk and speedily tried to answer the questions. I didn't even get to the final pages. After class, I again tried to talk to Sister, to see if maybe there was another form of the test, if I could do it over. She wouldn't even look at me.

So. Fine. A lesson in paying attention and following orders. But what happened after is what influenced my own teaching career. For the rest of the year, the Sister who taught world literature said to me, "With your ability, you're doing very well in the course." I tried at the beginning to tell her I was the one who messed up on the qualifying exam, but she dismissed me, saying, "Keep applying yourself, dear."

Because the test was apparently in my personal folder, other future teachers of English classes also expressed their surprise at my initial work. They hadn't expected me to do well either. Some of them marked my work accordingly. A valuable lesson on the role of expectations was forever ingrained in my head.

During the year, the community tried to determine whether or not we had truly been called, and likewise, we, too, tried to decide whether we had a vocation to be a Sister of St. Joseph. Some realized they didn't and left after a few weeks or months. We never said goodbye to these friends. They just disappeared. We'd discuss it at recreation. We assumed others were asked to leave: some who always dreamed of becoming a nun, who acted too weirdly religious; others who played childlike pranks, short-sheeting beds and gluing things on chairs; and still others who talked at dinner about cutting their toenails or other unsavory details, sort-of social misfits.

Even for the well adjusted, a disciplined, unfamiliar way of life was difficult. Communal living—demanding trust, openness, and communication—was a challenge. You had to live peacefully with a variety of temperaments, personal histories, and styles. For those who loved to talk, the rule of silence was a colossal challenge. Except during recreation—one hour a day (a half hour each after lunch and dinner)—we were supposed to practice silence. Told it led to efficient work on *charges* (assigned duties of cleaning or cooking) and in studies, silence most importantly aided recollection, the development of a "living awareness of the indwelling presence of God in our souls." Night was a time of strict silence, Grand Silence; starting at 9 p.m., we were not to talk except in cases of emergency. During the day, we kept ordinary silence; we were to speak only out of duty, necessity, or charity. I practiced all three of these exceptions—a lot. No one reported my talking on campus, but I got into trouble for talking to Mary.

I'd see her going to church or coming from her dormitory and rather than say our community greeting, "Praise be to Jesus," or reply to her greeting with "Amen," I'd start right in: "Mary . . ."

She'd immediately turn from me and scurry away.

Then I'd get angry and raise my voice. "Where are you going? I just want to tell you something."

Mary finally reported me to my Mistress, who happened to be our former principal from Central Catholic, the one who had fired Miss Sexpot. Sister had been promoted to Postulant Mistress. Mary and I had always greatly liked and respected her. Attempting to straighten me out about Mary, she explained that Sister Rose Alice—my sister's chosen name, after my mom, Alice Rose—tried to observe the rule of silence, which I was clearly breaking. She also reminded me that novices and postulants lived as separate groups; unless they got special permission or were invited to one another's recreations, they did not carry on conversations with one another.

I scoffed, said, "Really, Sister, do you mean you can't talk to your own sister? That's crazy."

She smiled at me and said, "Just try."

I promised I'd try to walk past my sister without saying anything and even try not to make eye contact. I did improve, but not talking to your real sister still seemed silly to me.

In the postulancy, we were bound together by spiritual values and a common *horarium* (schedule): rising, Prime (part of the Divine Office, the Church's official liturgical worship), morning meditation, Mass, breakfast, breakfast charge, straightening our rooms and making our beds ("make it smooth enough to bounce a quarter on; pleat the curtains"), main charge, classes, Little Office of the Blessed Virgin (psalms, hymns, scripture and other readings said on Sundays and holy days), examen (an examination of conscience), dinner, dinner charge, afternoon recreation, Little Office, classes, prayer and lecture, recreation, rosary and meditation, supper, supper charge, evening recreation, Compline (also part of the Divine Office), study time, strict silence, taps, lights out. In private, we daily read fifteen minutes from a spiritual book and made the Stations of the Cross (the tradition of commemorating the chief scenes of Christ's sufferings and death by praying at fourteen small relief plaques on the walls of the chapel) and a short visit to chapel after meals. We received the Sacrament of Penance weekly with Confession.

Postulants and novices met with family and other guests in the parlors. My family could visit once a month, except during Advent, as we prepared for Christmas, and Lent, when we penanced before Easter. Mary could join us every other month. We gathered in the archbishop's parlor, one of the biggest rooms in the novitiate. A stiff and stuffy space. One of my duties was cleaning it—every day—and I could never find a speck of dust anywhere. Nothing seemed to float even in the beam of light streaming through the stained glass windows. Nuns did live by the old adage "Cleanliness is next to Godliness."

If our whole family visited, we took over the entire room, but we usually shared it, setting up clusters of chairs for several other families. Mom and Dad and Tom and Dan visited the most. The boys, in high school now at Cretin, were gangly; I couldn't get over how big they were. Each time they visited, they seemed to have grown up—in every sense. They always looked so uncomfortable sitting on the straight-backed chairs. Trying to balance glass cups on the scrolled wooden arms of the chairs, they recited the scores of their sports' games and talked about their classes in school, then they slouched down, stretched out their legs, and stared at the paintings on the wall of church and convent leaders—popes, women superiors—who sternly peered down at us, seated on our needlepointed chairs, clinging to our punch and cookies, until it was time to go.

I couldn't wait to talk, to tell them everything: how my Mistress would sneak in books from St. Catherine's library for me, when I told her I was dying for novels; how I'd read the novels late into the night, under my bedcovers with a flashlight; how we put on plays and musical programs for the novices on feast days; how my college classes motivated me; how I missed my old friends; and what my new friends thought of the novitiate. Too soon, the hand bell would ring, announcing the end of visiting hours.

Dad would ask his usual "Are you sure you're happy?"

And I'd always answer, "I'm fine, Dad."

Then he and Mom hugged and kissed Mary and me. The boys shrugged their goodbyes, their hands in their pockets. This formal visiting—taking place always in Mom and Dad's presence—was not conducive to a brotherly/sisterly give-and-take. There was no banter or teasing. No secrets shared. Every visiting day I felt I missed more of my brothers' lives.

The family all waved as they walked out the huge front novitiate doors, heading toward our home across the street. It was odd to be so close physically to them and yet so far away psychologically. When I walked out on the college grounds, I

Our home across from the convent in deep snow

could almost see into their living-room window. Again, I didn't pay attention to the rules; I yelled or waved if I saw anybody. But I never left the grounds. That would have been really breaking the rules in my mind—but strangely, Mary did once, and got reprimanded.

In that first year of the convent, I hated the 5:30 a.m. bell, Grand Silence at 9:00 p.m., and lights out at 10:00 p.m., but I loved the Liturgy of the Hours, especially morning Prime prayer and Compline prayer at night. The Psalms, like poems, deeply affected me. However, slowly, like a turtle tentatively peering out of her shell, I began to question if I should be a nun. I began to think I was mistaken about the call. I missed my family.

But then a strange and sad thing happened. My Mistress called me into her office one afternoon to ask if I thought I should go to the parlor to meet Tom Barrett, who had come to see me. I was dumbfounded; no single guys ever gained access to the convent. I said, "Of course I should see him. He's a good friend. It must be important."

I met Tom in one of the smaller side parlors. He sat balancing on the edge of a chair in the back corner and jumped up when I entered the room. He appeared tall and handsome. He looked surprised at my postulant outfit, but said, "I'm so glad to see you."

We sat next to each other in the corner. Tom had brought terrible news: our friend Matt, who had acted with us in *My Three Angels* at Cretin, had been killed riding his bicycle near St. John's University.

"I needed to tell you in person. I hitchhiked from St. John's. Will you pray for Matt?" Tom said.

I was deeply shaken. I don't remember if I cried or if Tom and I talked about anything else, but I do remember being very happy to see him. I think we hugged goodbye.

I had really liked Matt, and he was also the first friend of mine to die. It weighed on me. I took his death as a sign I was still called, still chosen, that I must not leave. I would go ahead and in the summer wear one of the beautiful wedding dresses kept for all of us to marry Christ in.

My mother, saver of writings, kept a few of the letters I wrote during the postulancy. We could write home once a month. Our friends could only write at Christmas, but we could receive mail every Saturday from family or relatives. Reading my letters, I recall how creative and fun living in community could be and how exhilarating it could be to escape that same community—even if it was to remove warts.

Nov. 4, 1963

There have been many big days around here. The night after visiting, the novices put on a big pizza party for us. Christ the King was a big feast day; we had a procession that night into chapel. All Saints Day was another recreation day and All Souls Day was a prayerful day sort of— said quite a few Our Fathers, Hail Marys, etc. for faithful departed. Sun. was a recollection day. I love those days. It is a time to think and pray by yourself. . . . Oh, I should tell you about my last trip to the doctor. I got to go with another postulant. She is a diabetic and she had to go to St. Joe's for a test so we went to the hospital 1st and had breakfast there and then went to the Lowry. Both of my warts are off now—Gee, I hate to write about them—they sound so ugly. Well, anyway, the trip was exciting.

June 17, 1964

. . . everyone is dieting to get into our wedding dresses that are now about 2 sizes too small. I haven't tried mine on because S. Rita Joseph has been on retreat. I've been swimming and playing tennis a lot. Also reading quite a bit. Oh, I forgot to tell you I just finished reading "A Man for All Seasons." We're getting quite a bit of Thomas More because we're reading a book on him for refectory reading. I've also been reading a lot on birth

control. "Jubilee" magazine had a whole issue dedicated to this–emotional letters, etc. An interesting problem and I imagine a heart-rendering one for many people.

Isolated from society—no radio, TV, or newspaper—we postulants still picked up the '60s upheaval in our campus classes, in our superiors' reports, and during our family visits. We knew about *The Feminine Mystique* and Betty Friedan asking, "Is this all?" We knew about the earlier Elizabeth Cady Stanton and Susan B. Anthony, and thought our sisters had been true feminists long before their time. They had earned PhDs and worked before it was acceptable for women to hold jobs. Early CEOs, they had owned and administered hospitals, schools, and universities. Working with men, they had raised funds, asking for money from male business owners and philanthropists. Being nuns had allowed them to act in ways highly unusual for women of their times. Serving as alternative role models and inspiring examples of what women could be and do, we enthusiastically followed their leadership.

As postulants, we thought about sexism, classism, pacifism, and racism. We knew that two hundred thousand strong had marched on Washington for Jobs and Freedom, and that Martin Luther King Jr. had delivered his crucial "I Have a Dream" speech there. We knew our sisters strongly believed in and taught racial equality. We knew about the Rondo neighborhood in St. Paul, broken by the building of Interstate 94, and how relocation exposed fundamental racism. We prayed for its resolution and celebrated diversity in our liturgies.

We knew of our fellow Minnesotan Bob Dylan, and his distrust of the growing U.S. involvement in Vietnam. We sang "Masters of War" and "We Shall Overcome" at sing-alongs in our postulate room. We also sang the music-defining Beatles' "I Want to Hold Your Hand" and "I Saw Her Standing There." And of course we knew of the assassination of John F. Kennedy, which signaled a cynical shift in our nation's frame of mind.

Nov. 27, 1963

Well, I'm attempting to get my thoughts gathered together to tell you what's been going on.

First of all, we all were very shook up about Kennedy's death. I watched T.V. for 2 days (we had a T. V. put up in the postulate and in the novitiate) and on Sat. we got to read the newspaper at St. Kate's library and also watch T.V. over there for a few minutes so we kept up on the news. And it sure was a drain—after the mass and funeral I think everyone was really tired and keyed up. . . . The whole thing seemed so fishy to me. I hope the Secret Service or someone still stays on the case.

I forgot to tell my family how we found out the news. An ancient Sister from St. Catherine's taught us history of western civilization. A kind, dear soul, she lectured softly and boringly, her head barely peeping over the lectern she stood at for the whole hour of class. On November 22, 1963, she was droning on when suddenly our Mistress flew into the room.

She whispered something to Sister, who grabbed her chest, turned stark white, and said, "Thank you, Sister."

Our Mistress then said in a shaky voice, "Girls, our president has been shot and killed."

We said a prayer for him and then our Mistress left the room. Our professor began where she left off in her notes.

I raised my hand and said, "Sister, we can't go on. We must stop our lesson. Our president has been killed."

She looked up, said, "Of course. Thank you," and slowly walked out.

I was always raising my hand, like the time our Mistress brought in a strange little, black, whiplike thing. Her face very red, she tried to tell us to use it on our legs and arms on Saturday night in our cells, a reminder of penitential practices, designed to help us lead disciplined lives. We all looked at her blankly. What? *What?*

Finally, I said, "Sister, we're supposed to use this thing on ourselves? Really? Self-flagellation, like what the Ecstatics and Mystics did? This is medieval."

Getting redder, she said, "Yes."

Well, we laughed heartily about it after she left, but truly I was a bit shocked by the *discipline*, as it was called. For the time we used it in our cells—the practice was discontinued in a year or so—we'd strain to hear others lashing themselves. Mostly we heard giggling. Then it just got boring and routine. I barely gave a switch over my arms and legs. I wasn't sorry about anything really.

Except not seeing my family: that I was sorry about. But I didn't tell them so. Stiff upper lip, conventional reporting, seemed to be how I communicated with them.

Nov. 28, 1963

Today was a really big day—I mean it was Thanksgiving and everything but we surely celebrated it big here. First of all, we got up at 6:00—never thought I'd see the day when I'd be thrilled about that—sang Mass and had a long breakfast, sang with the novices at 10:15—Mary and I played some duets on the piano at this time, played around in our postulate until our turkey dinner and then we had a treasure hunt—we went out on the hill and I said "hi" to you all from the middle of the field. Hope you got the "hi" from there. Then after the hunt we went over to Fontbonne Hall. I signed up for basketball. It has been 2 yrs. since I've played and you would laugh to see how stiff I am. Can't imagine what it will be like tomorrow.

Another thing to tell you, my charge was changed. I now clean the postulants' home, the postulate, along with 3 other kids and then I wash dishpans after supper so it really is much easier than the refectory charge although I liked that before. . . .

Say, guess I'd better close for tonight. My 3 dorm mates are all ready for me to snap off the light——to be continued.

Today, of course, nuns remain close to their families and participate in their events. They are not bound by rules of separation. But in my time: I missed Thanksgiving with my family. Postulants were not allowed to go home for a visit at Christmas either. I worked on becoming detached, the image of my father at games—standing apart—coming back to me. I wanted to believe in my vocation.

After we successfully completed our postulancy, the provincial superior and her council approved our entrance into the novitiate. The Feast of the Transfiguration of Christ, August 6, was our reception day. Dressed in our white bridal gowns, thirty-four of our original reception of forty-nine processed to the altar. Months before, we had had a great time trying on the gowns, saved in a room in the novitiate. We had picked ones that fit us. And then, as my letter said, we tried not to gain the "freshman fifteen."

On this day, I knew I still had a long way to go to reach humility because even though I had finally admitted I was near-sighted and bought glasses—for self-effacement purposes, wire-rimmed granny ones—I vainly didn't wear them processing up and down the aisle of the St. Paul Cathedral. I wanted to be beautiful on my wedding day.

I was also the only postulant who hadn't sewn her own habit, a rule of the Order. Sister Rita Joseph, a dear lady, kicked me out of the sewing room after I broke three needles and a few machines. It brought back memories of Muzzy trying her hardest with me. "You can't sew. It's OK, I'll sew yours," Sister kindly offered. "You'll be the only postulant I've ever let off the hook." She sewed my light, black cotton habit for reception day. In the winter, she also sewed a heavy, black serge habit for me.

At the ceremony, the archbishop received our requests to enter the novitiate:

Ordinary: What do you ask, my children?

Candidates: Your Excellency, I ask to receive the habit of the Sisters of St. Joseph of Carondelet.

Ordinary: Are you firmly resolved to serve God as a faithful spouse of

Christ in the religious state as a Sister of St. Joseph?
Candidates: Yes, Your Excellency, I am firmly resolved to serve God in the religious state as a Sister of St. Joseph.
Ordinary: Do you desire to renounce the vanities of the world, to strive after religious perfection, and to live according to the rules of this institute?
Candidates: I earnestly desire to renounce the vanities of the world and to become truly Christlike by living according to the rules of this institute.
Ordinary: I am convinced of your sincerity and approve of your being received into the novitiate. Go now, my children, to receive the holy habit.

We left then, with the congregation singing, "Come, O spouse of Christ, receive forever the crown which the Lord has prepared for you." Each of us received the religious habit we had spent so many hours making (except for me). Sister Rita Joseph gave me mine, along with my guimpe (a wide, stiffly starched cloth that covered the neck and shoulders) and forehead band, the starched linen cornet that framed the face, the black veil and underveil, the cincture extending to the knee, and the black braided belt with the rosary of five decades. Sister said she liked the name I chose, would like using it: "No, Sister Zoë, you cannot come into my sewing room. Pray for me in church."

I was proud to put on the habit. And I did put on my granny glasses when we reentered the cathedral, advancing to the communion rail while the congregation sang. The archbishop again addressed us:

Ordinary: As novices in the Congregation of the Sisters of Saint Joseph of Carondelet you wear the holy habit which you have so earnestly desired. You are now entitled to the religious name by which you will henceforth be known.
(He reads the name of each novice.)
Ordinary: I exhort you to study and to practice during your novitiate the principles of the religious life and the spirit and customs of the Congregation, so that you may prepare yourselves to become worthy religious.
Novices: I am grateful for the privilege which has been granted me today. I shall strive to cooperate with divine grace so that I may prepare myself to

pronounce worthily the vows which I hope to take in the Congregation.
Ordinary: May the blessing of almighty God, the Father and the Son and
the Holy Spirit, descend upon you and remain always with you.

Our new names symbolized our desire "to leave the
world" in pursuit of holiness. "Zoë" meant *Life* in Greek. Zoë
was also an African saint, a wife and mother who watched all of
her family martyred for Christ's sake. I wanted to be prepared
if the Greek word wasn't enough to justify my choice. And, of
course, for me there was *Franny and Zooey* of J. D. Salinger, who
was an introvert, not unlike a contemplative nun.

I saved our reception booklet. As I read it now, I'm a bit
creeped out by the wedding and virgin analogies. The opening
prayer: "Hear, O daughter, and see: turn your ear, forget your
people and your father's house; and the king shall desire your
beauty" (Ps. 44, 11-12). And the Priest's Prayer: "Let us pray: O
God, you are turning your servants away from worldly vanities
and making them eager for the prize of a heavenly vocation.
Pour your grace upon them so that, mindful of their profession,
they may accomplish with your help what you have inspired
them to promise."

Lines from the Epistle (1 Cor. 7, 6-8, 25, 29-32, 34) include "The unmarried woman, like the virgin, is concerned with
the things of the Lord, that she may be holy in body as well as
in spirit in Christ Jesus, our Lord." And from the Meditation
Song: "I hold the kingdom of this world and all its allurements
in contempt for the love of my Lord Jesus Christ, whom I have
seen, whom I have loved, and in whom is my belief and my de-
light" (Ps. 44, 2). "My heart overflows with a goodly theme; as
I sing my ode to the king. Alleluia, alleluia. My lover belongs to
me and I to him; he browses among the lilies. Alleluia" (Cant.
2, 16). The Gospel tells the parable of the ten virgins who took
their torches and went out to welcome the bridegroom. These
verses were beautiful, but the sexual allusions made me nervous.
I did not believe I was marrying Jesus Christ; I was committing

to a vision of Other-centeredness.

I was also hurt by the invocation to leave your family. Now I realize the importance of "forgetting your people and your father's house." In order to truly grow up, we must set out from our homes, from what our mothers and fathers wanted us to be or do, to find our own callings. The Gospel call, again and again, is to leave home and family. The opening cover of the reception booklet, "Live in My Love," and the ending, "And Love Is My Answer," is the essence of being *called*.

I believe I am still answering this call of Love.

AS A NOVICE

After our reception, we junior novices entered a parlor set up by senior novices in the attic of the novitiate, the 1890 beauty shop, to get very short haircuts. With only little mirrors, it was difficult to see how shorn we looked, but we could guess from our friends' heads. We accepted it as part of our commitment of two more years to determine if we were called to religious life. Prayer and dialogue would decide this through the process called *discernment*.

Prayer life in the novitiate, like that of the postulancy, included daily meditation, Mass, morning and evening prayer, and the rosary. In addition to common prayer, we spent a minimum of forty-five minutes in prayer and spiritual reading in the chapel. Added to our personal devotion was the *chapter of faults*, suggesting the last judgment. In the chapel on Fridays, we knelt before the superior at the communion rail and acknowledged our faults of the week.

I usually confessed how many times I broke silence or how many times I did not try hard enough to meditate—to let myself not think, to commune with God. I'd get caught up reading spiritual books instead. I would make an effort to understand my favorite theologians: Dietrich Bonhoeffer, Hans Küng, Søren Kierkegaard, Reinhold Niebuhr. I could get lost for hours in Pierre Teilhard de Chardin's universe, in his Omega Point. I also had to confess how impatient I might get with some of the other novices or how I raced through a charge. The superior would assign some prayer or action for me to do for penance, such as saying another rosary or performing the Stations of the Cross, or folding laundry or peeling potatoes.

Our new direction included a very structured program of studies, all held in the junior novitiate room. We took only written English and speech as nonreligious courses. God and His creation, church and community history, and liturgy were our other college courses, but we also attended classes in Scripture; moral, practical, and ascetical theology; prayer; customs and rules of the community; and religious vows. This first year as a novice, called the canonical year, was devoted to religious formation, which meant we were to read, write, speak, and think only things spiritual.

I missed creative writing and found strict silence demanding. But something happened over the course of canonical year. By my own volition, I gradually stopped talking. From silence, meditation and prayer flowed—but I still relished reading theological and religious texts, looking for and finding truth and beauty.

I saved some of my own writing from the convent. A letter to my family reveals how I was changing, growing more reflective. A nineteen-year-old's considerations:

Dear Family,

It is beautiful today. I'm sitting on the ground recollecting myself and my thoughts are turned homeward.

The trees just shimmer, glistening and whispering with the wind; the sumac bushes and the Japanese-like trees are bright red in some changing spots, the maple trees are beginning to redden and golden on the tops; the sky is blue, blue. It all equals one beautiful beginning-of-fall day.

Today is Recollection Sun. and I think I want to share a few thoughts with you . . .

God is in every person. Every man's speech is God speaking in some way. Man, we got to listen—

and we have to say to ourselves again and again "I am alive." I am living in a God-awful world of suffering and sorrow, conflict and war but also an exciting, life-giving world, a world where peace and joy and love can exist. In a pessimistic world with so many despairers, so many Camus' and Sartre's, we need to be optimistic like Mr. Blue or remember men like Kennedy or Dag Hammarskjold or Tom Dooley or look at each other—Mom and Dad, beautiful true Christians and Tom and Dan, good, good people and Jim and John, men who show Christ in a quiet way in the business world and Mary who bubbles over with enthusiasm and Patty, a special gift from our good God . . . .

When I think of the world, of the "whole vast army of living humanity," when I think of all those people in the world who need our help—those in Viet Nam, in China, in the Middle East, the dope addicts, the hippies, the drunks, the prostitutes, the children of all these; the forgotten old people, those suffering the changes in the Church, those suffering the fast changes in the world, those people sick inside because they don't know who they are—or can be; those physically diseased or dying—on and on—

but then I think—I can't take into myself the entire world—somewhat yes because someone—and I suppose it is the religious who must hold up to the Lord what He must see—but still Christ Himself did not work in the entire world; he limited Himself to one area. He was born and grew up and died, not making too much of an impact on the area of His life—"Is he not the son of the carpenter of Nazareth?" But again Christ did take on Himself the burden of His entire world and not only of His in year 1 A.D. but of all time—ambivalences, paradoxes, mysteries abound in the Christian life . . . .

Well, those are some things I thought about today. Thanks for listening. I love you all very much.

Sister Zoë

We saw our family every other month in the canonical year. Mary and I shared our time. By the end of the year, I had trouble talking even on visiting days. So quiet inside and out,

I didn't have much to say. It was almost a burden to engage in conversation.

I'd let my family ask questions: "How are you?" "What are you interested in?"

I'd answer: "I'm fine." "I'm reading a great book on prayer right now."

We were all probably relieved when the hand bell rang, announcing the end of visiting. As they left, Mom fussed, "Please promise you'll eat." Dad still always looked me in the eye, held my hand, and asked, "Is this what you want? Are you sure you're happy?"

As a novice, I tried not to look at my family's house when I was out walking in the fields. If they spotted me, they didn't call out either. They were trying to be supportive, to let me be. It was also certainly easier for them to have picked me out the year before, because I had looked more like my old self, wearing just the short skirt and cape of a postulant. In full habit, it was hard to tell us nuns apart.

I felt especially separated from my family when I realized Mary and I could not attend our brother John's wedding. When I asked, the Mistress of Novices told me a novice might be permitted to go only to the ordination of a brother or the profession of a sibling, at the discretion of the provincial superior. That did not mean a wedding. I was so disappointed. John and his wife, Lois, a friend and alumna from St. Catherine's, came to see Mary and me, but that visit could not take the place of the wedding itself. I hated missing it.

My main charge in the summer of canonical year was working at Bethany, a home for elderly sisters, next door to the provincial house. We helpers cleaned and cooked. We also organized games and crafts, visited, read, and sang to the nuns. I learned so much that summer about pain and suffering and humility and kindness and intelligence and how to have fun. A few of the seniors complained about how we cleaned their rooms or served their meals, but most of my charges were great role models on how to grow old graciously.

By the second year of the novitiate, as senior novices, we all took classes on campus: classes in liturgy and theology and psychology, philosophy of nature, and, in the summer, language classes and music appreciation. That year I did not seek out old friends on campus. I talked mainly with those I sat next to in class. Actually, I always felt some estrangement from other students who thought of us nuns as *curve raisers*. "What else do you have to do?" I was asked several times. I didn't think these women would understand my regimen of work, study, and prayer.

I also found the faculty not particularly interested in us as students. Perhaps the professors were trying to help us with silence and holiness; perhaps they didn't want to be accused of favoritism by the other students. In any case, we were seldom called on. In the last class of the only creative-writing course I took, the professor said, "Those who have talent, keep up your writing." I didn't know if she meant me. She had not encouraged or discouraged me in grades or remarks on my papers. It was interesting—and a bit hurtful—to me that faculty sisters wouldn't acknowledge sister students as they would college women. It didn't make you feel part of the community. But perhaps I overreacted; when I recently asked Mary if she had found this to be true, she said, "No, except for the students calling us *curve raisers*."

My charge as a senior novice was to read aloud during silent meals. All meals were silent except for Sundays and feast days, when Mother Provincial concluded the prayers before meals with "Let us bless the Lord." We'd all then happily answer, "Thanks be to God," and talk away. At silent meals, we indicated the beverage we wanted by the position of our cup— upside down meant we didn't want anything; upturned meant coffee at breakfast and dinner, and milk at supper; on the side meant tea with supper. To get milk in the morning, we left our water glass empty and filled it from the milk for the cereal.

On ordinary days, after the blessing by Mother Superior,

I would climb the four steps behind the podium, like a pulpit, placed in the middle of the enormous refectory—filled with twelve long tables covered with white cloths. The provincial-council members, the governing sisters of the St. Paul Province, sat at a head table. I stood over everyone. Reading into the tall, snaky microphone, I couldn't breathe too close or lean too far away—I'd get screeches or whispers—and I had to watch my sibilant *s*. Everyone listened seriously, particularly the council members. The books often were a challenge; I had to look up a number of words for pronunciation and meaning.

I can still remember some of the texts I strived to read perfectly. Caryll Houselander's *The Reed of God* showed the human side of Mary, Mother of God, as an empty reed waiting for God's music to be played through her. Houselander shared her vision of Mary as an anxious but believing teenager whose sacredness grew with her *Yes* to God. Another book was about Blessed Charles Eugène de Foucauld, a French priest living among the Muslim Tuareg in the Sahara. He was assassinated in 1916 outside the fort he built for the protection of the Tuareg. His inspiration and writings led to the founding of the Little Brothers of Jesus, among other religious congregations. Still another book, *This Tremendous Lover*, by Dom Eugene Boylan, posited a practical program of humility, charity, and abandonment to the will of God. Through humility, one accepted herself with all her faults; through charity, one "adjusted" herself to other members of the Church and lived for them as well as for herself; through abandonment, one tried to accept all that God allowed to happen in her life.

I was too nervous to eat much after reading. I had lost my postulant chubbiness, now refusing the seconds and left-overs I used to say I was *charitably helping get rid of* at meals. Seconds were passed "down the side" of the table. We were to look to see if the person across from us was interested, then pass on the dish. I still tried to take some of every food at the table, as we were asked to, but I actually became quite thin, often eating very little of the nutritious meals—meat or fish, potatoes, vegetables, bread or rolls, and tasty desserts.

A charge I did enjoy that year: working as a "sincere bat catcher." Our massive building's extensive attic housed a number of bats, who'd swoop through the lower floors at night. Every floor had tennis rackets and gloves for those assigned to fight off the enemy. Someone would shake my cell's sheet whenever a bat was spotted. To be a member of the Bat Brigade meant you weren't a Francis of Assisi type who would never harm a single creature of the Lord. We catchers sometimes hurt these mammals as we caught and carried them outside. It was a strange scene: white-bonneted women (we wore caps over our shorn heads at night) in black robes and slippers lunging in complete silence at the tiny, black, webbed-winged, squeaking beings. A black-and-white pastiche.

We junior novices loved being awakened on Christmas Day morning by senior novices softly caroling in the halls. "Still, still, still / One can hear the falling snow" and "I wonder as I wander out under the sky . . ." The next year we sang these tender songs to the new novices. This special custom and liturgies of Christmas with quiet prayer and candles, mighty hymns and dance and ribbons and banners—the organ with all stops pulled out—and breathtakingly beautiful Gregorian chant, helped me get through another huge disappointment: missing our brother Jim's wedding the day after Christmas.

He and his wife, Jacque, came to see us directly after their reception. Mary and I oohed and ahhed over Jacque's lovely gown and Jim's handsome tux. Jim hugged our superior at the door. She smiled, gently pushing him away. Grateful to feel at least a bit involved in the wedding festivities, I was still angry about our missed attendance. To this day, I greatly regret not being able to attend my older brothers' weddings. Of course, that ruling changed shortly after my time in the convent; nuns are now totally free to go to all family events.

That second year in the novitiate my dad wrote a short

letter to me, displaying his continual enthusiasm over new ideas. His request for me not to tell Mom meant something was probably wrong with his plan.

Hi Sister Zoë, I'm alone this pm—Dan is bowling and Mom's out with the girls for her birthday luncheon . . . new scheme to give a third of the profits from Pat Rogers Associates to charity. Plans to have Mary and you involved. Ask your superiors if you can own stock in our corporation. Don't say anything to Mom as I want it to be a surprise for her—I tried dyeing my hair so I will become 20 yrs. younger to get the strength to put this over. Ha Ha. It's fun having you girls in my dreams—I owe a lot to you kids for helping me find the way to happiness. Love, Dad.

Making vows was the focus of senior novice year. From our studies, we understood public vows to offer oneself to God went as far back as the Israelites and early Christianity, and as time went on, the Church drew up canons, or rules, to govern the practice of poverty, chastity, and obedience. The 1955 *Constitution* of the Sisters of St. Joseph on poverty included fourteen entries on legal matters, such as possessions before entering and wills—one explained why Dad couldn't give us stocks. The emphasis was clearly on common life: "The vow of poverty relieves a religious of preoccupation in her personal needs and enables her to better carry on special work of the congregation which is entrusted to her." Everything was shared; no one was more privileged with goods or money than another.

The vow of poverty was my favorite vow. I wanted to live a simple life, to be equal with others in possessions, to not worry about making money or keeping up with the Joneses. Although as I look at it now, the 1955 definition could also foster an immaturity about income and selfishness about mission. Why didn't we have to worry about personal needs? Didn't that foster naiveté? Or elitism, because someone had to worry about them? Better to think of poverty as sisters do today: living a simple life, which includes the wise use of material and spiritual resources. Upbeat rather than downbeat: the ability *to give* rather than *to not have*. I remember the words of my dad: "Peggy, love what you do. Don't worry about how much money you'll make. Love to go to work because it isn't really work."

The vow of chastity in the 1955 *Constitution* was described as an obligation to "abstain from every interior and exterior act opposed to chastity and contrary to the sixth and ninth commandments of God." Sisters were also asked to use self-restraint to control their thoughts and passions and to practice mortification and self-discipline. Conversation with seculars—especially those of the other sex—"should be regulated by what is in accordance with business relations and social courtesy." We were warned to avoid "particular friendships," dangerous because they might mean an exclusive emotional attachment to another person that lessened our commonality with other nuns.

Our instruction in the novitiate broadened this limited definition by saying chastity was an embracing love. But what did that mean practically? I found chastity the most difficult vow to understand, though I really wanted to. I wanted to know how my former interest in boys and boyfriends would be superseded by a general love for all mankind. I wanted to understand sublimation. I believe what I absorbed, though, was a certain caution about any dealings with males, as well as the Church's and convent's fear of lesbianism.

I tried to form what nuns now would say is the essence of chastity: strong communal connections and meaningful personal relationships. I got along with everyone in the novitiate and was a close friend with several novices who were talented artists and writers. They gave me many gifts: cards with quotations or original poems decorated with striking symbols; hand-carved candle holders; homemade pottery; an original burlap-and-yarn cover for my Bible; creative bookmarks for other books. Lovely presents from vital presences; we laughed, cried, discussed, argued, prayed, and sang together.

As for obedience, the 1955 *Constitution* stated: "We were,

in a spirit of faith, to submit our will and judgment to the will and judgment of the superior in the belief that the will of God was manifested through her." We were required to ask permission from the local superior for all decisions, minor to major. Because I admired my superiors in the novitiate and usually charged ahead without asking permission, I wasn't anxious about keeping the vow of obedience. But I was reminded how we kids grew up fighting our parents sometimes. We needed to stand up to those in charge, to test our mettle. We needed rules, but we needed to butt up against them, too. It was our job. Questioning authority helped us to understand it. We discovered discussion was better than blind surrender. It was important to come up with our own suggestions and solutions; sometimes our parents actually changed their opinions and positions based on what we had to say. I figured that was how I would deal with my superiors and the vow of obedience, too. The juniorate would soon prove that untenable.

Before taking first vows and moving to the juniorate, four of us novices traveled that summer of 1966 to North Dakota to teach religious education to junior-high-school students. A young and spirited priest had requested that we come. He met us at the train station in Jamestown and drove us to the tiny town of Tappen. On the way, he asked if we could play any instruments. I said I could play the piano and the cornet. I didn't tell him I played the cornet badly. Mom and Dad had purchased two instruments, the cornet for John and the clarinet for Mary. The rest of us kids could choose either of those instruments as our own. I played second cornet in Marshall Central's band, my best piece the "Notre Dame Victory March."

Delighted to have a variety of musicians—the other novices could play bongo drums, a clarinet, and a piccolo—Father said he had all of the instruments at the rectory. He could hardly let us get settled there, he was so excited to begin band practice. We had no idea why we were practicing.

Well, it was for Sunday Mass at different churches spread

miles and miles apart. We four novices stood in the back of the church at one town, in the choir loft at another, in the front of the church at still another. Each church owned a pump organ. I had never played one before. Father said not to worry. He asked one of the other novices to kneel on the floor and pump the pedals. I reached across her to play the keys. Awkward but functional.

The congregation sang strong songs, "A Mighty Fortress Is Our God" and "Holy God, We Praise Thy Name," and soft string songs, "Kumbaya" and "Michael Row Your Boat Ashore." The closing song was the "Notre Dame Victory March," with me blaring the cornet with a lot of farting sounds. The congregation clapped in rhythm. Processing out, Father's face was one big grin.

We celebrated by going to lunch at a farmer's home near Steele, another tiny community of about seven hundred folks. An enormous table was set up in the farmhouse dining room. We joined the large group of churchgoers already seated, men and women dressed in clean jeans and pressed dress shirts, many of the men sporting bolo ties. They all laughed and pummeled each other, pointing at us. Father beamed at us, his band. After a terrific turkey meal, like Thanksgiving, the group announced it was horseback-riding time.

"C'mon, Sisters. Who's going first?" the biggest, oldest guy said.

One of the other sisters said, "How could we in full habit?"

"I'll try it," I said.

I got put on a horse and was told to keep him moving and focused because he was spoiled and had a mind of his own. Others followed us out to the pasture and down the cornfield rows. Suddenly my horse turned and headed back to the barn. Wildly. I couldn't get him to stop or slow down. He galloped so fast my veil flew off. The white cornet around my face shifted. My rosary beat into my thigh. I bent down to stay on the saddle—and on the horse. I looked up as we neared the barn. It had a half door and the top was closed! I quickly lay flat on the horse as he stormed into the barn, immediately halting at his corral. I was jerked back, upright. A sight. The church group came running, concern on their faces. Someone handed me my veil. I laughed, then everyone cheered. Someone said, "Where'd you get these nuns, Father? They're the best."

These friendly, generous people were *the best*. Their children, too. It was a pleasure to teach them Sunday school. The only sad remembrance—saying goodbye to Father. He seemed so isolated in his big rectory, and we had watched him drink a lot that week. It was the first time I thought of loneliness as the most difficult challenge for someone who is called to religious life.

In August, after completion of our two-year novitiate program and acceptance by the provincial and her council, we novices professed our religious vows of poverty, chastity, and obedience and became part of the juniorate, located at the Provincial House, 1880 Randolph Avenue, adjoining the novitiate by way of the chapel. We would be there for another two years as part of the training for sisters. At our profession, we received the crucifix we hung on cords around our necks. Our habits were now complete.

Twenty-eight of our reception of forty-nine made first vows.

Ordinary: What do you ask, Sisters?

Novices: Your Excellency, I ask to make my temporary profession as a Sister of St. Joseph of Carondelet.

Ordinary: Have you seriously reflected on the obligations which you contract in making your profession in this institute?

Novices: Yes, Your Excellency, I have seriously reflected on these obligations during my novitiate, and I promise with the grace of God to be faithful to them.

Ordinary: You have heard the earnest request of these novices. Do you, Sister, give consent on the part of the Congregation?

Superior: Yes, Your Excellency, these novices may pronounce their temporary vows and become members of the Congregation.

Novice: My God, all-powerful and eternal Being, I, Sister Zoë, desirous of living entirely for you, make to your Divine Majesty, in the hands of our Provincial Superior, until the sixth of August, 1968, the vows of poverty, chastity, and obedience, according to the Constitutions of the Sisters of Saint Joseph of Carondelet.

Ordinary: Receive, Sister, this crucifix as a visible sign of your profession: wear it as a mark that in your heart you share the burden of the cross of our Lord Jesus Christ. Faithfully observe the obligations of your way of life as a Sister of Saint Joseph that you may ever become more closely united with your Divine Spouse.

I accepted the cross signifying my commitment to act poorly, chastely, and obediently, the way God wanted me to live.

AS A SISTER

In the juniorate program, we continued to live with our reception sisters and to study theology, prayer, rules of the community, and vows. Added to these classes was instruction in canon law, the system of laws made and enforced by the hierarchical authorities of the Church to regulate its governance. All of us were engaged in the liturgical movement that followed the Second Vatican Council in 1963. The Council had adopted the *Constitution on Sacred Liturgy* to help Catholics understand and participate more actively in worship. The *Constitution* stated that common-office prayer was always preferable to individual prayer, and liturgies were to express the local culture of church members. For the first time, Mass in English rather than Latin was permitted. By the time our group entered, our forward-thinking nuns had, of course, already incorporated all these changes.

We young nuns faithfully read *The Catholic Worker* newspaper, published seven times a year out of New York City. The newspaper, started by Dorothy Day and Peter Maurin to make people aware of the Church's teachings on social justice, has always been priced at one cent. Day said the word *Worker* in the paper's title referred to "those who worked with hand or brain, those who did physical, mental, or spiritual work. But we thought primarily of the poor, the dispossessed, the exploited."

Ade Bethune, a vibrant liturgical artist, volunteered her

illustrations to improve *The Catholic Worker*. What she had to say about her brush-and-ink drawings of female saints: "I thought it was only fitting to show working saints, since the paper was called *The Catholic Worker*. Then I began to realize there were no other saints. All saints were working saints." Her drawings included *St. Margaret, Queen of Scotland: Those who instruct others to justice shall shine as stars for all eternity*. Later in life, Bethune gave her personal papers, books, and artwork to St. Catherine's. On a visit to the novitiate, she had become close friends with a former Mistress of Postulants and then later with a college art-faculty member and the director of the library.

I thought of her and the *Worker* when I asked permission to tutor young African American girls in the Mt. Airy public-housing projects in St. Paul. The projects were in a hilly area off a major interstate north of the Capitol. I asked for approval to go there by bus, unaccompanied. I reported to the recreation center in the high-rise building and planned something fun to do every week in its activities room.

On April 4, 1968, the girls met me at the bus stop, crying and yelling, "Sister, Sister, our King is dead. Our King is dead."

An elderly man stopped me as the girls and I walked to the center. "Sister, maybe you shouldn't be here today."

"Sister, stay with us," the girls cried. "What's going to happen?" They looked around their neighborhood with frightened eyes.

We talked about the assassination very briefly. The girls asked, "Why did he get killed, Sister?"

"Because he was changing our world. And some people don't want to change," I said. "He was a leader and a hero."

We talked about leaders and heroes as we baked cookies in the beat-up, old oven of the center. Each girl took a plateful home to her troubled family. I returned to the juniorate, where we had special permission to watch Martin Luther King Jr.'s funeral. I cried; *my* King was dead.

During the first year of the juniorate we continued to

attend classes at St. Catherine's, taking American society, metaphysics, and a summer-session science class, but the majority of our classes now centered on preparation for our future ministries. The choice of ministry was made by the provincial and her council according to the aptitudes of each sister and the needs of the community. After earning our undergraduate degrees, we would be assigned to schools or hospitals or to other work. We had made temporary vows for two years after the novitiate experience. Three years later we would profess final vows, consecrating ourselves forever to the service of God and others. That made a total of eight years to become a fully professed Sister of St. Joseph, five at the provincial house and three on our first ministry.

Mary had been assigned to teach history in secondary schools for her ministry. I was assigned to teach secondary English. I began reading and writing in earnest to prepare for teaching. I took principles of learning and teaching, the first class of a total of eighteen credits in education, including the teaching of religion and student teaching. I wasn't entirely sure about my ministry. Early on, I had to make peace with not becoming an actress—impossible to do in a habit. If I hadn't entered the convent, I might alternatively have considered psychology or social work or public policy.

Sorting out myself and the world, in 1966 I wrote:
Me—Or Not

I am a paradox; I am a changeable, unpredictable person; I am a mystery even to myself.

I always have been this paradox. As a little, freckle-faced, pigtailed girl I was a picture of innocence, and yet I can remember being the leader of the gang who attacked the boys on the school playground. As I grew up and continued going to school with the boys, I again played the leadership position but this time not away from or against them but toward them. I was the chief flirt, and me and the boys were always held in detention after school. But in my classes I wasn't afraid to show up the boys, to lose dates. I was too interested in all kinds of knowledge; I couldn't waste time pretending to be dumb. I couldn't waste time in anything: I wanted to be in everything. I joined the choir, the glee club, the drama club, the pep club, the marching and dance band. I was in G.A.A., Student Council and other organizations. I was an activist and I loved it. And I hated it. I wanted time to do my homework, time to sleep, time to be home with my family, time to just be. No one knew this. My family thought I loved talking on the phone for hours, loved being at school for long days. And I did, and I didn't.

During the summer of my sophomore year, my family moved from our small town to St. Paul. My father had been thinking of moving for several years, but every year there was something to wait for: my brothers winning that "most valuable player" award or beating that tough team or my older sister playing her senior piano recital or graduating valedictorian. But I could be moved. I could leave my activities; I could adjust; I could fit in anywhere. So they thought, but I am a mystery even to my parents and friends. They label me extrovert and I agree with them—but not all the time. Many times I discover my shyness. Moving was one of those times. I felt alone, friendless, afraid, but again paradoxically, willing and excited to experience a new, bigger life. I loved my small town but found the big city full of new opportunities. I missed my old friends but found new faces, new ideas, new experiences, stimulating. I found life both unbearable and worth living for.

In college now, I continue discovering my fickleness. My discoveries are quiet little findings. I find that I want and don't want something. I find I want to be alone, to look at trees, hear birds, feel wind—by myself . . . sometimes. Other times a talk with a close friend appeals to me. Still other times I enjoy talking with someone I know very little. Sometimes I want to do all these at the same time. I find that I am a queen and a servant at the same time; I like to help others but feel very happy to be persuaded to take it easy and let others wait on me. I find that I am the greatest talker . . . and the shyest listener. I find that I'm finding and losing myself. I find that I am a paradox, a changeable, unpredictable person, a mystery even to myself.

During the juniorate years, I worked at my studies, my

Sister Zoë in full habit and Sister Rose Alice in a modified habit with Mom and Dad, Dan and Patty

duties with the retired Bethany sisters, and my prayer life. I still resented lights-out at 10:00 p.m. because I couldn't find time to complete all my tasks. By the end of senior year, I hated reading and writing because I'd had to take all of my English classes in a little over a year. A grueling schedule.

We were allowed to spend a week at home the summer between the two juniorate years. I went with my family to the tiny cabin on the St. Croix River they still rented for the summer. It was delightful to be back near water and to snuggle in close with family members. My vacation began shortly after I had spent time sitting and reading on the grass in the college's backyard and getting bit by what I thought were chiggers. I had little bites all over my body. At the river, someone suggested applying fingernail polish to the bites. I did, and soon my entire body was one big, angry rash. Added to this discomfort were the facts that it was very hot, we didn't have air-conditioning, and I, of course, was dressed in the full habit. Miserable. A family friend, a priest, came out to visit one day of that vacation week and said, "Take the habit off. Let yourself air out." I couldn't. I was too embarrassed and by this time too paralyzed by rules. I did eventually go to our family doctor, though, and got a cortisone shot for poison ivy.

Later that summer, the juniorate sisters were allowed another vacation at Timberlee, an old lodge the Order had purchased on Big Fish Lake, about eighty-five miles north of the Twin Cities. We had to wear our habits except when we were actually swimming, but we could relax, sun ourselves on the dock, dive off the raft, fish from one of the rowboats, and hike in the woods and around the lake. At Timberlee, the rule of silence was dropped. We talked away. It was heavenly.

In the evening, as the sun set, casting a rosy-orange haze on the lake, we all congregated around the huge stone fireplace in the lodge—the swimmers, showered and smelling of soap and crisp, clean lake air; the pray-ers finished with chapel; the supper cleaner-uppers done with the dishes, smelling of hamburger, ketchup, mustard, and Palmolive.

The fire blazed, crackling and snapping like a huge frying pan full of bacon. The pungent-sweet smell of birch and cedar logs mixed with the knotty pine fragrance of the lodge walls. Smoke escaped from the sooty hearth, filling the room, bringing tears to our eyes. We threw open the windows, forcing the heavy smoke out, encouraging the refreshing, light night air in. We were at Timberlee for fun, not for weeping.

The old phonograph played waltzes and square-dance tunes, enticing us to dance—laughing and clapping, twirling and swirling, we jostled the bridge players and interrupted quiet conversations, filling the room with feeling and being.

Then quietly, quietly, the guitar, ukelele, and bongo players began, the lapping of the water sounding during the rests, the hiss and sputter of the dying fire between songs. Sipping from mugs of steaming hot chocolate with melted marshmallows, thinking and dreaming, we sang softy, watching the flickering flames, while the big white moon cast shadows through the windows. Timberlee entranced us all.

By second semester of my final year in college, I was initiated into Delta Phi Lambda, the honorary creative-writing society. I was pleased to work with other English majors on the yearbook and honored when asked to write the yearbook dedication to Sister Antonia McHugh, the first president of the college. I wrote the *La Concha* 1967 dedication using her great phrases: "Energize yourself." "It's terrible to have a stagnant mind." "She who would be a woman must avoid mediocrity."

I was practice-teaching at Derham Hall, my mother's alma mater. I learned a great deal from my supervising teacher about Greek mythology, the freshman English subject we taught, and how to engage students—and also how to respect and enjoy them. Mrs. Dokken and I appreciated each other's enthusiasm and support. My practice-teaching supervisor from the college didn't share these qualities. In our conference after her on-site observation, she said, horrified, "Do you remember your first words to the class?"

"Didn't I say something about Zeus?" I said.

"No, before that," she said, shaking her head, her stiff white hair not moving an inch. She was dressed to the nines, fancy suit, high heels, painted fingernails.

"I guess not," I said.

"Well," she said, pointing to the classroom door, "you said, 'Will someone get it?' *Get it*—appalling from an English major. *Will someone please close the door?* That's proper English."

"Oh . . . well . . . what about the lesson?" I asked, biting my tongue.

She said she thought it went well enough. I didn't care to ask her for any guidance; she had missed the essence of teaching.

In the second year of the juniorate, a big change took place in our outward appearance: we discarded the habit. The provincial leaders told us that the first Sisters of St. Joseph in France wore widow's garb so they could go out to serve the poor without male chaperones, and their head covering and long sleeves and skirts made them blend in. But we had kept this style of dress for three hundred years, and our black-and-white habit had become more conspicuous as time passed. The movement to modify the habit, to not separate us from "the dear neighbor," was underway. Soon sisters were wearing clothing indistinct from those of other laywomen. But that took a little while. My outfit in the juniorate: a creamy, double-breasted suit with a short black veil. Definitely dumpy.

The Rogers family

With the sweeping changes of the Second Vatican Council, it seemed discussion developed into our mode of being. The upheaval in the Church led to questions about how we lived and acted; we scrutinized ourselves and our ministries, as well as the larger culture. Many public conflicts competed for our attention, particularly the civil-rights movement and the Vietnam War protests.

Some of us became active in the political process. I served as a delegate at the neighborhood caucus for Eugene McCarthy, a poet and a Minnesota senator who opposed the war in Vietnam. The DFL caucus was packed and rowdy because McCarthy was running against fellow Minnesotan and former Vice President Hubert Humphrey. It was the beginning of the "walking caucus," which meant those attending moved to join others in the room who supported the same candidate or the same issues, and together they picked delegates to represent them in the regional and then state conventions. We convened at an elementary school where classrooms were designated for the various platforms (peace, antiwar, antipoverty) and candidates (HHH, Clean Gene, Dump Johnson) or combinations (McCarthy and peace). There were choices. Options. A new idea, especially for women, most especially for religious women.

For some sisters, change was occurring far too fast; I avoided talking with Sister St. Edmund, my former eighth-grade teacher from Marshall, at community gatherings because she had become so negative about the behavior of other sisters. She particularly took offense at those who discontinued wearing the habit. I was surprised and saddened by her reactions.

I was an example of those who wanted change to happen faster. Once Pope John XXIII flung open the Church's door, I rushed through, full of ideas and demands. Always the one with her hand up, I believe I drove the Mistress of the Juniorate batty with my questions: Why did we limit our ministry? What about social work? What about other professions besides teaching and nursing? Why did some sisters take trips and spend money on fancier clothes, overlooking the vow of poverty? What about particular friendships?

The Mistress didn't like to be challenged and several times suggested my constant inquiries could mean perhaps more serious problems of doubt, that maybe I wasn't called to this life. I went back to my former Mistress of Postulants and asked her about this. She said, "Questioning is good. It doesn't mean you don't have a vocation. It means you're thinking."

But the seed had been planted. Perhaps I had needed the goading of my superior to consider my feelings. Maybe I questioned too much because I was thinking I didn't belong. Sometimes I dreamed of seeing and talking with Tom Barrett again, and of getting married and having children someday. I also considered: Do I need to be celibate to serve others? Why would a superior curtail enthusiasm? Would it be more advantageous to work with the poor outside the convent walls than living in basic comfort within community?

And then my brother Tom came to the convent one

night. After Grand Silence. I was in my juniorate dorm room studying when my friend, the Mistress of Postulants, knocked on the door. I was utterly surprised to see her.

"Your brother Tom is here to see you," she said.

"Why?"

"Because he needs you," she said.

She and I walked through the darkened building past the atrium and chapel to the novitiate side. Tom was pacing in the archbishop's parlor. My stomach clenched when I saw him. Gaunt. Ashen. Searing eyes. I knew immediately something was terribly wrong. The Mistress left, saying, "I'll leave you two alone. Take as much time as you need."

Tom furiously talked, very loudly, gesturing wildly, not making sense.

"Tom, what happened?" I said.

He continued to shout, getting more and more agitated. I knew I had to get him home somehow. But of course I couldn't leave the convent. I deeply resented this restriction. "Tom, let's walk out by the chapel. You can go home to Mom. Is Dad home?"

He didn't stop to consider what I had said but followed me out the door, down the hallway, swearing. We came to the vestibule of the chapel. On a table in the back stood the ciborium, the box holding the communion wafers for Mass. Tom swept the ciborium off the table, scattering the wafers, shouting, "Fuck the hosts."

I eventually got him out the door. He leaped off the steps. I called out, "Promise me you'll go right home, Tom."

Not looking back at me, he strode off, shouting obscenities.

I asked the Mistress if I could call my mother. Sister led me into her dark office. Quickly, I turned on a light and dialed home.

"Mom, did Tom get there? He's really sick."

"He's just tired, Margaret. That's what the priest from St.

John's said. He's very tired. He apparently hasn't been sleeping."

"Mom, he's very sick. He needs to go to a hospital immediately. Is Dad there?"

"No. He's away on business."

"Tell him to come home, Mom. Can you get Tom to St. Joe's?"

Somehow she did. I assume this first time must have been like the other times I saw her take Tom to hospitals over the years that followed. He'd yell, cry, swear, open his car door while she drove. So small, Mom seemed to have superhuman strength. She'd pull in his tall, strong body next to hers and pull up to the emergency door, saying, "We need an orderly. We need help. My son needs help." To Tom, she'd say what she'd whispered to the escaped lady from Weiner Memorial many years ago: "Don't worry. You'll be all right. They'll take good care of you."

Shortly after Tom's visit, I finished my last classes at the college and decided for certain—or almost certain—that I would leave the convent. Maybe I'd reconsider after a period of time, but I was so distressed that I could not take Tom home after his visit or see him regularly during his hospital stay. And when he returned home, it greatly troubled me that I couldn't offer him or my mother and father any physical or emotional help to cope with his shattering illness.

The need to help Tom might have been the final catalyst for me to leave, but I had been nervous and shaky over the decision for some time. I had prayed on it for weeks, begging for insight, for reassurance. My prayers always seemed to end up pleading with God to show me some sign. I remembered being at the slough in Marshall playing with milkweed pods, pulling them apart—"He loves me; he loves me not"—the game calling to mind how nimbly and capriciously one could choose the direction of one's life. *Please, God, help me decide.*

I couldn't imagine what it would be like on the *outside*: what I'd do; where I'd live; what I'd wear. Some days I felt insecure and placed the decision on a back burner. Other days I summoned up courage but then got bogged down again: Was I meant to stay? Could I leave with an open heart and mind? Finally, I just decided: I could give and receive love in teaching, and hoped I could do the same with a husband and children.

I felt I had my *Who am I?* question down, and the *What should I do?* question would take care of itself. I had mulled over these questions, weighing the values of earlier influences: parents and grandparents, brothers and sisters, Catholic education, rural and urban environments. I considered how my parents and teachers lived their lives. I wanted to imitate them, to be competent and responsible, creative and flexible, courageous and loving.

My upbringing had shaped me into a gutsy doer. That doer grew up in the convent, leaving behind family and friends and parties and dating. Giving them up had not been easy. I had longed for all. But I had become comfortable with myself, which would serve me well for the rest of my life. Imagining the future, I hoped to obtain achievement and adventure; balance and beauty; family, friendship, and fun.

When I informed the Mistress of the Juniorate of my decision, she did not try to discourage me. I wasn't surprised— she had suggested it, after all—but still I was a little hurt she didn't seem very sorry to see me go. We picked a date—a few weeks after—and a time of day—when everyone would be over at the college for a special lecture. Leaving was still secret. I waited until the last week to tell the Mistress of Postulants; I knew she'd be disappointed. She tried to talk me out of it, saying the Order needed women like me. I thanked her, but said it was too late. I needed to go.

I left at the beginning of a larger movement out of the community. Within about five years, the province lost over 250 of its 1, 200 members. There were 49 in my reception group; 17 took final vows; 4 sisters remained in the Order.

Mary left a few years later. She continued to teach high-school social studies, received advanced degrees in both Asian and pastoral studies, and worked in Catholic parishes for many years after the convent.

My last week in the convent, I approached the bursar general, a tall, tough nun in the administrative offices, realizing I would need a transcript of my classes to apply for a job. I explained to Sister I would be leaving the Order and asked if I could please get a copy of my transcript. She reacted viscerally. "What? You're leaving? After receiving a college education? We provide for you and then you leave. You take advantage of us. You get a free education."

I knew my face was bright red. I was shaken to tears but didn't want to cry in front of this woman.

"What's your name?" she said.

"Sister Zoë Rogers," I whispered.

"Who? Speak up for pity's sake."

"Sister Zoë Rogers," I said more distinctly.

"Oh . . . you are a Rogers. Well, what I said doesn't apply to you. Your parents have paid the college for you in contributions."

That did it. Brought my voice back, my twofold sense of justice. "Please don't ever talk to anyone else leaving the Order as you did to me, Sister. Others might not be as blessed as I am to have parents able to give money, but no one should be told they stayed in the convent for a free education."

I could have added that it wouldn't have been worth the sacrifice if you hadn't really believed in your vocation, but I was starting to cry. I turned away, left the office, made it down the steps and out of the building. I even got as far as the woods beyond the Dew Drop Pond before I broke down. I was so angry and hurt. I'd never been shamed like that before. Later, I could be somewhat more understanding of this nun. She, too, was angry and hurt: a sister was leaving.

Bound by tradition, I told no one I was leaving. The day of departure, I found my trunk in the basement. I got out my old clothes, put them on, and walked out the double oak doors. My parents were waiting. Dad helped me carry my trunk down the steps to their car. I had told my parents of my decision on their last visit, whispering to them in the parlor. They had looked surprised, anxious, happy. We concentrated on when and where they'd pick me up.

"We can talk about everything later, honey," Dad said.

"Yes, Margaret, we can discuss it all when you're home," Mom said.

I knew I'd miss the convent, particularly celebrating liturgy, singing Gregorian chant, practicing silence. And enjoying good, smart, dynamic women. But feeling both liberated and constrained—knowing who I was in the context of a larger whole—I felt I could do anything within the strictures of society and culture. I had defined my true self, an identity that couldn't be changed by any system, suggestion, principle, or procedure. I was free and in control of my life, ready to move on.

An Essay on Definition
  by Sister Zoë Rogers

What is life? Is this a foolish question, a cliché, a hackneyed phrase? Perhaps—but it is a question to be asked at different times in our life: in a youth's time of newness, during our active, middle years, in reflective old age. This piece is a 21-year-old's definition of life.

Life is the birth of nature.
Spring springing herself—
opening herself wide—wide.
Warm earth, warm sun:
the warmth of birth.
Life is the birth of an idea,
an idea growing, maturing in our heads—
until suddenly,

Oh, I get it. It's like this—the birth.
Life is a baby's birth,
the pain of one echoed in the scream of another.
An ugly, bloody, yet beautiful,
oh so beautiful birth
is this life.

Life is death.
Life is the death of nature.
Winter closing the flowers and covering the leaves,
stripping, enclosing herself.
Damp, snowy earth—
Crisp cold air:
the cold death.
Life is the death of an idea,
an idea voiced too often, no longer accepted.
Life is a person's death,
the pain of one mirrored in the pained faces of others.
An ugly, yet beautiful death
is this life.

Life is love.
A young child sitting in her mother's lap,
relating the adventures of the day,
cuddling close;
two friends endlessly discussing,
continually discovering each other;
lovers looking, planning ahead;
parents waiting, worrying . . .
Life is love

And life is hate.
A young soldier peering
into the face of an enemy;
a young Black student

encountering his enemy;
a prisoner staring at bars,
remembering his enemies;
a psychotic looking at himself,
hating his enemy—
an ugly, yet beautiful life.

War and peace
are two polarities of life.
The shouting and whispering done in the home;
the fences and the open land cultivated by neighbors;
the injustice and the acceptance practiced by a nation;
the violation and the fulfillment of treaties by countries—
an ugly, yet beautiful life.

Life is joy and sorrow.
Discovering, sharing, giving is happiness:
sadness is losing, holding back, holding tight.
Seeing is joy: closing our eyes is sorrow.
—and ugly, yet beautiful life—

Life is birth, love, peace and joy.
Life is death, hate, war and sorrow.
Life is gray, ugly, beautiful—a mixture of all.

III. CALLS

We will love all, but especially those who need help. . . . We will love
our time, our technology, our art, our sports, our world.

– Pope Paul VI, Second World Congress of Lay Apostolate, 1957

FROM A FRIEND

I was home with my parents for less than a week when Dad called to me in my room: "The phone's for you, Peggy." It was Tom Barrett. Somehow he'd heard I'd left the convent. He asked if I knew Spanish. I couldn't speak it very well but could read it, so I said, "Sure. Why?"

"You could come work for Gene McCarthy with me in New Mexico. It's all paid for. What do you think?"

"Sure," I said. "When do we leave?"

"Saturday. Two days from now." He gave the details of the flight. "Can you get a ride to the airport? I'll meet you there."

I hung up: What was I thinking? From the convent to New Mexico?! I calmed myself: I knew Tom, and I wanted to help get Eugene McCarthy elected. I'd be fine.

The next day my sister-in-law Jacque took me out to buy clothes. Miniskirts! I remember buying two very short, striped dresses, navy and red, and black and white, along with underwear and sweaters and belts and shoes. I went to a hairdresser to shape my short hairdo.

I got on the plane with Tom, excited and nervous. He introduced me to others who'd be campaigning with us. Loud and confident, they made me feel quiet and insecure. I bought some cigarettes when we landed and started smoking to look more assured.

In New Mexico, Tom flew around the state in a small plane doing advance work; I was assigned the Santa Fe precincts. I walked miles through the dusty city, knocking on doors, speaking halting Spanish, trying to connect the pictures hanging on the walls in almost every household—Jesus and John F. Kennedy—to the Catholic Clean Gene. At the convention itself, I was horrified by the bribing of delegates—non-English-speaking families were paid to come to the caucus and to stand when leaders stood; other caucus leaders had already established a standing vote rather than a written ballot. Disarmed, unable to do anything about it, I was disillusioned by this political process.

Even though we didn't win, the campaign workers celebrated with a final, special dinner together. Seated next to Tom, I was disappointed he talked all night to another graduate student from the history department at the University of Minnesota. That left me stranded with a lawyer from Washington, D.C., who had tried to get me to go to dinner with him every night of the trip. On the plane the next day, I sat next to Tom again, but this time he talked to a history professor all the way home. We said goodbye at the airport. I told him I'd be leaving in a week for Cleveland, Ohio.

I left with another former nun, my friend Judy, to work for the summer at the Student Health Organization of Case Western Reserve. We had applied and been chosen for this position as nuns. When we arrived in Cleveland, the other health workers (Judy and I were the only teachers hired) acted solicitous towards us. Surprised at our dress (I wore my miniskirts) and where we chose to live, a roach-infested apartment where prostitutes worked and hung out (Judy slept with a knife under her pillow), the nurses and doctors-to-be seemed disappointed when we told them we'd left the convent. They seemed to want us to be contradictions to their hippie lifestyles. They wanted us to be different.

Judy and I were very different from those who lived on Maple Court, a one-way, dead-end street. On this street, kids drank Coke and ate potato chips every day, all day long. Snotty noses ran over raw open sores. On this street, there was one stereo, and at any time, day or night, out of any window might come the shout, "Put on the Supremes" or "the Mamas and the Papas."

Carl B. Stokes, who was elected in 1967 as the first black mayor of a major city, a symbol of a changing America, was severely challenged in governing Cleveland that summer of '68 with a shootout between a group of black men and the police. In the Hough area, riots raged, and in the barbwired downtown, National Guard army tanks rolled and soldiers brandished machine guns. Ordered out of the Hough area, our project concentrated on transplanted Appalachians and Puerto Ricans. I worked with a graduate student from University of California, Berkeley, gathering information from the poor and uninsured on how emergency rooms of major hospitals refused to admit them; regardless of their illnesses or injuries, they were told to get on a bus—for a long, long ride across the city to the one welfare hospital.

I got to know a number of welfare mothers. Warned of possible police brutality as a McCarthy campaign worker, I ended up coaching those who planned to participate in the Chicago DFL convention: "Watch out for the billy clubs, the human wedges. After the mace, breathe through your masks. Get down. Get down."

My aunt Rose and uncle Frank, who taught at Case Western Reserve, would come every Sunday with their family to pick Judy and me up, take us back to their home, and feed us a homemade dinner. They worried about our housing and our work. We'd have animated dissenting discussions. Yet it was reassuring—and nourishing—to have family watching over us.

In the middle of the job, I flew home for an interview to teach English at the senior high school in a conservative town in central Minnesota. My mom drove with me to the town in my brother Jim's car, which I had borrowed for the day. In the interview, the superintendent said, "We'd like you to take on some extracurriculars and to take a cut in salary [six thousand dollars!], because you're single, and we've got a male faculty of breadwinners here." (!)

I said, "I'll help with the plays but not give back any money."

The superintendent went on, "We've never hired one of your kind before. You're an experiment."

I didn't know if he meant because I was a former nun or a Catholic or a woman—but in any case, he hired his *experiment.*

After the interview, driving out of town, Mom and I discussed women's rights. I was driving too fast in the dark with a drenching rain on a two-lane highway. Suddenly, the left turn signal of the car in front of ours started flashing. The car stopped. Panicked, Mom shook her hand at the driver. "Move up! Move up," she shouted. I slammed on the brakes, never thinking to look behind—my dad later would say, "You should have gone on the shoulder. And why didn't you look in your rearview mirror?" The car behind us charged into Jim's Buick at over seventy miles an hour—our insurance company claimed the driver froze with his foot on the accelerator. We crashed into the first car then skidded off the side of the road, down an embankment, and into a tree. I hit the steering wheel and was knocked unconscious.

Coming to, I looked over at Mom in the passenger seat. She was bleeding from a cut on her head. Ambulances with lights and sirens blared on both sides of the highway above us. I shouted out my window, "Help my mom! We're down here. Help my mom!"

The last to be extricated, Mom and I were helped onto stretchers—and into two ambulances. The drivers, young guys, immediately began racing each other. They shouted through walkie-talkies: "Hey, we're hitting seventy-five." "We're doing eighty." "On to ninety." I couldn't say anything, my head and back aching. I wanted to shout, "Why are you doing this?! My mom is in that other ambulance. Be careful!" When we pulled up to the emergency door—safely, thank God!—our stretchers were pulled out and placed side by side. A nurse took a quick look at Mom: "This woman is very red. Check her blood pressure." They whisked Mom away. I didn't get to say her blood pressure might have risen because of the ride.

I didn't see her until the next morning. The car crashes overloaded the hospital—each of the other cars had five passengers. I was placed in a room with a woman who hadn't been in the accident, but who must have had some mental issues. She kept getting out of her bed, coming over to mine, talking to herself: "Oh, look at this. Beautiful girl in a bloody yellow dress. Blood all over. It'll never come off. She'll never walk again. That's what they're saying. Dark hair. Yellow dress. Never to walk again." I couldn't move because of the pain.

Sometime in the night, I was taken for X-rays; I had several compressed vertebrae in my upper back. As soon as it was light, I asked to see my mother. A nurse pushed me over to her room in a wheelchair.

Mom was in bed but busy. "I hope you didn't say anything about the accident to anyone, Margaret. Don't talk to State

Farm. I don't know about the other insurance company. Just don't talk to anyone until we talk to ours. I've called the superintendent. He'll be coming over soon for a visit. I want him to know you're all right. I haven't called home yet. Your dad's still on the road. I don't want to call Jim. I don't want to upset Jacque in her seventh month."

"Mom, are you OK?"

"Of course, honey. I'll be fine. A little high blood pressure, this cut from the rearview mirror—she pointed to her bandaged forehead—and a compressed vertebra in my neck, but I'll be fine. They say you will, too. We'll both get braces to wear. They say the car is totaled. I guess we'll have to call Jim soon. We have to find a way home."

Mom finally called Jim, who picked us up, after stopping and checking on his Buick. "Damn, Mom, you said this was a little accident. I thought it was a fender bender. You two are lucky to be alive."

Before we left, the superintendent stopped by with flowers. Embarrassed, I thanked him and said I would see him in the fall. Mom and I uncomfortably rode back to St. Paul, exclaiming with every bump on the road. I stayed home with pain pills and a brace for a few days, and then flew back to Cleveland. I didn't want Judy to be alone, and I wanted to finish our project. I slept flat on my back on the floor of our scary apartment for the rest of the summer; it was the only way I could be comfortable. I called Mom often to make sure she really was all right.

Exhilarated and tired from my work in Cleveland, I flew back to the Twin Cities the day before I was to report for orientation at my new school, a two-hour drive from St. Paul. My parents picked me up at the airport and we drove directly to the duplex that I had rented from a kind elderly lady who lived downstairs. It was across the street from the high school—ideal since I planned to get along without a car, saving every penny to travel to Europe that summer. I would have a roommate, another teacher at the high school, who had written earlier asking if I'd like to share lodging. That night she greeted me, "Hi, you must be Marge. I forgot to ask in my letter, where'd you go to college?"

"St. Kate's," I said.

She shrieked, "Are you a Catholic? Oh my God, I can't live with a Catholic!"

I gave her an incredulous look. "You must be kidding. Listen, I'm beat. I'm moving in."

We unloaded the car and Mom and Dad headed back to the Cities.

The irony was that my housemate was dating a divorced Catholic man from the Cities. He would stay over on weekends. On Sundays, he asked me to go to Mass with him. I did once and was embarrassed that people thought he was *my* boyfriend.

To get to my roommate's room, the boyfriend had to walk through my bedroom. The two of them openly made out everywhere. When we watched the DFL convention on TV together, they looked up briefly and then went on kissing as I watched in horror the graphic violence of the Chicago police on Michigan Avenue, at Lincoln and Grant Parks, where protesters and innocent bystanders were severely beaten. The news coverage showed smoke from the tear gas used by the police and "stink bombs" thrown by the protesters drifting into the Conrad Hilton, the headquarters for the Democratic Party. I knew that Tom Barrett was staying there, and I kept shouting, "Oh my God! My friend Tom is there. Oh my God! My friends from Cleveland are there. Oh my God!" My roommate and her boyfriend kept making out.

Usually I tried to get out of town on weekends, taking the train to the St. Paul Depot and staying with my folks. I started dating a guy I had known in high school. When that ended, Tom Barrett came back into my life. He called asking if I'd like to go to a play at the Guthrie Theater with him. It just happened: our relationship changed from friendship to something more. But

Tom Barrett inoculating against tuberculosis in the Peace Corps

in a couple of months—too soon—very disturbed about Vietnam and the draft lottery, Tom decided to leave graduate school and enter the Peace Corps. He said he needed to do this himself. He didn't ask me to see him off, didn't call to say goodbye. I waited to hear from him the day he left, the words, "I'm leavin' on a jet plane . . . " running through my mind. "Don't know when I'll be back again." It brought back memories of Tom in high school, when a group of us went to see Peter, Paul, and Mary at Northrup Auditorium. I had felt so alive, so happy, at that concert.

Tom and I exchanged a few letters, but aware of his distant tone, and still hurt, I stopped writing. I didn't know if this upset him, but he stopped writing, too.

I threw myself into teaching at my conservative high school. The whole faculty thought I was a raving liberal, a radical SDS-er (Students for a Democratic Society, a representation of the New Left). The American history teacher asked me to team-teach a black-literature unit with him. We focused on the civil-rights movement. It gave me the opportunity to explore the writing of Zora Neale Hurston, James Baldwin, Richard Wright, Ralph Ellison, Gwendolyn Brooks, Langston Hughes, Lorraine Hansberry, Martin Luther King Jr., and Malcolm X with the students. Our class was popular, the kids hungry to know and experience a world different than their own. My own courses: a sophomore class of so-called *slow learners*, who were my favorites—not slow, just not turned on; two junior American-literature classes; and two senior European-literature classes. And, of course, I was in charge of costumes and makeup for the plays. A grueling first-year schedule.

With very little free time, I still volunteered at the state hospital in town, going on a walk every week with a young boy who wouldn't speak. I alternated silence with storytelling as we strolled the grounds. One day, the boy pointed at some black-birds flying overhead. "We eat 'em," he said. A major break-through.

At the end of the year, the superintendent asked, "How can we keep you here?"

I smiled. "Up my salary and hire some single male teach-ers." I knew I would leave the small town and return to the Cities. I had interviewed for and accepted a position at a high school in St. Paul.

But first: travel. After that first year of teaching, Marsha, a friend from St. Catherine's who also taught high-school Eng-lish, and I toured Europe, living on five dollars a day. We spent a few days in New York before flying to London. Hicks from the Midwest, we were chased through Central Park and ordered to leave Harlem by concerned bystanders. We hitchhiked through the British Isles, which was safe to do at the time, although in Ireland we did have an incident with a non-Irish guy (we threat-ened him with our umbrellas!) who dropped us off on a remote road, but our next ride brought us to a charming country dance. Drivers took us long distances because I shared my Marlboro cigarettes with them. After London, we used our Eurail passes through fourteen different countries."

We visited Hungary, during the Cold War, before *glas-nost*; crossed into East Germany through the Wall at Checkpoint Charlie. We were warned by Spanish women not to talk back to the Franco militia and saved from a marauding gang of teenag-ers by a fascist policeman in Athens. We traveled from Munich to the concentration camp at Dachau on a raucous commut-er train, flirting with a New York Jew and a handsome Israeli. We initially made plans to go "hofbrauhausing" with them that night, but after Dachau, our train was absolutely silent. Departing, our new friends told us they were immediately leaving Germany.

We watched Neil Armstrong become the first man to set foot on the moon on small TVs set up on Parisian streets and dined at famous Maxim's—which we had scrimped for on the whole trip and almost didn't enjoy so worried we were about looking elegant and drinking wine parsimoniously because we couldn't afford a second carafe. We attempted to ski in Switzerland near the Matterhorn; I knew only how to "snowplow" and came barreling down the mountain so fast I deliberately fell before careening off the cliff. With a racing heart, I managed to get up, take off my skis and carry them to the chalet up some distance from the edge. I went in and bought an *I skied Zermatt!* emblem to sew on my new, pink ski jacket.

Coming through customs on our way home, believing—hoping—that what we wore was exempt from taxation, I had my pink jacket on over a Scottish blouse and kilt skirt underneath a leather coat from Spain; I also had adorned myself with a Swiss watch, jewelry from many countries, and a wool hat from Greece. Other gifts I carried in a bulging Italian purse. Marsha was likewise dressed to the hilt. The customs officer saw us coming, laughed out loud, and waved us through.

We returned to Minnesota in time for the opening of school. I began teaching—in an *Up the Down Staircase* time, 1969 to 1970—in a medieval fortress, an inner-city high school in St. Paul, a far different place from the small-town high school where I'd been. Here intercom messages with different codes interrupted all day long: "Teachers, please bring Form 001 to the office at the end of the day." That one meant, "Protect the kids in your room. Lock your door from the inside; there's trouble in the hallway." The kids, of course, knew the codes, and by the time the announcements were over, every kind of weapon was spread out on their desks—chains, ropes, knives, knuckles—though thankfully, at this time, no guns. Girls, hugely pregnant, sat on the bathroom floor discussing having their second and third babies. Kids popped pills. "Hey, Teach, the *reds* shipment just came in. We all bought at lunch. Everybody's out of it."

Yet I liked it. I liked the kids. I had a junior honors class for American literature and four *regular* senior literature classes. One of these classes was made up entirely of boys who had been to Totem Town. Some had made it to St. Cloud Reform School, and some were certainly on their way to the Big House. That was the talk—*Who's made it to Stillwater Prison?* They couldn't read or write, and the curriculum called for Chaucer and Shakespeare. I decided to teach them how to fill out a job application, how to dress for and how to talk in an interview.

I took the kids on buses to *The Learning Tree.* Gordon Parks was an alumnus of the high school, and his movie was showing in downtown Minneapolis. A North Minneapolis gang apparently heard we were coming, showed up, threatened my students with a gun in the theater, and slashed lettermen jackets in the parking lot. I stood—knives held up to my face—between the two groups, shouting, "Stop! Stop!" Gang members eventually, reluctantly, sulked away. No police showed up, but they were waiting for me in the principal's office when we returned to school. The principal said, "Officers, Miss Rogers won't be taking any more field trips like this. Right, Miss Rogers?"

A complicated year. A married vice principal threatened to give me a poor teacher rating unless I went out with him. In a time before sexual-harassment suits, I countered with "Get out of here. And don't you try this with anyone else on the faculty. I'll report you to the principal, to the superintendent, to the school board."

That same year, 1970, I fell in love with a likeable poet with a sense of humor and adventure, a teacher who taught at the same high school. We had known each other for a very short time, meeting in August and getting married in April. I remember wondering several months before our wedding if we were doing the right thing. I didn't entertain the thought long; the idea of canceling a big wedding seemed overwhelming. We had sent out many invitations and had already received a plethora of presents. I found out years later that my mother had sent a wedding invitation to Tom Barrett in Bolivia. I don't know how she got his address. And I don't know why she invited him. Did she want him to write and make a claim on me? Tom told me later that he had wandered the streets of La Paz that day wondering if he'd done the right thing by not letting me accompany him.

At the end of the school year, my new husband and I moved from St. Paul to Asheville, North Carolina. He knew a family who lived there, and it sounded romantic and exciting to go south and into the Blue Ridge Mountains. He bought a large red BMW motorcycle with our wedding money and rode it to Asheville; my mother and I drove the car, packed with all our possessions. She and I found an apartment above a gas station. Mom stayed and helped me buy used furniture to outfit the place.

But my husband immediately insisted on taking a trip to Nova Scotia, Canada. It would be a lark, going with the family he knew from Asheville. We'd help the mother drive her children to meet the father in Halifax. We would babysit the kids in a house the couple had purchased in a tiny, lovely village. After discovering the mission of this trip—his friends were buying up seaside property cheaply from poor elderly folks—I wanted to leave. Very early on a still morning, I walked in rubber boots down a dirt road, my husband by my side, arguing as we tromped to the ocean. Our angry voices reverberated across the wild daisy fields and over the barking of the seals.

A few weeks later, we drove back to North Carolina with the opportunists. In Asheville, I got a job teaching at a technical institute. The director had been educated at Rosary College in Illinois and said she felt comfortable hiring someone from Up North. What I was to accomplish: to improve the basic reading and writing skills of county employees so they could obtain better salaries. I had a group every morning who needed very rudimentary instruction. One older student, Dora Knuckles, the institute's laundress (who had huge knuckles), so desired to write a letter to her daughter. She eventually did—her first writing ever. She and I both teared up when she tucked it into an envelope to mail.

My afternoon group needed intermediate help. We worked on literature and more structured writing. On the first day of this class, a self-appointed spokesman greeted me, "Why do we get a Goddamn Yankee for a teacher?"

After a minute, I said, "Who won that war anyway?"

After another pause, he said, "She's all right. OK, what are we going to do?"

At night I taught at a business college. Another teacher, a young, beautiful woman with long black hair, who taught typing, sometimes came barefoot to school. Her father, she said, ran a still in the back country. One weekend she asked me if I'd like to go *brooming* downtown with her and her boyfriend.

"Sure," I said. "What's *brooming?*"

"You don't know *brooming?*"

"No."

"Well, you bring a broom into your car, stick it out the window, and see how many niggers you can knock off a corner."

"Oh my God!" I gasped. "No. How horrible! No." I was utterly shocked.

Somewhere in the back of my head, I knew this uneducated woman was just following her crowd of hillbillies, doing what everybody else did, but I could never speak to her again. I hated what she symbolized. I still hadn't gotten over African Americans stepping off the sidewalks for me in Asheville. When it first happened, I stepped off, too, saying, "Please walk here with me," but the look of fear the man shot back stunned me. I was making this more difficult for him. I couldn't believe the difference from my inner-city school in St. Paul, where African American students took charge, where the white students feared getting into trouble with them.

We stayed in North Carolina only until the middle of winter. My husband rolled a vehicle doing construction work, and he couldn't find another job. His father flew out to see us and offered him a position in the family business. My husband set off on the motorcycle to work on a project in a small northern Wisconsin town. He had an accident on the way, totalling the BMW, but he was unhurt. I again packed up our belongings and met him at a remote resort about fifteen miles north of the construction site. We rented one of the log cabins from a nice older couple.

I stayed at the cottage without a job or a car. The owner came over every morning, knocked at my door, and invited me for coffee in the main lodge. I'd put down my cross-stitching, or whatever else I was doing. I slogged over to the lodge behind the owner, who shuffled along with his big buckle boots, and took my place on the end of a long trestle table in the dining room. Over a steaming cup of coffee, I'd listen to the couple talk about their children and grandchildren, about fish and deer, rain and snow. Then I'd trudge back over to my cottage, pick up my *Kwitcherbellyaking* cross-stitch, and watch soaps.

My husband came home later and later. He had to enter the resort on a very narrow, circular road. He got stuck often and demanded help from the owner, who patiently shoveled him out. I was beginning to wonder why I was married to him, but I had taken vows for better or worse.

One morning I drove into the small town with him and noticed its biggest building, a state-owned nursing home. It dawned on me that I could volunteer there. The folks on the bottom rung of the employment ladder were people with disabilities; they were so happy to have someone beneath them. They assigned me chores. I chatted with residents and emptied bedpans—and discovered that a volunteer had no clout. When I protested a heartless rule to the administration, that married couples living in the home were not allowed to sleep in the same room together, they said, "Who are *you?*"

The building project completed, we moved back to Minnesota, to a surburban apartment complex in the Cities. I was hired by a principal to design a reading and study-skills class. One day he called me into his office. "I know you're trying your best to get them to read, but when you tell them to bring in anything they want to read, anything at all—Marge, *The Happy Hooker*?" It worked, though. The student, embarrassed to discuss this book with me—that was the deal; they had to discuss the book—eventually brought in a book on hunting and fishing. We discussed the first book he'd read since early primers. This elective English class, which drew kids who couldn't read as well as college-bound kids who wanted to speed-read, became very popular.

Things kept getting worse between me and my husband. I realized how little I knew about him. Naïve, inexperienced, I didn't know how to make it work. I went to marriage counseling and then finally decided it couldn't succeed. In the spring, just a little over a year after our wedding, the divorce was final. The marriage ended with a sense of relief but also of failure. My confidence crashed. A train wreck. Like the caboose on a crack-the-whip train, I was flung this way and that. It was all the harder to be sad and lonely inside when outside everything was springing up new and fresh, blooming alive.

I was glad to be busy that summer, working with Hallie Q. Brown Community Center in St. Paul. Hired as a camp counselor, I rode in and out of the city on a bus with six- and seven-year-old campers to a shelter on Square Lake near Stillwater, Minnesota. I looked up information and then created a little booklet I tucked into the pocket of my shorts. I checked it often for help with the next challenge of the day, finding: songs, song-words, game-songs, rhymes, rhymes and actions, games (without materials), mental games, games with materials, pantomimes, water stunts, rainy-day activities, crafts, tag games and relays, one-pot meals, desserts, salads, non-utensil meals, plant life, and animal life. As much as I loved these kids, my skills were better suited for high-school and college-age students.

After teaching for three years at the suburban school, my contract was not renewed. The district had to make cuts; I was last in, first out. I was accepted into a graduate program in education at the University of Minnesota, working as a counselor-teacher and later as an administrator of the extension division's outreach program for *locked-out populations*. During the day, I counseled at the reading and study-skills center on campus and at night with adults in the poorer communities of St. Paul. I hired faculty to teach in the community, offering legislatively funded tuition-free courses from the University. One day a week, I taught a class with other women professors at Stillwater Prison. The men welcomed our composition class enthusiastically. It was a pleasure to teach them but not a pleasure to go through the security measures and the occasional lockdowns. And one of the inmates somehow got my phone number and taunted me, "Ms. Teacher, I'll see ya; when I get out, I'll find ya." I found out he had murdered several women. Disconcerted, I searched for a new apartment; my phone number would change, too.

I took a break from my University job in the summer, joining two other teacher friends in the game preserves of Africa. But before we left, my roommate Mary and I threw a party. I asked my friend John, from high school, to come. He did and brought Tom Barrett with him. Tom and I talked and talked and walked around a nearby lake together until early morning. I told him I would be leaving for the summer in Africa. He wanted to know when I would return.

Part of an international group tent camping from northern Kenya to Johannesburg in 1973, the year when two Canadian girls were shot to death at Victoria Falls, we were ordered out of Uganda by President Idi Amin Dada and chased by stone-bearing Masai because one of our group had taken their pictures (stolen their souls). A young, friendly, white man from Rhodesia (now Zimbabwe) wanted to give me a tour of his family's enormous farm, complete with a church and school for the blacks who worked it. He explained from early pioneer days his family had taken care of the indigenous people. I told him I had to be moving on. At night around the campfire, our traveling group had fierce arguments over racism and apartheid. The New Zealanders discussed the Maori; the Canadians, First Nations, Métis, and Inuit; the Australians, the Torres Strait Islanders. We Americans talked about Native Americans and slavery.

Almost the entire trip we suffered dysentery and mostly could only wash up in bathrooms of resort hotels or local bars. But the whole 6 week trip—including air and ground transportation (in an old army truck with old airplane seats), and food (bought in local markets and cooked over our campfires) cost $965! And there was no better way to experience Amboseli, Lake Nakuru, Serengeti, Ngorongoro Crater, and other national parks. No forgetting bolting out of your tent in the morning to see a giraffe or monkeys or a mongoose or a herd of gazelles or wildebeest looking at you!

When the tour ended, I hitchhiked through South Africa with two other women because we wanted to hear reactions to apartheid—it was difficult to find any public venues (bars were even segregated by gender) to discuss the topic. We conversed with British, Scottish, and Irish drivers until the Afrikaaner police patrol picked us up and escorted us through the Transvaal.

A postcard I sent home:

Dear Folks,

Am writing this from Cape Town, SA. It's been an exciting week. We arrived in Johannesburg last Wed. the end of our camping trip. Then a Canadian and New Zealand girl and myself decided to hitchhike from Joburg to Durban, Port Elizabeth and then to Cape Town. Wouldn't have written that until the end so you wouldn't worry but it was great. Had many nice drivers (about 30) and picked up much knowledge about the scenery, politics, govt., etc. Yesterday we arrived in Cape Town, rented a car and drove down to the Cape of Good Hope. We're now flying back to Joburg and will leave tonight to Nairobi and then to London. Will have a week in

Wales and then home . . . Having just a super time. Hope everyone is fine.
All take care. Love, Marge

When I returned home, Mom asked, "Margaret, were you safe?" Dad said, "What did you find out, Peggy?"

The day after I returned, Tom called. Did I want to go out with him? I flashbacked to several years before when Dad had asked me, "What about Tom Barrett? Is he back from the Peace Corps? Hell, he was a smart guy, beat the pants off us in *Jeopardy*. He never got married, did he? You ever see him?" At the time, I wasn't interested; I was going out with both a banker and a realtor. I had bought a duplex of my own. I felt like a mature businesswoman. I'd answered, "Oh, Dad, I don't know. Tom's an intellectual. He's still a student. I heard he's now in law school." (I didn't say, "You remember don't you, Dad, waiting with me the day he left for the Peace Corps?") "Oh, I see . . . " Dad had said.

I said yes to Tom. We went to *The Way We Were*, with Barbara Streisand and Robert Redford. At the end of the movie, I couldn't stop crying. Humiliated, I couldn't stop myself. Tom waited patiently, giving me a side look now and then to see if I'd gained control. Finally, we went for a nightcap at the Commodore Hotel in St. Paul, a place where F. Scott and Zelda Fitzgerald and Al Capone and Fred Barker once hung out. We had drinks in its elegant art-deco bar, and Tom asked me about my marriage. I tried to be as honest as I could, not excusing myself of responsibility, but also not accepting the fault. I ended by saying I'd probably never get married again.

So intent and focused—and affected by the movie, and probably still impacted by my series of plane flights from Cape Town to Johnnesburg to Nairobi to London to New York to Minneapolis—when I excused myself to go to the bathroom, I fell flat on my face. Tom did not laugh but reached out solicitously, asking if I was all right, if I could stand up. At that moment, I thought: I could love this man again. When he brought me home, he kissed me goodnight and, walking away, leaped off the steps of my duplex—and in a short time, leaped back into my heart.

We dated for two years. He finished law school and began clerking for the Minnesota Supreme Court. I continued working for the University extension program. I hired him once to teach a law course at the Martin Luther King Center. He also acted as my lawyer when I sold my duplex. The realtor representing the buyers had assigned additional costs for me to pay. At the closing, I said, "My attorney has studied the documents." The realtor immediately dropped his charges.

My friend Ginger and I moved into a high-rise apartment in Minneapolis overlooking the Mississippi River. When Tom and I got engaged, we made arrangements to rent another apartment in the same building, moving from the more expensive tenth floor to the cheaper fifth.

Tom wanted us to be married in the Catholic Church. And of course so did our parents. I applied for a Church annulment. Though glad to do it for loved ones, I didn't love the process. It again brought out my twofold judgment call: you had to have money to apply; those from a *good* Catholic family got served more quickly; you had to use the Church's reasons for the dissolution. I had to say my ex-husband didn't want children (which he didn't, but I hadn't known if that would change over time). As I had explained to Tom, I felt equally responsible for the breakup, but the process sought evidence solely against him, an official blaming of the other party. For me, the annulment chipped another fissure into the rock that is the Catholic Church.

Tom and I were happily married in the beautiful Abbey Church at St. John's University. We honeymooned in Ireland: went to museums in Dublin; dug up our roots in County Mayo and Donegal; stared into the turret of a huge British tank in Enniskillen, Northern Ireland; and relaxed on a hot day in a small coastal town. It was only seventy-five degrees in Clifden, but

Tom and Marge Barrett with the Rogers family on their wedding day

the Irish were sweltering: long lines at ice-cream carts, gallons of swallowed pints, talk of highs, records being set. We were comfortable, sitting shoulder to shoulder on rocks jutting into the sea, laughing at seagulls and sandpipers, listening to the lilting banter of the Irish and the lapping of the waves. We walked, hand in hand, out into the country. On a hilltop, we discovered an abandoned, centuries-old castle. We became the king and queen, stepping through a bailey and kissing in the keep.

My mother and father met us in London on our way from Ireland to Paris and then Spain. They were en route to Scandinavia. It would be a treat, they said, for us to lead them around London for a few days. They traveled a great deal but on planned tours, in big buses. They were looking forward to being with just us and getting around on the Tube.

We picked them up from the Cunard Line Hotel, shaped like a huge boat, on the far outskirts of London, where Dad said he hadn't yet seen a Brit. We took them to the National Gallery to see a special Rembrandt exhibit. As soon as we entered, I was lost in the dark, luminous paintings, and Dad got lost in the building. Mom was worried. Who might he be talking to? Tom and I set out looking for him.

I finally spied his white head. "Dad, where were you?

We've looked everywhere. Did you find something you really liked?" I was thinking, *Yes, he, too, loves Rembrandt's portraits.*

Bending down, astonishment on his face, he pointed to the mosaic floor of the Gallery. "Hell, yes, Peggy. Look at this. Perfect. Each little square perfectly set next to the other. And it goes on for miles. Amazing."

That night in London, the four of us went to a theatre production, *Kennedy's Children.* Tom and I didn't know anything about the play, but thought it might be historically interesting. It turned out to be a monologue about the '60s, exposing the dregs of American society: sex and drugs big time, *fuck* almost every other word.

At the intermission, Tom and I sheepishly said, "We had no idea." "Should we leave?"

Dad said, "What? Hell, no. It's amazing. That guy hasn't forgotten a line. What a performance. All by himself out there."

Tom looked at me, smiled. I was so lucky.

FROM FAMILY

Following doctor's orders, I was in a rocking chair, alarm clock by my side, timing when I could next pick up my beautiful daughter. I'd given up my office chair at the University of Minnesota to stay home with my baby, who had colic. The baby cried and cried, and I cried, "Where's my secretary?" Having this perfect baby was far more challenging than I ever had imagined in the convent.

Eventually I became more of the happy, harried mom: the caretaker of a three-year-old, two-year-old, and a newborn. Wonderfully busy days of feeding, dressing, playing, bathing, cleaning, laundering, shopping, and cooking, but some days I felt pushed to the limit. Like the afternoon my suddenly albino, blue-eyed children emerged from the white tornado of their bedroom. *Oh holy shit. Everything white. A silky sheen on every surface. Oh holy shit.* But as usual, that evening, the mess cleaned up, I lovingly tucked my children into their beds. As I leaned down to kiss them good night, from their bodies rose the most marvelous smell of baby-powdered children.

An industrious homemaker, I renovated and restored our first home, an older duplex. I found our second home, built at the turn of the century, on a walk with my children. Tom and I had only one car, an orange Rabbit with no air-conditioning. At the time, Tom worked for migrant legal services and traveled during the week in the hot Red River Valley of Minnesota and North Dakota. I pushed the kids around in a double-decker stroller for play, groceries, doctor appointments, and hunting real estate. We eventually also bought triplexes, two old rental properties, and an unfinished cabin in northern Wisconsin. The kids played around me as I stripped wallpaper and woodwork, painted, fixed, and maintained. A landlady, I found occupants for the apartments and collected the rents. The kids helped me clean. When they started school, I also led parent associations and served on the school board of their Catholic school—a trying time because of a conflict between the school and the parish.

In the summers, the kids and I would go to the cabin. We stayed all week. Tom would come up on weekends, oftentimes with other family members. The cabin was modest, and we didn't have air-conditioning, TV, or a telephone. I remember watching the kids whenever we arrived at Lake Du Bois in northern Wisconsin. For the first few days, they picked fights with each other and complained about being bored. By the third day, their neighborhood friends and their favorite TV programs were forgotten. They played cards and games; they hid in the tree fort. They swam and boated. They fished with our next-door neighbor, Bill, a funny older gentleman. They frog- and turtle-hunted, caught butterflies, read and read. They grew up loving nature and discovering how to make their own fun.

For a week every summer, our family drove or took the train out west—to the Black Hills and Badlands in South Dakota; Yellowstone National Park and Jackson Hole in Wyoming; Glacier National Park in Montana; Banff National Park in Alberta, Canada. We once drove all the way to British Columbia, to Victoria and Vancouver Island. The kids, eager sightseers, hiked the hills and mountains, swam in the lakes and oceans, and rode the horses at ranches.

Every winter, right after Christmas, we would drive to the mountains to ski, mostly at Big Sky, Montana, or Steamboat Springs, Colorado—we could make those trips in a day. A long day. As the kids grew older, we started flying with them to other ski resorts in Colorado and Utah. All fun trips, except the one to Winter Park, Colorado, where our youngest child, Norah, at seven, broke her femur doing "a little blade skiing." Her boot caught a tree stump and didn't release. The ski patrol tobogganed her down the Mary Jane run alongside Tom. The other children, Katie and Tommy, skied me down (I was in shock after watching Norah lift up her ski pants and say, "I don't have a leg").

Norah and I flew over the Rockies in a helicopter to the Denver hospital. Tom and the kids packed up our rental place and drove to Denver in our car. The doctors wanted to keep Norah in traction for months—they worried about the growth plate. I said I couldn't stay with her; I had to get the other two back in school. We decided to rent a propeller plane. The pilot, a registered nurse, Norah, and I filled the cabin. Norah was in terrific pain because her leg was not set. The pilot opened his little curtain at some point and said to the nurse, "I can't bear to hear her moaning. Can she have a little booze? I've got some." The nurse said, "She can't, but maybe her mom could."

Children's Hospital, in St. Paul, admitted Norah, and a fine surgeon set her leg. But she woke up from surgery in a full-body cast, which terrified her. She learned to live with it. She had to stay in it for three months, in a hospital bed in our living room. Our terrier, Bailey, who never obeyed unless he wanted to, spent every night under her bed. Once a week, her teacher brought her lessons to the house, and I home-schooled. Norah eventually got crutches and went back to school. The next winter, she "got back on the horse" and went skiing again. I was always awed by our children's resiliency.

When they were in junior high school, I signed up for a writing class. The night my work was read, I came home, after bedtime on a school night, to find the house all lit up. The kids greeted me at the door.

"Mom, did you get an A? Can you stop writing now? No? Oh gosh. No? Well, promise me one thing: you'll write at off times."

"Mom, it's so scary." (*Why scary?*) "Because you had a life."

"Promise me you won't publish. If you're thinking of doing that, just forget it. I'd have to move away."

I did continue to write, *off times* and *on*; to edit and publish; to earn a Masters in Fine Arts in creative writing at the University of Minnesota; to study in Prague and St. Petersburg, Russia; to teach at the University of Minnesota, the Collegeville Institute for Ecumenical and Cultural Research, the Jewish Community Center, and the Loft Literary Center.

Busy, lovely times with children, homes, and careers.

Through those years of raising our children, Tom and I watched over my brother Tom and sister Patty. Our children grew up realizing my siblings were part of our family and accepted their differences. The kids must have been annoyed at times by the number of phone calls from Tom and Patty and by our time spent on them, but we didn't hear any complaints. Even as teenagers, the kids weren't embarrassed when Tom or Patty came to watch their athletic or school events. Today our children say what a great influence their aunt and uncle had in their lives and how they never questioned our desire and effort to help take care of them. Always guiding lights, Patty and Tom gave back tenfold to all of us.

There's a theory that even though one has the genetic chemical imbalance of schizophrenia or bipolar disorder—my brother Tom was diagnosed as having both—if the individual does not suffer major stress, he can avoid a critical breakdown. More to the point these days is that help, by way of medication and support resources, can be plugged in at the very onset of the disease, helping to alleviate cataclysmic episodes.

"How could I have let this happen? I had the rest of you to watch, of course. But still. I should never have let this happen." Mom remembered Tommy staying with friends for a week when he was two years old. She and Dad had taken us four older kids on a vacation. Tommy cried the whole week and couldn't be consoled. Two years later, he had surgery at the Mayo Clinic for a lazy eye. "He was too young to be at the hospital by himself. Even though Muzzy would come visit him, read to him, sing to him, he was all by himself with both of his eyes covered for a week. It was too much."

When he was five, his appendix ruptured. Mom had nursed him for a week, with what she thought was the stomach flu. Tommy was a happy-go-lucky kid, not a complainer, so she didn't know how sick he really was until his temperature rose to 104. She placed his limp arms around her neck and lifted him from the living-room sofa. Tommy's feet almost dragged on the ground as she carried him to Weiner Memorial. He stayed there for a week. Children couldn't visit at the hospital so every day we kids packed up a bag of messages, pencils and paper, crayons and coloring books, and comics and storybooks for Mom and Dad to deliver. A few months later, we took turns reading to him when he broke his arm falling into a large construction hole in the neighborhood. Mom had warned him, "Don't go near the hole."

"But that's the first place my friends and I headed for," Tommy said.

He was the brother next to me in age. One night Jim and John, babysitting us, hosted a wild party while Mom and Dad were in the Cities with the other kids. They had called a few friends, saying they had the house to themselves. Soon it seemed all the young people in Marshall had stormed our house with cases and kegs of beer. It got very rowdy.

Tommy rushed into my bedroom, saying, "I'm scared."

"Should we call the police?"

"Let's call Father Dolan."

We didn't call anyone, but we did go downstairs to see the damage happening around us. I remember yelling at Julie, a friend of Jim's, that she couldn't wash a frozen turkey from the basement freezer in a sink full of cigarette butts. She swore at Tommy and me, but Jim told her, "Let them be. Put the turkey back." Tommy and I soon began enjoying ourselves, watching all the carrying-on.

Jim and John made their friends come back the next day to help clean up. Tommy and I didn't snitch, but Mom and Dad knew something was wrong as soon as they walked in the door—maybe by the looks on our faces or maybe by the broken lamp staring at them. Jim and John suffered serious repercussions at home and at school—loss of leadership roles, suspensions from sports teams, talks with the priests and nuns. No one asked Tommy and me what we thought, but we would have said it wasn't all our brothers' fault. Lots of older kids crashed the party. It just got out of control.

That summer, Julie of the frozen-turkey episode was our instructor at the Legion Pool in town. Tommy and I, young to be in junior lifesaving classes, held our own, knowing how to leap off the diving board with our clothes on, legs spread wide, our eyes focused on the pretending-to-be-drowning person. We knew how to remove our clothes underwater and how to blow our pants or shirt up as a flotation device. We could tread water for forty-five minutes, and we knew how to release a drowning victim's desperate holds. We were doing fine, even though Julie, now one of Jim's *former* girlfriends, took her scorned love out on us. She'd make us swim extra laps and tread water longer than others.

The day we were supposed to put all our learning and exercises together and really save someone, Julie picked me first, as usual. "OK, little Rogers, get in the deep end." As I started out, she swam up underneath me, grabbing my head, squeezing my neck like a vise. "Hey, little Rogers, you big enough to handle me?"

My first reaction was to panic, then I quickly figured she was probably testing me on a hold so I sank for an escape, whipping her arms up and off me. But she grabbed my hair and pulled me under. Tommy dove in and down, trying to loosen her grip. I thought I'd drown, but then Julie suddenly let go of me and seized Tommy by the throat. I couldn't help him; I needed to go up for air. Once I caught my breath, I screamed, "She's drowning my brother." The teacher of the intermediate class heard me, jumped in, and swam to Julie. "Stop it," she yelled, and brought Tommy over to the side ladder in the normal over-the-chest lifesaving hold. Once Tommy caught his breath, we left the pool, racing home on our bikes.

We told Mom about Julie. Mom closed the kitchen door so we couldn't hear what she said on the phone, but Julie never bothered us again.

In high school, Tom and I double dated a few times. After I entered the convent, Tom finished high school at Cretin and received a scholarship to St. John's University, where he worked on a double major in pre-medicine and humanities. He was selected for a unique opportunity to study abroad, but was sent home by St. John's before the departure date—and immediately came to see me in the convent. And flung the communion hosts on the floor.

Tom had suffered a complete psychotic breakdown. We saw him the day after his convent visit; Mary and I were allowed to go because Dad had called to say Tom thought he was dying and wanted his brothers and sisters there. In the hospital room, he alternately paced back and forth, bellowing and beating his head, and curled up in bed, crying in Dad's arms. Dad kept saying, "What's wrong, Tommy? What's wrong?" We all looked at each other, shocked and scared.

After his initial break, Tom would be in and out of hospitals for years. He could be manically keyed up, hysterically laughing and yelling, or severely depressed, sometimes catatonically so. I remember visiting him one Christmas in a locked psychiatric ward. He sat on a chair, making no movements. His head hung down. I tried to get him to look at me. I asked questions, told stories. Eventually he raised his head, but his eyes stared through me, haunted. *He's in hell*, I thought. He stayed in that unit—like that—for weeks.

He'd get better, then worse again. Over and over.

In the worst times, he would fight, sometimes with my brothers. He would make Patty and her staff nervous and receive orders not to visit her group home. He would get kicked out of apartments, get put in jail. He'd refuse to bathe, to cut his hair, to dress properly. He'd hoard newspapers, magazines, and requests for donations. He'd scream. He'd swear. He'd talk to the TV. He'd cut himself.

In better times, he would take classes, get a job, make new friends, see old friends, date, practice photography, paint, read, and write.

He was in touch with me through the worst and best of times. He would join the family for holidays and gatherings. We both lived in St. Paul. I took him to doctor and dentist appointments. I stayed close to him always, visiting him when he was sick, going to plays or concerts or movies when he was healthy. We ate out. He called me often, just to talk. He played soccer with my children in our backyard, though I was always nervous about it. I could never be sure how Tom would be. I wanted to protect my children and, at the same time, to protect Tom. I didn't want my children to fear him.

Only once did he actually threaten me. He came to my house with some volatile friends, and I kept them all playing basketball in our driveway so they wouldn't come inside the house with my kids. Tom got angry about that and threw a Coke bottle on the cement. Glass scattered everywhere. I asked the men to go. Tom got more belligerent. I then said, very anxious and upset, "I'll have to call the police if you don't leave." They finally left. When Tom was better, he apologized, saying he never wanted to trouble me. He loved me.

Tom died in 2012. At his funeral, my brother John gave a very moving eulogy, telling of Tom's struggles in life. John called Tom the bravest man he's ever known. I, too, spoke at the funeral. I began by saying Tom lived life as my father said we should all live: 100 percent. His life exemplified giving it your all: physically, mentally, emotionally. He grew up a fun, kind, smart, engaging boy, who enjoyed life with his family, neighborhood buddies, and classmates at Holy Redeemer Grade School. At Cretin High School, he graduated with the highest academic, athletic, and leadership honors: member of the top ten and National Honor Society; All Conference and Honorable Mention All-State in football; All Conference, MVP, and captain of basketball; a winning member of the golf team; first vice president of his class. Tom was also named Cretin's Cadet Colonel, the highest honor based on all endeavors.

As a sophomore at St. John's, he was one of twenty top North American students selected to participate in the 1967–68 international honors program, traveling and studying with three professors in Japan, India, and a country in western Europe. That plan derailed, of course, but Tom eventually graduated from St. John's. He did further study at the University of Minnesota and University of St. Thomas and received a master's in English education.

Over the next thirteen years, Tom taught high school and worked for Control Data Corporation briefly. He worked for short times as a janitor, a survey analyst, a clothes sorter, a delivery person, a carpenter, a taxicab driver, and a reporter for the *Highland Villager*. He wrote stories and poems and two novels, lost in his many moves. Running for public office once, as mayor, he garnered a lot of votes—Rogers must be a popular name in St. Paul (as I told Tom when I visited him in the hospital)!

At the time Tom was afflicted and diagnosed with mental illness, it carried a terrific stigma. Families were blamed—my mother was told it was her fault—and often discouraged from helping with recovery plans. But our family followed the example of our parents and always stayed involved with Tom's care. We stood by him as he endured various solutions: medications of all kinds (his generation—guinea pigs—tried out all sorts of drugs at all sorts of dosages), megavitamin therapy, electroshock therapy at Mayo Clinic, a special treatment center in Connecticut. Throughout all these therapies, Tom never complained.

In 1990, when our family heard about a miracle drug, clozapine, we demanded Tom try it—at that time he was in danger of being committed to the state mental hospital. Clozaril (the brand name) gave Tom a semblance of a new life. He evened out—and then had over twenty years of equilibrium. He lived an independent life in a secure home, Safe House, intended for critical care of people with persistent mental illness. They let Tom live there permanently.

He coached sports teams for Apollo Resource Center, part of People Incorporated, an umbrella organization for folks with mental illness. Apollo's teams won big in softball, volleyball, and basketball. Tom volunteered at Catholic Charities' Dorothy Day Center, which provided food, shelter, housing, and other services for those in need. He engaged in other church activities and played softball for a church-league team for years. He sent donations to a multitude of organizations—usually twenty-five or fifty dollars—keeping a ledger of the check number and date he issued it. He wrote personal letters to accompany some of his gifts and would help anyone in need.

He published pieces in *Mississippi Musings*, a book of "Voices of Minnesota Mental-Illness Survivors." He wrote birthday cards.

Sonnet #10 (for Margie)

So you're constantly told
That you're incredibly old
And have only fifty more years
To imbibe with Barrett some billion barrels of beer.

But just stop and think that at your young age
You are still gonna be in on the latest rage,
Whether it's hopscotch or jacks or betting your dough
On the Vikes or the Twins or the Stars, or maybe their foe.

Hell, yes, baby, take it from the Boad,
You have plenty freeways and that dusty old road
To go on down before you're ready at last
To start looking back at the glorious distant past.

So please don't be melancholy, be jolly & free,
And never be a slave to the hour-glass's trickery.

Tom got around, taking buses everywhere. Every week
he went to the hospital to check his blood because of Clozaril's
possible adverse affects, but he didn't have to be admitted—until years later, when he had prostate cancer. He survived that
surgery and recovery, again never complaining. On dialysis—the
legacy of lithium, a drug he had taken in the early days of his
illness—when the nurse asked him if he had any serious medical
issues, he said, "Well, I have an allergy to strawberries."

As an alternative to dialysis, Tom deperately needed a
kidney transplant. He put his name on a donor waiting list at a
Twin Cities hospital. The call came to my house very early one
morning: a young woman had died in a car accident; her kidney
was compatible with Tom's. I picked Tom up and drove him
to the hospital. John and I—the in-town siblings—stayed with
him, as we had for his cancer surgery, until he was wheeled into
the operating room. I said to Tom what Mom had once said to

him, "Don't worry. You'll be all right. They'll take good care of you." Suffering from hospital delirium after the surgery, he pulled out all his medical tubes.

Recovering from that, he was sent to a rehabilitation unit in the hospital. There he was taken off Clozaril abruptly (against my objections) because it was contributing to his lowered white-blood-cell count, and the doctor felt Tom's physical health was in jeopardy. Tom totally decompensated. After all the years he had worked to stay out of hospitals, Tom was committed to another locked psychiatric unit.

He asked me, "Do I have to go, Margaret?"

"Yes, you have to, Tom. I'm sorry."

He nodded at me, his red-rimmed eyes, deeply socketed, showing such pain. That moment, that vision, will stay with me forever.

In the unit, Tom was heavily medicated with various drugs—Seroquel, Risperdal, Zoloft, Oleptro—each being tried at different dosages for several weeks then slowly withdrawn, the psychiatrist trying to decide which drug or combination of drugs would bring Tom back—if he could come back. Tom was unable to even hold utensils to eat. He was transferred to a nursing home for further rehabilitation.

There my husband and I experienced something remarkable. We came to visit one night and found Tom transformed from the unresponsive condition he had been in for months. He greeted us with a smile, offered us chairs, asked Tom, "Do you have any jokes to tell?" Tom and I stared at each other, astonished. My brother continued, "I'm at the end of my current drug. They've been withdrawing it for a while. Before they start another one tomorrow, I need you to tell me things. Marge, what happened? Can you tell me about surgery? How did I get here?" We talked into the night, the two Toms telling jokes, talking about sports, my brother asking about our siblings, our children, his other nephews and nieces. That night he was the brother I knew from before his initial breakdown.

The next morning, when I excitedly came to visit, he was once again unresponsive. Weeks later, John and I decided to move Tom back to his apartment—maybe his own place, with his own things, with his own friends, might help bring him back. We found a fine psychiatrist. He invited John and me to attend his sessions with Tom.

I asked this doctor about the clarifying evening my husband and I had with Tom. "Why did this happen? How can it be explained?"

"I have no idea," he said.

Over time, Tom rebuilt his life once again. He called me to go to plays and movies, to readings, to restaurants. He bought gifts for family members. He read new books. He started to write again. He took walks. He went to church. He was happy. He chose the time to take care of removing the hernia he had developed after his transplant surgery.

It was dreadfully ironic that Tom died from complications following this simple surgery.

After his death, I found a booklet of photographs and poems in Tom's apartment. In one picture, he sits on a lawn lit by the sun, dark shadows playing around him:

With the sky so clear
And the air so pure,
I sit here along with my friends,
And experience a comfortable day.

As I write these lines
I feel a sense of peace
Because my soul is calm
And my feelings resonate nicely.

On this beautiful afternoon
There is beauty to behold,
And a feeling within myself

That this is a special kind of day.

So I celebrate being alive on a day
Like this day, and am thankful for happiness.

When I read it, I cried, not only for the sentiment expressed—that he could be thankful for his life (he always told
me how lucky he was)—but also for the simplicity of the poem.
Tom's earlier writing had been so intellectually expressive. Here
was a poem honed by years of suffering: plain and uncomplicated.

Tom had a friend, George, an older man who had also
lived for a time at Safe House. George was a character. I remember him as a teller of wickedly funny stories.

People with mental illness change addresses a lot, but I
took Tom to visit George, wherever he was, about twice a year.
At one point he was living in a nursing home in Minneapolis,
which he did not like. After visiting that cheerless place, I vowed
to myself that the next time we visited, I'd get things to brighten
George's side of his double room. He had only a single bed,
a gray metal chair, and a sort of cardboard dresser on which
rested a tiny, beat-up TV with taped rabbit ears.

The next year, Tom and I found George, bald and beard-
less, with a walker, on the second-floor hallway.

Tom said, "Hi, George."

George looked blankly at us, but said, "Hello, Tom."

We moved very slowly to George's room.

Tom said, "Here. Take this chair, Margaret."

I sat by George's bed. Tom cleared off some stuff from
George's roommate's chair and brought it over. He sat on it,
clasping a plastic grocery bag to his chest. George sat in the
middle of his bed, staring vacantly. I suddenly remembered my
promise to bring something to liven up this sad room, but I had
brought nothing. The TV had even disappeared. A shabby sheet

covered the bed. George collapsed on it, folded into a fetal position, closed his eyes.

Long minutes went by.

I finally said, "Tom, should we go?"

"Ah, no, Margaret, we just got here."

"But George's sleeping . . ."

"Ah, he might be but maybe not." Tom went on to say that when we had visited him in the hospital—when he himself was unresponsive—he could still hear us talking.

"Should I talk now, Tom?"

"If you have something to say, Margaret."

We briefly discussed the upcoming holiday. I told him what the family's plans were, when we'd pick him up.

Tom leaned back in the gray metal chair.

More deep silence.

I glanced at my watch, worrying about all the things I needed to do that day, that week.

George eventually sat up, said, "Hi . . . Tom."

"Hi . . . George," Tom said.

Long pause.

I rushed in. "How's the food here, George?"

"Awful," he hissed.

"They seem to take good care of you."

No answer.

"Want to walk with us, George?" Tom asked.

George shuffled the twenty or thirty steps to the elevator. On the first floor, Tom said, "Hello, happy Thanksgiving," to everybody. He offered them gum. They looked nervously at him, saw George and me, and relaxed a bit. We took the elevator back up, lumbered to George's room. He dropped back in bed.

Silence.

"Tom, are you going to give your gifts to George?" I asked.

Moments passed.

Tom finally said, "Here, George, here's something to

drink." Tom reached into his grocery bag. He drew out a large Coke and placed it on the bed. George left it balancing there. Tom rummaged in the bag again, then handed George a huge Hershey's bar.

George shook his head. "I can't eat nuts."

"Oh, I'm sorry, George, I'll take it back," Tom said, shoving the candy back into the bag. He took out a book. "A mystery, George. I think you'll like this." Tom set the book on the bed next to the teetering Coke.

Later, driving Tom home, I said, "Let's go buy something for George's room right now."

"Ah, he'll be there for a while, Margaret. You're busy. We can do it another time." Several beats later he added, "Maybe I shouldn't have given that book to George. I don't know if he can read it."

I didn't know if Tom meant because George had lost his glasses (he told us he had a year ago) or was too sick now and couldn't concentrate.

After dropping Tom off and driving back to my house, I realized I had watched an amazing scene. Tom had simply accepted George's condition, offering him unconditional love. He might have hoped George would come back to his former feistiness, but he acknowledged his present place as not necessarily bad, just different. He gave his friend room to *be*. I realized that we could all emulate this behavior. We could listen to people, spend time with them, especially the sick and the vulnerable. We could respect all people.

I closed my funeral eulogy with comments from some of Tom's many friends who called or wrote e-mail messages about him after his death.

"I can honestly say I knew no one who did not like Tom."

"He has always been one of my heroes in life—so kind, so gentle, so loving, so genuine, so generous."

"He was a loving gentle giant."

"'Great soul' is the perfect description for him. With all

Tom Rogers

his burdens, his first concerns were always for others. Can't think of a time when I ran into him that the first question wasn't 'How's the family?' or 'How are you?' He was just a terrific person, and everyone who knew him will be very sad when they hear he's gone." (When I received this email, I thought of Ralph Waldo Emerson's "Over-Soul," how Emerson believed humans come from the biochemical stuff of which we have been made, and how we should look to ourselves and each other because God is living in everyone's mind. While one part of my mind recalled Transcendentalism, however, another sang soul song titles: "Soul Man," "He Was Really Sayin' Somethin'," "You Lost the Sweetest Boy.")

"I know God sent the finest angels to take Tom to heaven. It was a smooth ride, and your mom and dad welcomed him with open arms. He is smiling down on his family who cared for him and loved him so much. He was a remarkable man who always faced adversity with hope and greeted life, family, and friends with his heart and a piece of gum."

Mom welcomed him. She's now catching up with Tom, as she did every night for so many years. And Dad's smiling, happy to have his son free of burdens. And Patty is singing and dancing with Tom. They both died on October 30, the day before Halloween, four years apart.

When Mom and Dad had asked my brother Jim and me to become legal guardians for Patty, we assured them we'd always watch over her. We both lived within driving distance of Hammer Residences in Wayzata, where Patty moved when our family left Marshall. Jim was a lawyer. I was a teacher. Together, we seemed right for the job. The state required the court hearing to take place in the county in which Patty was born. We three traveled back to Marshall in May 1987.

"It's too loud," Patty complained from the rear seat.

Jim didn't hear her. We drove past the Marshall city-limit sign. When we moved to St. Paul in 1961, Marshall's population had been about seven thousand; in 1987, close to twelve thousand people lived in our old hometown. We noticed the many hotels and restaurants that had cropped up along Highway 19. In 1967, Southwest Minnesota State College was built over the boggy bottom of the slough we kids used to play around. I wondered how many trucks had dumped how many loads of dirt to cover that hollow? I didn't see it happen. I've only been back to Marshall a few times since my family moved away.

"It's too loud, and it's too cold," Patty grumbled again, shivering in an exaggerated fashion.

As we drew closer to town, Jim put Beethoven's "Ninth Symphony" in the tape deck. He pumped up the volume full blast and cranked open the sunroof of his new Buick.

"And too windy," Patty shouted. "I just got my hair set, Jim." She placed her hands over her hair, over her ears.

Jim turned and laughed at her. "We're announcing ourselves, Patty. We're back home."

"Some people!" Patty grinned.

We decided we had time to look at our old house. "Go for it," Patty cheered. Jim turned off Highway 19 and sped up Minnesota Street.

"Oh my God, look at the hill," I gasped. "It's so flat. It's so nothing."

"Look at the house," Jim said. "It's absolutely miniscule. Goddamn, it looks trashy."

"Watch it, Jim; that's a bad word," Patty said.

"Sorry, Patty, but it looks BAD."

"I know, Jim." She poked me in the back. "Jim knows

everything, Marge."

The shutters hung loose, brown rather than Irish green. The whole house needed paint. The yard, too, needed attention: dandelions growing in the peony bushes, the apple tree dead, no sprouting green spring grass, no remains of tulips or smell of lilacs.

We knocked on the door to see if we could get a glimpse of the inside. No one was home. Feeling like trespassers—glancing over our shoulders—we walked into the backyard. I peeked in the garage-door window, and my face stared back at me. Because I was feeling like a freckle-faced, pigtailed girl, the image of the pale, forty-two-year-old woman with short, colored hair shocked me.

I looked past the reflection to see that the fort was still there. But the swinging ladder and dormer window seemed so small, and the pigeon coops had vanished.

We watched cars drive up Minnesota Street and park in the visitor's lot of the hospital. "All the fields are gone," Jim said slowly. Then, brusquely, "Let's go. We still have plenty of time. Let's go see stuff."

Jim stopped the car at Liberty State Park. We hiked to the river to check out our old haunts. The Redwood flowed high again, threatening its banks. The perfume of apple blossoms mixed with the moldy stink of rotting twigs and leaves. Our favorite elm trees still spread out their limbs for us. We raced— "Beat you back!"—to the car and continued on our way, past the Marshall Theater and Post Office, the Lyon County Library, down Main Street, and out to the American Legion Field. We got out and wandered around. It was May 18, and though it was too early for the swimming pool, the tennis courts were crowded. We didn't know any of the sweaty players.

Doubling back, we followed the familiar gasoline and greasy frying smells into Mike's Truck Stop, where we celebrated our return with an early lunch. We didn't know anyone there, either. We were strangers, tourists now, from the big city.

"Better get over to the courthouse." Jim wiped his face after devouring one of the *Best Hamburgers in Town*.

"I'm scared," Patty said.

"Nothing to it, Patty," I said. "Just tell the judge what you think."

The hearing moved quickly. A lawyer presented the legal papers, which Jim and I had already signed, to the judge, who nodded and signed his name. He, in turn, presented the document to the clerk, who stamped the order. A simple, uncomplicated case. No one even asked Patty to speak.

"All rise."

Jim and I stood. The judge swept out of the room in a hurry, his black robes flaring like bat wings.

"Congratulations, Patty." I leaned over and gave her a hug.

"Great. It's all over." Jim reached for her hand. "Let's go."

Patty wouldn't take his hand. Wouldn't move.

"C'mon, Patty, Peggy and I are your legal guardians. The judge gave permission," Jim said.

Patty refused to budge; she sat, her heavy body solid on the wood bench. She glowered, her cheeks almost the same color as her pink sweat suit. Behind clear, plastic-rimmed glasses, her eyes stared straight ahead. She held a dry, callused hand over her mouth.

"People are waiting. We've got to go, Patty," I said.

She refused to budge.

It had dawned on me by this time that Patty had wanted to talk to the judge. I was weighing our options when Jean Moon, the social worker, approached. Could she help? I took her aside and asked—if the judge would be so kind—could he please come back in and ask Patty what she thought of his legal decision?

The bailiff announced the judge's reentry. "All stand, the Honorable George I. Harrelson *again* presiding." The judge swept in, bat wings flapping.

Patty stood. And answered his questions: "Yes, Judge, I am me." Smiling broadly, "Patricia Jane Rogers. Yes"—nodding quickly—"you got that right, Judge. I am thirty-three years old. Oh, yes, Judge, I want my brother, Jim, to be my guardian. And, Marge, too, she's my *guardian angel*. Whoops. Just kidding." And then seriously, with emphasis, "I want her to be my guardian, Judge. Thank you, Judge. I know everything."

She shot through the swinging, slatted door of the railing up to the bench to shake his hand. "I'm me, Patty. Thank you, Judge." Then she happily spun around, large hips swaying, and charged out of the room.

The bailiff and reporter smiled. Judge Harrelson, his robes hanging quietly, walked over to Jim and me, smiling too. He shook our hands. "You've got quite a sister," he said.

We walked out with Jean Moon. "Patty's obviously pleased to have you as guardians." She asked Patty how she was getting along at Hammer's Carlson Apartments, if she was eager to move into her own house, if her work at Opportunity Workshop was still satisfying. Patty was enthusiastic—as usual—about everything. She was excited about moving into the community; still plenty busy with church, social, and athletic activities; still enjoyed folding towels at the Radisson—but employment at McDonald's was her favorite goal.

"She could also consider a simple clerical job," Jean said to Jim and me. "Her reading and writing skills are quite advanced, you know." She finished by saying she was sorry we'd had to drive all the way to Marshall to become guardians.

Leaving town, Jim punched Beethoven back on. Majestic melodies pounded through the car. We drove by the old house for one last look, this time going up the back way. The worn metal gas tank still stood out in the backyard, purple thistles growing tall around it.

"Let's buy the house, Peg, and keep it up," Jim said, driving fast out of town. We didn't hear the siren—the patrolman must have been following us for some time—until Patty spied him. "Jim. Jim." She pointed out the back window.

Jim got a speeding ticket. Patty grinned. "Some people!"

In 2012, I took a trip to Marshall. Excitedly driving up Minnesota Hill, I stopped dead on the road: our house and garage were gone. The hospital's parking lot had been expanded right over its footprint. At my fiftieth reunion, in 2013, classmates told me they thought maybe the house had been moved. Tom and I looked for it in the housing development they suggested, but it wasn't there. Perhaps Jim was right: we should have bought the house.

When Hammer downsized, Patty moved to a single-family home in Plymouth with three housemates. Years of summers, and holidays, and family picnics, and annual meetings followed. Patty never missed calling all her brothers and sisters, and nieces and nephews, on their birthdays, and was in charge of the guest book at family weddings. She was the proudest bridesmaid at our brother Dan's wedding. Whenever we got together, Patty sang, danced, and played her harmonica. She read her poetry, offered toasts, and orchestrated riddle contests: "What does one light say to another light?" She would pick winners, usually from the newest members of the family, those marrying in, but often she'd choose me because I'd sing my answer, "You light up my life . . ."

Dad was often the first person chosen to give his answer in the riddle game. To be chosen first meant you were the big loser. Patty would smile at Dad's answer. "Close, Daddio. Close." She joked with him, her Daddio. She poked fun at his big stomach. She called him "old man," and then would giggle, covering her mouth. Dad would ask, "*What* did you say?" and she'd giggle some more.

When Patty became a young woman, my parents asked the Church for advice on Patty's sexuality, specifically on the

Patty Rogers, bridesmaid for Mary Ann Rogers

issue of sterilization. Worried that Patty couldn't reliably perform birth-control measures and might be taken advantage of or initiate sexual relations herself, they consulted the pastor of their parish church. Monsignor said my parents couldn't alter one of God's creatures; Patty would have to bear children if she got pregnant. But, as they had done when told to give Patty away, my parents decided for themselves. They sought a legal decision for surgical means. When they explained what would happen to Patty, she said they'd better hurry with it, because she was going to see her boyfriend that night.

In her last five years of life, Patty descended gradually into the depths of Alzheimer's disease. Statistics show that the majority of folks with Down syndrome will develop this terrible disease, oftentimes suffering with it when younger than fifty, which was Patty's age when we observed a noticeable decline. Patty was fifty-four when Mom died.

Because it was quite late by the time we got the funeral director out the hospice door, the out-of-town family members called, and all of Mom's stuff packed up, I suggested to Patty's staff that we visit the next morning to tell her in person that Mom had died. Patty had visited Mom the day before at N. C. Little Hospice, where Mom—dying of pulmonary fibrosis, hardly able to breathe—in an unbelievable display of strength and courage, worked to appear normal to Patty, asking the usual questions, ones she had asked for years—about the other residents at Queensland, Patty's group home; about Patty's work program; about her massage at the spa. Patty hugged her and said, "I love you, Mom. Get better."

The morning after Mom's death, Mary and I drove out to Queensland. I worried about how to approach Patty. Dad's death, sixteen years earlier, was still difficult for her. Up until recently she'd ask, "Why did Dad have to die, Marge?" I also wasn't sure how we'd reach her. At this point, she wasn't able to track conversations or to verbalize much at all, but that day she greeted us at the door, gave us hugs, clearly knowing who we were. I was amazed.

"Let's sit down on the couch, Patty," I said. "Mary and I have something to tell you."

"OK, Marge," she said, sitting down close to me.

Again, amazed she had called me by name, I put my arm around her. "I have something to tell you," I said again.

She looked right into my eyes. "I know, Marge. Mom died last night."

I looked over at the staff person sitting across the room, her eyes big, her eyebrows raised. She said, "Patty came down to breakfast this morning and told everybody her mother had died last night. The other residents gave her hugs and told her how hard it was for them when their parents had died. Patty thanked them. Then they all went on eating cereal."

Stunned, I felt Mom's spirit surrounding us.

Patty was able to attend our mother's funeral on St. Patrick's Day, March 17, 2007 (in the packed Our Lady of Victory Chapel at the College of St. Catherine), but soon after, Patty's mental state deteriorated rapidly. Confused and depressed, she didn't know how to say my name. I wasn't sure she knew who I was. She stuffed paper and a telephone handset into her clothes. Because of that, her physique appeared bulky, but she wasn't big anymore; all her foods were pureed, and her appetite had changed. Her gray hair had grown long and lanky because haircuts had become difficult; she either pushed the stylist or jerked herself away. She had a large bald spot on top of her head, but she wouldn't wear hats anymore. She didn't want to wear jackets or gloves either. I bought her a sweatshirt because at least the hood could be thrown over her head when she went out in the cold.

She used to let me smooth lotion on her hands. And give high fives. Now she often wouldn't let me touch her. She just looked down and rubbed her teeth and gums with her index finger. When she did glance up at me, it was with scared, vacant eyes. But, sometimes, when I visited, she might glance at a game on TV or a DVD we made about her life or the musical *Annie*. "Tomorrow" was one of only a handful of words left in her vocabulary. She'd sway or march to a song I played on the piano or simply to her own internal rhythm. Sometimes she would let me get close, even give me a kiss.

She was unresponsive most of the time. One day she forgot how to walk, holding her head and moaning, and her staff rushed her to the hospital because they thought perhaps some vein had exploded in her brain. She returned to her group home in a couple of days, able to walk once more. A couple of weeks later, she developed a bad cold and didn't seem to remember how to blow her nose. Her staff took her to the hospital again because they worried she would aspirate. Again, they brought her back home, with orders to wipe her nose on a timed schedule. On weekdays, she went to Community Involvement Programs, a day care, where she parked herself on an occasional chair and peeked at others engaged in activities. She stole paper and stuffed it into her underwear. She was incontinent all of the time.

I hated to see Patty in such a state. I hated to see her suffer.

I was grateful for the one time she came out of her disease, just for a moment. A little gift. My husband and I picked Patty up to take her to a niece's house for a baby shower for our daughter. It was in the winter, snowy and icy on the street where we parked. Patty, with a replaced knee, was a bit clumsy getting out of the car. I took her hand. We both slipped and fell down, me on top of her.

Underneath me, Patty laughed. "Marge, what happened?"

"We fell down together."

"Two staff, Marge. We need two staff for this."

I laughed as Tom helped both of us get up.

But then the cloud descended again. Patty would only say my name one more time, minutes before she died.

A great number of people came to say goodbye to Patty as she lay dying in her cozy bedroom at Queensland: folks from Hammer Residences, church groups, work buddies, friends, family members. John and his wife, Lois, and Tom and I stayed with her the final day and night, sitting on chairs in her room, talking with everybody, and catching some sleep on the living-room sofas. In the middle of the night, we were startled the instant she died by a multitude of birds—who must have nestled in the bushes around her bedroom windows—flying away with a loud, rustling call.

Patty taught us so much. I shared my parents' point of view—maybe not that Patty was an angel, but that she was a special person given to us. An antidote to arrogance in our bright, competitive family. We learned empathy and sympathy from Patty. And love. Love of music and laughter. Love of being and doing.

Song for the Kind
by Patricia J. Rogers

Thankful for love peace for joy
Thankful for God thankful for joy I live upon
Morning star of love light saints of God
Bring all people together in trust
And love peace Lord hear our prayer

Angels walk to water beautiful warm love song
Thankful beautiful blue bird come light
Of the world thankful for food
Bright red and blue white dove in sky
Bird sing a song love for joy to share

Thankful bright blue star in love
Truth peace for beautiful love of my family
I feel happyful warm love light
Beautiful words fill my mind
As I write this song for the kind

FROM FATE

I was late. I was always late, trying to pack too much into a day, a week, a lifetime. I grabbed my red scarf, hat, and gloves from the top shelf of the front closet; wound the long scarf twice around my neck; crushed the hat down over my dark-dyed hair; jerked the leather gloves on; scooped up a red book bag and a big black purse from the front entry chair; and pushed out the heavy oak door of my house.

I didn't think twice rushing down the slippery concrete steps I hadn't salted. I raced to the car parked in the narrow driveway alongside my house. Snow was mounted on either side, almost as high as the black ski rack on top of my car. The banks were spoiled, the snow mixing with soil from the flowerbeds next to the driveway and the grime leaching off the car. Dirty white banks I had added to, shoveling last night, throwing the snow high up, over the top. Hard work, but I had wanted to be able to get out early this morning. The job had been left for me to do, with Katie and Tommy away at college and Norah in her last year of high school, busy and never home, and Tom having late and early meetings. Too tired last night to completely finish the job, and not wanting to dig out the rock-hard snow today, I decided to power through, letting my new Ford do the work.

I tried to kick snow off the front tire flaps with my high black boots, but it was frozen on, dirty stalactites that didn't drip. Squeezing by the snow embankment, I awkwardly climbed into my red Explorer, threw the book bag to the passenger seat, and ruffled through my purse for keys. I pushed the car key, hanging on a heart chain, into the ignition, twisted the switch, and pumped the accelerator. Revved the engine. Not allowing the car to warm up, I jerked the gearshift into reverse, and, centering my eyes on the rearview mirror, bombed back out of the driveway. Crunch. Whoosh. The Explorer shook, skated widely into the street. I straightened the wheels, sped to the corner, swung a turn onto Hamline Avenue, and barreled down the street toward the freeway.

I had trouble seeing—the heater and front-window defroster and fancy wired back window couldn't keep up with the heavy demand; no number of coils could erase the ice and hoarfrost building up on either end of the car. I rubbed my gloved hand across the misted windshield to clear a space to look out. My glove was wet, and my fingers tingled with the cold.

From every car a small cloud of exhaust hung in the air—strange butt-breathing from exotic arctic animals. Or the speech balloons of a cartoon. The exhaust pooled with the gray sky drooping over the road. Remarkably dreary. And extremely cold at 8:30 a.m. on the twenty-first day of January in St. Paul, Minnesota. Twenty degrees below zero the raw temperature. Crazy cold the wind-chill factor. Crystallized. Brittle.

Occasional danger warnings interrupted the music on 107.9, the oldie-but-goodie station I listened to on the radio. Sometimes I listened to 97.1 or 94.5, the ones the kids chose, but I never listened to public radio, to anything that might demand my attention while I drove, anything that might distract. I played loud rock and roll, or pop, songs I grew up with, could sing along with, swing my shoulders to, or beat out on the steering wheel. The touted stereo system bounced the sound around. My car boogied down the street.

I punched the volume up another notch for "Unchained Melody." Bobby Hatfield of the Righteous Brothers reached the high note on *mine*—and that was what I desired; to somehow achieve that exquisite peak in something I did in my lifetime. To attain it in music, art, writing—especially in writing. To touch some chord, some nerve. Some perfection. Reaching the top. Then I could roll down the scale like Bobby did. *I need your love. God speed your love to me.*

I was on my way to Poets of the British Isles, a University of Minnesota outreach course taught at the Women's Club in Minneapolis. I loved meeting in the old brick building with its rich awning, like a stylish New York apartment, and stepping into its interior elegance: manteled fireplace, mahogany moldings, leaded-glass windows, library full of books by and about women, the dining room overlooking Loring Park. But most of all, I loved its aura, its spirit, joining in with all of the women who had graced this place since the turn of the century. I couldn't wait to get there, for the warmth of its roaring fire, for the tea and crumpets the instructor promised to bring. I sang along with the Righteous Brothers.

The freeway was packed. I waited impatiently in the metered entry lanes, inching up to the light somewhere beyond the long line of cars. The exhaust enveloped them all, "haunches" as in Carl Sandburg's fog. I tried to remember lines from Menna Elfyn, the featured poet of the day: "A man said from his pulpit / 'thanks to the women who served' / 'and would the women stay behind?'"

I began to relax. It happened when I was alone in the car. I enjoyed the intimacy the car offered when I was with Tom or the kids, especially on long car trips, away from the telephone and the TV, when they shared their innermost thoughts. But I relished time for myself, in this private place, this Virginia Woolf room of my own.

Still waiting, I picked up a fleck of Kleenex from the tray holder and crumbled it into the small plastic bag hanging from the glove-compartment knob. I looked over the car, proud of my work. I tried to keep it as clean as my home, vacuuming even the far back, where the dogs ride. I picked up and threw away gum wrappers and paper scraps and leaky pens left by my daughter and her friends, and picked up and stored loose change Tom inadvertently dropped on the floor. I placed the coins in their appropriate spots in the holder underneath the ashtray. I didn't have to empty that out anymore, now that I had finally quit smoking—no need to disguise any rancid smells in my new jewel of a car, ruby red with ebony upholstery.

I finally got the green light and flew onto the freeway. *Like a bat out of hell.* What an old simile, I thought. What's something new? Fresh? Another weather report on the radio interrupted, a broadcaster warning of *black ice*: on days this cold any moisture, even exhaust from cars, can coat the asphalt with a fine sheet of ice that's invisible. "Watch out. Take your time," he said.

Right, I said dismissively, zipping over to the left lane. Cruising along, I finally let surface what I had been trying not to think about—the trip Tom and I had returned from the day before. Our good friend John had married a Swedish woman and moved to her village near Stockholm. They had four daughters. Recently he had been diagnosed with terminal cancer. He had been calling me long distance, ranting about pilgrimages to Lourdes or Fatima or Medjugorje, all the holy sites for Catholic blessings and cures. "Do you think I should go?" he had asked.

Tom and I had been to Fatima. The huge square in front of the enormous cathedral reminded me of the Red Square in Moscow or Tiananmen Square in Beijing, where thousands of believers had gathered, full of idealism, getting ready to be shot down. In Portugal, people crawled on their knees the length of the square to the sacred shrine of the three poor shepherd children whom Mary had appeared to in the fields near Lisbon. There were thousands of votive candles and collections of relics—bones of saints—and crutches and staffs of those purported to be cured. On the surrounding streets, souvenir shops advertised cheap religious tchotchkes—*buying your way into*

Heaven. It was all the stuff I distrusted and disliked about Catholicism.

Tom believed in the Church, in its theology and social mission. He faithfully attended Mass. In Sweden, when John murmured about spirits and angels, and his mother led the rosary, Tom prayed along. I nodded, mouthed replies, faking it. I had stopped going to church.

Speeding by the Waldorf paper plant by the side of the freeway, I glimpsed its heating exhaust filling the air like an atomic mushroom cloud. It dangled in the sky. A huge worry made manifest. Shivering, I remembered the coldness of Sweden, and was suddenly aware of my freezing hands inside my soaked gloves. I began to pull off the right glove with my left hand, leaning my arms slightly on the steering wheel. The car shifted, then skid sideways. Alarmed, but an experienced Minnesota driver, I reminded myself: *Don't brake. Turn into the skid. Roll into the slide.*

But I was spinning out of control at seventy miles an hour. Whisking through traffic—from the fast left lane into the slower right lane. Shit, I could collide with a car. But I didn't. No impact. No collision. I was beginning to realize, bit by bit— everything moved slowly now, a suspended moment—that this wasn't any normal skid. I wasn't approaching the wall of snow I was expecting. White soft snow, the Edelweiss flower, "clean and bright." This edge of snow was streaked black, hard as glass, and didn't "look happy to see me."

I was not aware of my body. I was trying to use my head: what was happening? It was quiet in this moment. Utterly, totally quiet. A hole in time.

And then the sound. So fast I couldn't wrap my head around it. The smash of breaking glass, the thud underneath. I thought: *This is serious.* I was rolling over, upside down. Up again. The high peak. *Very serious. With extensive, expensive damage. Tom is not going to like this.* I said his name, and then the children's, just their names—that was all the time I had—because I was down again, more glass splintering, the car crunching, bouncing, and somewhere in my mind, I thought I might die. Then I was up again. I thought of my dying friend. Of my father who had died recently. I said *Dad* and reeled over one more time.

I woke up. I hadn't been sleeping, but that's how it felt. And Goddamn it, I was alive. *It wasn't my time yet*, I said to my dead father. But the next brain wave entered on that one's back: I must be injured. Slowly, very slowly, I tensed and released parts of my body, as in the relaxation exercise in yoga class, when the instructor turned off the overhead lights and murmured soothing scenes in lulling tones—water ebbing back and forth on warm sandy beaches ("Lonely rivers sigh . . . 'I'll be coming home, wait for me'"). Even though I saw the crushed dial of the heater and the glassless windshield and felt the dangerous wind whipping though the car, I stayed mentally focused on my body: beginning with my toes, slowly, methodically, moving up, until I reached my thighs, hips, and breasts, where I stopped. How could you tense and release these parts? In yoga, I must have been asleep by my knees, I thought.

Don't move, I told myself—I knew of Christopher Reeve—but I turned to look at the zillions of tiny glass rainbow flecks on my purse and bag. A study in black and red and confetti. I looked down to see my lap covered with the same prism specks. *Don't move,* but now I thought of frostbite and looked in the backseat for a wrap. There was nothing. It was too neat; no old blankets or pillows messed up my tidy, organized car. Gritting my teeth, I determined that if I lived through this, I was not going to sweat the small stuff; I was going to live large and messy.

"Oh my God, are you alive? I was behind you. Oh my God! You rolled over four times!" I turned to see the face of a terrified young woman in my open window. I wanted to reach out to hug her, or shake her, to relieve her fright.

"It's all right," I said, "I'm alive. But I shouldn't move. I don't know if I've broken anything."

She looked as if she was going to throw up.

I need to be in control, I told myself. "Listen," I said, "you must stay calm. I need your help. *I need your love. God speed your love.* Do you have a cell phone?"

She shook her head. She was crying now. "No."

"OK," I said, "we'll just have to wait for someone to come help us. Is there anything you can cover me with? I'm very cold."

She looked into my car, disappeared, and then quickly reappeared with a homemade quilt. She tried to open my door, but it was sealed shut. Through the window she spread the quilt of wedding circles over me. I tucked my hands under it, thinking of red gloves in a gray sky, Snow-White fingers in the night, a gigantic Georgia O'Keeffe painting: razor-sharp ice entwined in warm rounded carcasses. A north and west fusion. Hands across the land.

"Are you all right?" A huge man in a heavy down jacket yanked on the car door. It tremored but held fast. The man leaned into the window. "Ma'am, are you all right? Don't you worry. We'll get you out in no time. I saw you roll over. I was over there, across the other side of the freeway." He pointed, but I couldn't see out; his frame filled the window. "I turned right around. I've got emergency supplies in my truck. Don't move, ma'am. I'm going to be right back. Don't you worry. Don't move!"

I obeyed his command, not turning my head to follow him, and he disappeared from my peripheral vision. I could sense the nice, scared woman still out there, shaking and crying by the car.

"An ambulance is coming." The big man's voice again. "We're going to get you out of here." He put something on my head. A collar around my neck. "There. That'll help you not move, ma'am."

I didn't know if he put it over my scarf or even if my hat was still on. And then I didn't know much at all. More people.

A siren. A loud crack and a blast of cold air when the door was pried open. Then a wooden board, like a toboggan sled for ski accidents; somehow I was placed on it, and me and my board— Sesame Street's "Me and my llama, me and my llama" ringing in my head—were inside a bright, warm ambulance.

Screeching sirens, and out of the corner of my eyes, red flashing lights. I was strapped to the board, like the one in a children's illustrated Bible. "Get up, take your pallet, and walk": Jesus directing the lame man. The board was slid onto a metal bed, like those in morgues on TV. The action was also like transferring a patient from a gurney to an operating table. Carter—no, Abby—from *ER* or McDreamy or Steamy from *Grey's Anatomy*: "Defibrillation!" "Cardiac arrest!" "Clamps!"

I didn't say anything. I watched two young paramedics take my pulse and blood pressure, counting, and inflating pressure on the cuff around my arm. I tried to remember the names of pressure. Systolic. Diastolic. Which was the high one, the one putting you over the top? I tried to read the numbers on the gauge graduated in millimeters of mercury, but I couldn't, and then wondered if my contacts were still in my eyes, wondered if I was seeing "through a glass darkly."

The thin paramedic with a light goatee and a dark-maroon *Go Gophers!* cap covered me with a heated blanket—God bless him—folding my hands in. I thanked him with my eyes, and then closed them. Strangely, the ending of Elfyn's "Will the ladies please stay behind?" played in my head: " . . . if Christ came back today / He would surely make his own cup of tea." I resolved from this point on—because I had been given a reprieve on life—to be totally my own person. Not a lady staying behind. I would step up, reach for the high note of "Unchained Melody." I would write my book about all that had been given to me.

Frigid air. The paramedics jumped out, their boots clunking on the pavement. That sound, all sounds, amplified: clanging doors, booming voices. The paramedics pulled out the stretcher, snapped open its legs and railings, and pushed it—and me—through the huge doors, into a room bright with florescent lights. I squinted at a whole slew of medical staff.

A nurse leaned down to me. "Is there anyone we should call?"

When I said, "My husband," she said, "I'll let you tell him. We think that's best; if our patients can, we want them to talk to loved ones themselves from the emergency room."

She got Tom on speakerphone. He was on a conference call, said, "Can you wait, honey?"

I did, with the nurse frowning. When he clicked back to me, I said, "I've had an accident. But I'm all right."

The nurse then told him I was at United Hospital.

Two aides—who believed I was out of it—pushed my cart to the X-ray lab, careening by shadowed walls covered with Thomas Kinkade imitations. Floating on stale air, I caught whiffs of antiseptic cleanser and the aides' tobacco breaths. I was pushed and pulled in and out of elevators. I heard the ding of announcing floors, the exhaling of pneumatic doors, intercom messaging, the clanging of trays. While I waited outside the lab, the aides whispered to each other. I heard everything.

"Hey," one said, "I read somewhere each time you roll over in a car, your body actually rolls over three more times; all the organs apparently go through a cycle."

"Man! Didn't they say she rolled over four times?"

"That's what I'm saying. Add it up."

"Her body made *sixteen* revolutions!"

"Fuck. She's going to be screwed up."

I thought I might be.

Back in the bright light. White-gowned doctors and nurses moved around quietly. I thought I saw one of the doctors pin up my X-ray skeleton. There seemed to be a hushed silence descending in the room. I imagined he pointed to, and called out, my cervical vertebrae: *C1, C2, C3, C4, C5, C6, C7.* The doctor had a deep voice, like James Earl Jones. *Star Wars.*

After each of his calls, I believed I heard an echoing female voice, light like Princess Leia's. *Check. Check. Check. Check. Check. Check. Check.* Their ominous and promising voices swelled like musical counterpoint.

"OK, folks, now the thoracic," I believed the doctor said, and began to count down twelve more vertebrae. I assumed the tense nurses and doctors showed tight lines on their faces, the same fear as the woman behind me on the road. I stiffened, too. And waited.

And then, finally, the lumbar: *L1. Check. L2. Check. L3. Check. L4. Check. L5. Check. Sacrum and coccyx. Check.*

I sensed a nurse saying, "Yes!"

But Darth Vader announced, "Internal organs."

I was back wheeling with the aides, talking about what they were going to do that night, about their girlfriends. One of them said, looking at me, "Man, it'll be like a miracle if nothing's wrong with her."

Tom was with me now, walking somberly beside the cart. He tried to hide his anxiety, smiling whenever our eyes connected. "You're fine," he kept repeating. "You're fine." Again, I wondered if I was, but in any case, as I was being escorted hurriedly to CT scanning, I concluded I'd stop rushing through life. I would live more deliberately. Like Henry David Thoreau. Or maybe Annie Dillard, closely observing, although I thought sometimes she went over the top.

A week later, tentatively, in Tom's car—"getting back on the horse"—I drove to Sal's Wrecker Service, where the Explorer had been held until all the insurance inspections and paperwork were completed. I wanted to make sure there was nothing left in the car now that it was going to be demolished for parts and scrap. The woman at the scene of the accident had put my book bag and purse into the ambulance, along with a note and telephone number: "Please let me know if you're all right."

Exhausted, with pain emanating from all my joints, I still had called her as soon as I returned from the hospital the night of the accident, wanting to reassure and thank her. Telling her what a policeman had said about the rollover rates of SUVs, I added, "So. I just want you to know. Don't buy one, OK?" When I had hung up, I wondered why I hadn't done any research. Why hadn't I checked *Consumer Reports* for rollover statistics? What materialistic hype caused me to buy a death trap?

Horrified at the sight of the Explorer, I could hardly breathe. Feeling asthmatic and claustrophobic, I panted, panicky, my gloved hands sweeping over the glass on the dash, then rummaging through the glove compartment. I remembered the dog bed in the far back, looked for it, and spotted a book lying on the backseat. It was a Bible. I wondered how it got there: The woman? The trucker? The presence of Dad again swept through the car. I took the Bible, deciding to send it to John in Sweden. I would tell him about my accident and the Bible's mysterious appearance in my car. I would tell him how I should have died but didn't. How I was watched over.

AFTERWORD

You are called by name . . . Become what you are!

– U.S. Conference of Catholic Bishops, Pastoral Letter, "Marriage: Love and
Life in the Divine Plan"

I've been called by a number of names: Margaret, Peggy, Peg,
Margie, Marge, Marjorie, Mag, Mags, Sister, Zoë. Tom calls
me Marge or Margaret, occasionally Margaret Ann. We've been
married now for forty years. We've raised three children and
welcomed six grandchildren into the family. We've traveled the
world.

For the past thirteen years, we have supported the Hill
Museum and Manuscript Library at St. John's University, which
is engaged in the photographic preservation of ancient manuscripts. HMML works to provide web access to digitized manuscripts and concentrates its work in countries where access to
manuscripts is difficult for outsiders as well as countries where
there is palpable risk that irreplaceable manuscript collections
will be destroyed. As part of this endeavor, we have traveled to
Lebanon, Ethiopia, Egypt, Armenia, Romania, Ukraine, India,
Turkey, Syria, Georgia, Israel, Jordan, and Malta. Our next trip
will be to Mali, close to countries our son-in-law was raised in,
Liberia and Ghana.

In the countries we visit, we go to the monasteries and libraries where preservation takes place, see the books, the rooms and methods of storage, even the gloves the technicians wear to protect the parchment pages. We meet with church or civil leaders who have given us permission to photograph and computerize their holdings, written in languages such as Aramaic, Hebrew, Arabic, Ge'ez, Greek, and Syriac.

We also sightsee. In Ukraine, knowing my other son-in-law's ancestors lived somewhere near Kiev, I told the group I wanted to visit Babi Yar to pay my respects. On a gray, misty, cold day, we got off at the last stop and walked out of the Kiev subway station into a large park, eventually finding the "Valley of Death," where the Nazis executed more than one hundred thousand people. I stared down into the huge ravine, silently mouthing words from Yevgeny Yeytushenko's poem "Babi Yar:" "Here all things scream silently / and, baring my head, slowly I feel myself / turning grey . . . "

Suddenly, my hair stood on end. There was a dead man— a present-day dead man—lying at the bottom. Crumpled, head over chest, wearing something like a tattered lumberman jacket and worn boots, he looked like a large puppet. Tom ran down the side of the ravine and then up the other side, calling out, "Margaret, we have to notify the authorities."

Standing on the rim, aware of the rain dribbling into the muddy chasm, the habitual beliefs of my childhood instantly surfaced. Surprising myself, I prayed. I prayed for this man who had joined thousands of others. I prayed for all those who had died, crossing over from darkness into light.

Our children, who call me Mom, Maggie, Nano, or Nanpan, also call me the holder (hoarder?) of memories for our family. I have stored boxes, bags, plastic bins of pictures, cards, letters, documents—births, graduations, weddings, deaths—in closets all over our house. I've made the kids help me haul *stuff* to our cabin on the St. Croix River, tangible objects of family members who have died: Muzzy's old Singer sewing machine;

Uncle Pat's now-split oak side table; my parents' first maple set of furniture—the bed Mary and I drew the line down to separate our space; the old oak table; Patty's silver-and-turquoise '50s radio; a painting by Tom.

Old memories mix with the new at the river. The grandkids (I'm their Nana, Nan, or Nannie) will remember building a tree fort and a go-cart, using scavenged parts and a new battery-powered motor; playing checkers and chess with pieces and boards their parents brought us from Mexico; having parties on the little red metal table and chairs handed down from older cousins, which they helped paint. Shopping with me, they bought a red-checkered tablecloth and napkins and a tiny wicker picnic basket to hold their new dishes and silverware.

Next summer we'll add the youngest grandchildren's names, Grace and Louis, to the wall of the tree fort. Gracie's letters will be yellow, her favorite color. Louie, who will be a year old, will probably not have formed a color preference. The letters of the older grandkids' names shimmer in their distinct choices: blue Caroline, yellow Maxwell, red Charlotte, green Teddy.

The kids had celebrated the original naming ceremony with a tea party in the fort: tiny red-and-white ladybug cups and saucers passed among them as they cheered, toasted, sipped.

Below them, lounging on chairs overlooking the water, their parents, Katie and Matt, Tom and Analisa, Norah and Cooper, had called out to look at the old blue heron and the baby eagle flying over the water. Geese had called. The dogs had barked.

Like their great-grandparents, grandparents, and parents before them, our children and grandchildren will experience their own ordinary-extraordinary lives.

I'm grateful for mine.

The Barrett Family

See the Girl with the Red Dress On

She can do the Birdland all night long. She
can do it with her pedal pushers on,
pet red vest—buttons-missing—swinging loose.

She can do that dance hopping in saddle
shoes—laces untying—blue plaid jumper
bunched and rolled over a crispy starched blouse.

Marrying Christ, she does it in a white
plastic bib, black serge habit, a banging,
hanging cross on her roped rosary belt.

See that girl with the red dress on, she's gonna
dance all night long. Strutting her stuff (tweet!
tweet!), mini-skirts jig and jag. Tweet! And tweet!

In pale pink and pearl wedding gown—repeat—
red hat and polka-dotted wedding dress,
her hands click and clap. And the beat goes on . . .

the beat goes on. She Birdlands with babies
in her arms, leopard-skin nursing robe freely
flowing. In reams of Eileen Fisher,

in dreamy chiffons, stained ripped jeans, in suits
and sweaters, she springs forth—scarlet, ruby,
rose, cherry—dips, glides, twists, and turns for her

family, friends, students. Donning Nana
wear, her grandkids tweet. Tweet! At the last, she
sashays to Birdland in her high-end sheath.

(after Ray Charles, "What'd I Say")

REFERENCES

Archives: Cretin and Our Lady of Peace High Schools; St. Catherine University; Sisters of St. Joseph of Carondelet.

Books: Dom Eugene Boylan, *This Tremendous Lover*, Christian Classics, Allen, Texas, 1996 (original, 1947); Jane Lamm Carroll, Joanne Cavallaro, and Sharon Doherty, *Liberating Sanctuary, 100 Years of Women's Education at the College of St. Catherine*, Lexington Books, Lanham, Maryland, 2012; A Collaboration by the Sisters of St. Joseph of Carondelet, St. Paul Province, *Eyes Open on a World, The Challenges of Change*, North Star Press, St. Cloud, Minnesota, 2001; Robert Ellsberg, *Charles De Foucauld*, Orbis Books, Maryknoll, New York, 1999; Arthur P. Rose, *An Illustrated History of Lyon County*, Northern History Publishing Company, Marshall, Minnesota, 1912; Caryll Houselander, *The Reed of God*, Christian Classics, Revised edition, Allen, Texas, 2006, (original, 1944); Arthur Miller, *Death of a Salesman*, Penguin Books, New York, 1949; G. H. Sneltjes, *The Marshall Civic and Commerce Association, Marshall . . . . The Agricultural Emerald of Bountiful Minnesota,* 1959.

Newspapers: Pat W. Rogers, "Guest Editorial," *The Marshall Messenger*, Marshall, Minnesota, 1945; Pat Rogers, "If I Were an Editor—I Would Write This Editorial," *The Marshall Messenger*, Marshall, Minnesota, March 25, 1955; "Half-Drowned Marshall Battles Flood with Will," *Minneapolis Morning Tribune*, June 18, 1957; "Unique Program Aids Good Young Drivers," *Minneapolis Sunday Tribune*, July 16, 1961; Lee Schafer, "A major new study of income mobility nationwide asks, 'Where is the land of opportunity?'" *Star Tribune*, January 28, 2014.

ACKNOWLEDGMENTS

"The Slough" was incorporated into a St. Croix Festival Theatre stage play in 2015 and "The Flood" appeared in Minnesota Historical Society's anthology *The State We're In*, 2010. Other essays and stories, in slightly different versions, have appeared in the following publications: "Princess," *Dust and Fire*, 2009; "Song For The Kind," *SN Review*, 2008; "Papa," *River Images*, 2001; "The Canning Jar, *Minnesota Parent*, May 1999; "Blackie," *Sidewalks*, 1995-96; "Mom in Memoir," *Gypsy Cab*, 1995; and "The Ironing Board," *Community Connections*, 1994-95.

The dates of these pieces demonstrate how long *Called* has been in process. From the very beginning, I've had help from individuals, groups, and institutions to bring it to fruition. When I first began to write, I took classes at the Loft Literary Center in Minneapolis. Later, I taught classes there. I learned to write better in both. I joined writing groups with other students from Loft classes: Brian Cabalka, Mary Sheedy Kurcinka, Brian Newhouse, and Bonnie White; Sara DeLuca and Sharri Kinkead; Beryl Singleton Bissell and Sonjie Johnson. Sonjie and I teamed up with Rosa Maria Peterson and Margaret Hasse to form a St. Paul writing group. After a summer program at the Iowa Writing Workshop, I continued working with two writers from Illinois and Wisconsin, Ricky Peterson and Jerry Schroeder. I met in the Loft's Writing Studio with Vicky Lettmann, Patricia Salwei, Connie Szarke, Beth Waterhouse, and Kasi Williamson. After receiving an MFA in Creative Writing from the University of Minnesota (a great experience with faculty and fellow students—I thank them all!), a number of us worked together: Kate Freeborn, Kate Hopper, Rob McGinley Myers, Rhena Tantisunthorn, and Francine Tolf. Francine and I would continue critiquing our writing for years, along with Ricky Peterson when she moved to Minnesota; for several years, we convened with Gay Herzberg and Carol Whitman.

My students have inspired me along the way, from the early days of teaching literature and reading to more current years. I've treasured the creativity, compassion, and constancy to the craft of writing from my University of Minnesota students, Loft classes, various workshop participants, the group at the Jewish Community Center, the pastors of the Collegeville Institute—especially the Wholly Writers, People Incorporated's Artability writers, Jerry Mevissen and the Nimrod members of the Jackpine Writers' Bloc. I gained experience in teaching and writing short-shorts as a blogger for MINN-POST.

I discussed *Called* from conception to completion with friend Dee Dee Van de North over her kitchen table. She saved my original documents and commented that I often came full circle with my stories, ending up as I had started years before. Other friends, Annette Atkins, Mickey Madigan, Rosalie Maggio, Mary Nantell, and Bonnie West, read my work and offered comments and support over time. Still others read *Called* in different stages and helped move it to its final version: Madeleine Van Hecke, Yvette Nelson, Niomi Phillips, Marney Wamsley.

Thank you to Sister Mary E. Kraft, CSJ, for her assistance in researching the archives of the Sisters of St. Joseph of Carondelet, and to her, Charles Baxter, Patricia Hampl, and Kathleen Norris for their endorsements of *Called*, Joey McGarvey for her careful editing, and publisher Robert Rennie McQuilkin and his wife Sarah for liking my story enough to publish it and for such magnanimous collaboration.

I remember my grandparents, parents, sister Patty and brother Tom, nephew Jean Paul and niece Megan Marie, and aunts and uncles. I'm grateful for my brothers, Jim, John, and Dan, sister Mary, and their spouses, Jacque, Lois, Mary Ann, and Pete, the Barrett family, nieces and nephews, grandnephews and grandnieces, cousins, and in-law families.

Finally, I thank wholeheartedly my husband Tom, our children, Katie, Tom and Norah, and their spouses, Matt, Analisa, and Cooper, who offered advice and encouragement for years. And I look forward to our grandchildren, Caroline, Maxwell, Charlotte, Teddy, Gracie, and Louie, reading this book one day.

MARGE ROGERS BARRETT has published a book of poems, *My Memoir Dress*, and her poetry and prose have appeared in numerous journals. She received an MFA in Creative Writing from the University of Minnesota, teaches at the Loft Literary Center, and conducts workshops around the country. She and her husband live near the Mississippi River in Minneapolis.

This book has been set in Garamond, a typeface created by Claude Garamond in the first part of the Sixteenth Century. He based his font on types cut by Francesco Griffo for Venetian printer Aldus Manutius in 1495. Garamond created a typeface with an unprecedented degree of balance and elegance, for centuries standing as the pinnacle of beauty and practicality in type-founding. Italics for the Garamond font are based on those cut by Robert Granjon (1513–1589).

To order additional copies of this book
or other Antrim House titles, contact the publisher at

Antrim House
21 Goodrich Rd., Simsbury, CT 06070
www.antrimhousebooks.com
860.217.0023, AntrimHouse@comcast.net.

•

On the house website
in addition to information on books
you will find excerpts, upcoming events, and
a "seminar room" featuring supplemental biography,
notes, images, poems, reviews, and
writing suggestions.